Meaning and Structure:
An Essay in the
Philosophy of Language

D1104688

Studies in Language
Noam Chomsky and Morris Halle, Editors

Meaning and Structure

An Essay in the Philosophy of Language

Bernard Harrison

The University of Sussex

Harper & Row, Publishers

New York   Evanston   San Francisco   London

MEANING AND STRUCTURE: AN ESSAY IN THE PHILOSOPHY OF LANGUAGE

Copyright © 1972 by Bernard Harrison

Printed in the United States of America. All rights reserved. No part of this book may be used or reproduced in any manner whatsoever without written permission except in the case of brief quotations embodied in critical articles and reviews. For information address Harper & Row, Publishers, Inc., 49 East 33rd Street, New York, N.Y. 10016.

Standard Book Number: 06-042671-3

Library of Congress Catalog Card Number: 79-174521

TEXAS WOMAN'S UNIVERSITY
LIBRARY

In memory of my mother and father

323265

Contents

Preface

This book attempts the philosophically unfashionable task of developing a systematic and general theory of the nature of the conventions governing the semantics of a natural language, with the object of offering a conceptual framework within which semantic phenomena can be understood in relation to syntax and to the communicative and social aspects of language. The theory which it advances is no doubt something less than a final solution to the central problem to which it is addressed; that of saying, precisely and without reliance upon metaphor, what it is for a linguistic expression to possess a meaning. My aim has been more modest: to increase the range of conceptual models against the background of which the discussion of semantics by philosophers, linguists, and psycholinguists can proceed. The availability of alternative conceptual models, provided they are not merely or idly speculative, is often a potent factor in encouraging or retarding scientific imagination in empirical inquiries. With this in mind I have tried, in what follows, to temper speculation with a proper sense of the empirical realities uncovered by linguists and psycholinguists, so far as I am acquainted with and understand their work.

Earlier treatments of some of the problems dealt with in the book, and some further developments of some of its ideas, produced since the main work of writing it was completed, have appeared in article form in various places. An earlier version of the theory of semantic anomaly in Chapter 11 can be found in "Category Mistakes and Rules of Language," *Mind* (1965); and a more extended version of the attack on imagist theories of meaning (Chapter 2) in "Meaning and Mental Images," *Proceedings of the Aristotelian Society*, 1962-1963. "Translations and Taxonomies" in *The Journal of Philosophical Linguistics*, No. 2 (Spring 1970) and "On Describing Colors," *Inquiry* (1967), contain respectively an extension of the theory of taxonomies in Chapter 3 and an application of the idea of a language as a system of linguistic devices to the discussion of epistemological scepticism about color vision.

The ideas presented here have developed gradually over the past ten years, and I have been greatly helped by discussing them with many colleagues at various universities, here and in America and Canada, including particularly Charles Stevenson, Julius Moravcsik, William L. Todd, Ronald J. Butler, Charles Whiteley, Benjamin Gibbs, Aaron Sloman, and Timothy Sprigge. I am particularly indebted also to Noam Chomsky for some very penetrating and helpful comments on Part III of the manuscript. All alike have striven patiently to correct my errors and cannot be held responsible for the obstinacy of those that remain. My wife Dot, afflicted with a husband hopelessly given to metaphysics mumbling about the house, found it in her heart to encourage me.

B.H.

Kingston near Lewes, Sussex
May 1970

Every proposition must *already* have a sense: it cannot be given a sense by affirmation. Indeed, its sense is just what is affirmed.

—Wittgenstein, *Tractatus Logico-Philosophicus*, 4.064

part one
The empiricist theory of language

1 Meaning and recognition

1.1 Much of our thinking about language shares the assumptions and traces out the ramifications of a single traditional outlook, which has in one form or another been characteristic of Empiricism since Locke, and which I therefore propose to call the "empiricist theory of language," or ETL for short. The ETL is primarily a philosophical theory, but it has enjoyed a respectable extraphilosophical currency: mainly in behavioral psychology, but also to some extent in linguistics. It has provided, as we shall see in the Appendix, the conceptual basis for a number of attempts to construct stimulus-response accounts of the acquisition and use of language; and it is apt to dominate the discussion, often in rather complex and unobvious ways, when linguists attempt to understand the semantic aspects of language or the relationships between syntax, semantics, and phonology.

The reason for the influence of the ETL in these fields is not hard to discover. It offers a set of satisfyingly coherent and interconnected answers to certain very fundamental questions about the nature of language, to which the psychologist of language, or the linguist interested in semantic questions, must have answers of some sort if he is to be able—*qua* psychologist or linguist—to get on with his work. The most fundamental of these questions concerns the content of the conventions which introduce meaning into a language. It is obvious that the difference between a cuneiform inscription or the words the Tigris boatman shouts, and the tracks left by birds in wet sand or the cry of a gull, is that the former are enmeshed in some system of human conventions and that because of this they possess linguistic meaning, whereas the latter do not. But what sort of conventions are these? Again, what is the relationship between the semantic conventions of a language—whatever they may be—and the rules of grammar or syntax? Are syntactic conventions intrinsically related to semantic conventions, or merely superimposed upon them? And how is the knowledge of what a word or a sentence *means* related, on the one hand, to knowledge of linguistic convention and, on the other, to knowledge of the things to which the word refers or with which the sentence is concerned? How far is the capacity to use language correctly and intelligently to be understood as a function of the nature of some system of learned conventional stipulations; how far as a function of certain mental or behavioral capacities constitutive of intelligence itself? And if the latter, are such capacities common to all animals or specific to the human species? To the objection that these questions are not philosophical questions—although they have traditionally been discussed by philosophers—it must be replied that they are certainly not straightforwardly empirical ones. That is, they cannot simply be solved in the laboratory or the data-processing room by the application of fully understood and unproblematic methods presently available to the social sciences. What they require of us is, in fact, the construction of a general conceptual model which will enable us to understand the semantic aspects of natural languages. Conceptual models may guide and inform experimental work, and of course, any facts about the bodies of phenomena which they are supposed to systematize and reduce to order may be relevant to their construction, including facts established in the laboratory; but the task of constructing them remains essentially a conceptual and not an experimental task. As to who should embark upon such inquiries—this is to my mind a question of counterbalancing relative gains and losses. Social scientists know, no doubt, more facts than philosophers; philosophers possess, perhaps, a certain facility at constructing theories.

At any rate, the ETL has traditionally provided such a general model: one which has been taken to yield, in a principled and non-*ad hoc* way, persuasively simple and elegant answers to all the above questions, and others which we have not yet formulated.

The central pillar of the ETL is an associative-referential theory of meaning which functions simultaneously as a theory of language acquisition and use, and has in the latter guise been incorporated into associationist psychology. Different parts of the resulting complex of views have been subjected, during the last ten or fifteen years, to criticisms which, although they are articulated from the points of view of quite different fields of study and are directed at rather different aspects of the associative-referential theory, display a certain structural similarity. I am referring to the later work of Wittgenstein and to the work of Noam Chomsky and the school of linguists and psycholinguists associated with him. Both Chomsky and Wittgenstein claim, in effect, that an associative-referential theory is inadequate to account for the complexities of a linguistically competent adult's use of language because, in effect, a natural language is not just a system of associations but, wholly or in part, a system of *rules*. Once this has been said, of course, we have to grant that Wittgensteinians and Chomskeans understand radically different things by the expression "a rule of language." The concept of a rule of language plays a fairly crucial role in the type of conceptual analysis to which Wittgenstein's later work has given rise, but is nevertheless notoriously ill-defined. All that most conceptual analysts offer is an occasional attempt to give a sense to the notion of a linguistic rule by analogy—speaking a language, we are sometimes told, is like playing a board game, or like executing a country dance—but the limits of such analogies are generally left quite obscure.

Wittgenstein's critique of associationism concerns itself mainly with the semantic aspects of language: with the questions of what is involved in coming to know the meaning of an expression, of the nature of understanding, and of the limits of meaningful utterance. In his work, and in the work of a good many conceptual analysts more or—as in the case of J. L. Austin—less influenced by him, we have, it seems to me, a large number of quite precise and detailed semantic investigations which are at worst inquiries into the semantics of a particular natural language—English—and at best perhaps reveal universal semantic or conceptual relationships. None of these results can be assimilated with any ease by linguistics or psycholinguistics, however, and this is at least in part due to the fact that the concept of a linguistic rule employed by philosophers remains so obscure. Without some clarification of this notion it is impossible, for example, to say what precisely a competent speaker of a language is doing when, in the course of using that language, he observes all the fine distinctions which the conceptual analyst—no doubt rightly —says he observes. And what sorts of rule must a child eventually learn to obey if his linguistic practice is to come to approximate more and more closely to the adult practice in which these distinctions are honored? Without some clarification of the notion of a linguistic rule all such questions remain unanswerable.

Chomsky's attack on associationism, on the other hand, is directed mainly at behavioral psychological versions of the theory. Like Wittgenstein, he considers them inadequate because they fail to do justice to the fact that the intelligent use of language depends at least in part on the user's having assimilated a system of rules; but in Chomsky's case the rules in question are the rules of a generative grammar: that is, the system of rules which (ideally) suffice to generate all, and only, the grammatical expressions of a language. For Chomsky, therefore, the notion of a rule of language is relatively well-defined, but in purely structural terms. Generative grammars of the sort developed by Chomsky (transformational grammars) have proved a fairly powerful instrument for the description and explanation of many structural features of natural languages. Chomsky's work has opened up new perspectives in psycholinguistics, and some of it has proved to be relevant to conceptual analysis, as witness the work of Professor Zeno Vendler[1] and others. There ought, one feels, to be a good deal more gold to be mined in the regions lying between transformational grammar and conceptual analysis; but in fact it is not at all easy, except in a few special cases, to see how to extend Chomsky's insights in such a way as to make them relevant to semantic or conceptual questions. Indeed, the most obvious defect of Chomsky's account of language is its failure to suggest any fruitful

---

[1] Zeno Vendler, *Linguistics in Philosophy* (Ithaca, N.Y.: Cornell University Press, 1967).

or even plausible way of representing the semantic component of a language as a system of rules.

And yet, Wittgenstein's work suggests that it ought to be possible to represent the semantics of a natural language as a system of rules and to explicate the required sense of the term "rule of language" in some reasonably precise and non-metaphorical way. Now, however sharply we differentiate structure and meaning for the purposes of doing linguistics, there must presumably nevertheless exist some relationship between syntax and semantics. And hence one would hope that such a representation of the semantics of a natural language as a rule system might in some way link up with the results of linguistics so as to yield a unified conceptual model. And one would hope that such a unified model might then serve as a common conceptual basis for certain forms of conceptual analysis and for linguistics and psycholinguistics (so far as the latter concern themselves with semantics) and that, given a common conceptual basis, the results of each discipline might prove to be more readily assimilable by the other two than is the case at present.

The object of this book is to lay the groundwork for such a model. I shall try first of all to formulate as clearly and simply as possible the complex of assertions and arguments which make up the ETL, and to show that they really are intrinsically connected so as to constitute a theory which must stand or fall as a whole. Part of the success of the ETL has, I think, been due to the fact that the criticism to which it has so far been subjected has been of a rather piecemeal kind: displaced from one position, holders of the ETL find it quite easy to retreat to a closely (but not obviously) related one and ultimately to the claim that there is simply no conceivable alternative (or, if they are psychologists, no conceivable scientific alternative) to their theory. "If a child doesn't learn the meanings of words by ostensive definition, then how does he learn them?" is a question frequently taken to have devastating force against critics of some parts of the theory, for example. I shall try to show that once we are in a position to examine the theory as an internally connected whole, it becomes possible to subject it to criticism of a far more radical and destructive kind than it has hitherto encountered. The thrust of this criticism is toward the conclusion that the ETL is a wholly vacuous theory, so that if it were indeed true that it offered the only conceivable source of light on the questions with which it deals, the only conclusion that would follow would be that the darkness enshrouding these questions was not merely total but irremediable.

I shall then try to show that things are not quite as bad as that. The criticisms which we shall level at the ETL themselves suggest possibilities of reformulating the notions of a rule of language and of a language game (or linguistic device[2]) in quite precise and non-metaphorical ways.

Next I shall try to show that these formulations can be made the basis of a model of the rule structure of a natural language (my use of "model" is further explained in Chapter 6) and to derive from the resulting model new solutions for a variety of philosophical problems concerning category mistakes, certain forms of necessary truth, synonymy, the logical status of conceptual analysis, and so on. Finally, I shall try to show that the model enables us to suggest answers to a number of questions raised by the study of transformational grammars concerning the relationships between syntax and semantics, and that it also enables us to propose new interpretations of some results uncovered by recent psycholinguistic studies of language learning.

1.2 So far as the ETL can be said to spring from a central idea, it is, I think, the double thesis that (1) to possess a concept is to "know the meaning of a word" in some sense which involves knowing how to use and understand it in all (or most) contexts; and (2) that to come to possess any concept ϕ is essentially to learn to recognize members of the class of objects, events, states of affairs, and so on, of which ϕ is the concept.

A form of this theory can be found remarkably clearly and persuasively expressed in H. H. Price's book, *Thinking and Experience*.

---

[2] "Language game" is not a happy term: language games are not, as has often been pointed out, all that much like games. In general, any phrase which ties our conception of linguistic rules to a particular metaphor is to be avoided. "Linguistic device" seems to me to be *almost* neutral in this respect and to have the advantage of already possessing some currency in philosophy.

The concept is not *before* the mind as an object of inspection. It is at work *in* the mind, but not as one inspectable content among others, as the traditional Conceptualists supposed. It shows itself not as a detectable item of mental furniture, but rather as a guiding force....[3]

It is the fact that we possess concepts that "keeps discourse on the rails," but the business of talking intelligently is nevertheless not to be thought of as a matter of uttering a string of vocal noises, which utterance is rendered intelligent, or "intentional," by being always accompanied by the simultaneous production, in what Ryle would call the "shadowy theatre of the mind," of a string of relevant concepts. Rather,

> in verbal thinking our concepts manifest themselves as guiding forces, directing the flow of words both public and private; as in image thinking they manifest themselves by directing the flow of images, and in intelligent action by directing the flow of muscular movements which are the successive stages of execution. If the reader is inclined to complain that on such a view verbal thinking is 'not in touch with reality', we remind him that concepts can be regarded as *memory*-dispositions, and that possessing the concept ϕ is equivalent to having a memory of what ϕ things are like. At any rate, that is what our basic concepts are, and all other concepts . . . are dependent in one way or another on these.[4]

As Price suggests at the end of the above quotation, the thesis that to know how to use a word is to possess a concept, and that to possess a concept is essentially to remember what a certain sort of thing is like, commits anyone who accepts it to the belief that some concepts are in some sense "primary," or more "fundamental," than other concepts: that some words are, in Price's phrase, "basic words." For clearly, it is implausible to say that knowing how to use so-called syncategorematic words like 'not', 'unless', 'however', or for that matter very abstract words like 'heterological', 'chiliagon', 'subsume', 'heretical', is a matter of remembering what certain sorts of things are like. The words which Price's account appears really to

---

[3] H. H. Price, *Thinking and Experience* (Cambridge, Mass.: Harvard University Press, 1953), p. 342.

[4] *Ibid.*, p. 350.

fit are those which, apparently, connote the qualities of immediate sensory experiences, for example, 'red', 'hard', 'slippery', 'cold'. It seems almost truistic to say that having the concept of redness or coldness is a matter of being able to remember what red things look like and what cold things feel like and, remembering this, to recognize red or cold things as red or cold. But when we try to extend this account to a syncategorematic word like 'not', and try to say what it is to possess the concept of negation, we find ourselves in difficulty. "It is a matter of being able to remember what negation is like, and, remembering this, to recognize negated things as negated" will hardly fill the bill, since it is not intelligible English. We might indeed try to turn it into intelligible English by construing it as "It is a matter of being able to remember what the negation sign looks like, and, remembering this, to recognize formulae which contain negation signs as formulae containing negation signs." But while this sentence states what most people would be prepared to admit as a necessary condition of someone's having a complete grasp of the concept of negation, it can hardly be taken as stating a sufficient condition. Similar difficulties arise in the case of abstract words. No doubt part of what may be meant when we say that someone understands 'heretical' or 'heterological' is that he is able to recall certain doctrines which he correctly believes to be heretical and certain words which he correctly believes to be heterological; and someone who can do this may in a perfectly straightforward sense be said to know "what (some) heterological or heretical things are like." But this will not help him to recognize further doctrines or words as heretical or heterological unless he also knows *what makes* the doctrines and words with which he is already familiar respectively heretical and heterological. But knowing *this* cannot be a matter of "having a memory of what ϕ things are like": on the contrary, it must (obviously enough) be a matter of knowing, and knowing how to apply, the verbal definitions of 'heretical' and 'heterological'.

The amplification of his thesis which these difficulties compel the empiricist theorist of language to make is obvious (and trivial) enough. Certainly, he can say, there are many words whose use can only be explained verbally. But verbal definitions and accounts of the uses of words cannot be given wholly in terms of words which themselves require verbal definitions or accounts of use. If language is to have any contact with the world (that is, is to be something more than an uninterpreted formal system, or a complicated word game), we must sooner or later reach a point in the explication of our more abstruse concepts at which the explication begins to be carried out in terms of immediate sensory experience: in terms, that is, of concepts like 'red', 'cold', 'dry', which can be regarded as dispositions to remember what ϕ things are like and to manifest such dispositions in recognizing ϕ things as ϕ things.

Basic concepts correspond in the ETL, then, to the points in language at which we make what D. F. Pears felicitously calls "the exit from the maze of words."[5] This exit is conceived by ETL theorists as a sort of flying leap: bits of language somehow become attached in the mind of the learner to bits of "the world." Different theorists differ as to the identity of the points of attachment in language. Price talks most of the time as if they are single words: 'red', 'dog', 'sky', and so on. But one can equally well hold, as Quine has done, that the points of attachment are sentences. Quine has argued that any developed language contains, on the one hand, sentences which acquire meaning by being linked directly with non-verbal stimuli (*via* some mechanism of conditioning), and on the other, sentences which derive their meaning from being associated with ("conditioned to") other sentences. Thus in a well-known passage he remarks:

> the power of a non-verbal stimulus to elicit a given sentence commonly depends on earlier associations of sentences with sentences. . . . Thus someone mixes the contents of two test tubes, observes a green tint, and says 'There was copper in it'. Here the sentence is elicited by a non-verbal stimulus, but the stimulus depends for its efficacy upon an earlier network of associations of words with words; viz., one's learning of chemical theory. . . .
>
> The intervening theory is composed of sentences associated with one another in multifarious ways. . . . There are so-called logical connections, and there are so-called causal ones; but any such interconnections of sentences must finally be due to the conditioning of sentences as responses to sentences as stimuli . . . .

[5] D. F. Pears, "Universals," in A. G. N. Flew, ed., *Essays on Logic and Language* (London: Blackwell, 1955), p. 63.

Theory may be deliberate, as in a chapter on chemistry, or it may be second nature, as in the immemorial doctrine of ordinary enduring middle-sized physical objects. In either case, theory causes a sharing, by sentences, of sensory supports. In an arch, an overhead block is supported immediately by other overhead blocks, and ultimately by all the base blocks collectively and none individually; and so it is with sentences, when theoretically fitted. The contact of block to block is the association of sentence to sentence, and the base blocks are sentences conditioned . . . to non-verbal stimuli.

Our example 'There is copper in it' is an overhead block, along with 'Copper oxide is green' and others. One of the base blocks is perhaps the sentence 'The stuff has gone green', a sentence directly conditioned to the sensory stimulation got from the test tube.[6]

It seems clear that although Price and Quine differ on the question of the identity of the linguistic entities which occupy the terminal points (or one half of the terminal points) of the associations which link language with the world, they are in substantial agreement on two considerably more fundamental matters: (1) both make a sharp distinction between utterances which possess meaning as it were "in their own right" ("basic words"; "base block sentences") and utterances which possess meaning solely by virtue of standing in some kind of relationship to some utterance or utterances of the first type (Price's nonbasic, abstract, or syncategorematic, words; Quine's "overhead blocks"). Thus, although Quine seems at times to take the view that the meaning of any utterance might in principle be learned through the conditioning of that utterance to nonverbal stimuli, he would certainly say, I think, that in any actual language only certain sentences will be learned in this way, and he would presumably have to hold that unless *some sentences or other* were conditioned to nonverbal stimuli, language would involve merely the eliciting by verbal stimuli of verbal responses: that is, it would be a formal game which might exhibit structure or pattern, but would possess no content (its utterances, that is, considered as a corpus of text, might possess a syntax, but would possess, taken individually, neither sense nor reference in the Fregean senses of those terms).

[6] W. V. Quine, *Word and Object* (Cambridge, Mass.: The M.I.T. Press, 1960), pp. 10–11.

And (2), both consider that what confers meaning upon such utterances as possess it in their own right is the fact that there exist associative linkages of some kind (for example, S-R linkages) between such utterances and the members of some favored class of extralinguistic entities (sense-data, particulars, relations, "fixed ranges of stimuli," or whatever). Both (1) and (2) are in my view fundamental tenets of the ETL.

1.3 Conceiving of the points at which language is put into connection with the world as sentences yields certain advantages when the empiricist theorist of language comes to confront the problem of accounting for syntax, and in general for the element of concatenation in language.

The fact that a child learning language *ab initio* becomes, after a finite period of time, able to construct indefinitely many original sentences (that is, ones which he has never heard—and which have perhaps never been produced), and in such a way, moreover, that each such sentence is appropriate to the particular environment of discourse in which it is produced, is one of the most obvious and remarkable facts about language. The theorist of language must therefore ask himself what is the basis of the ability to concatenate. Price's theory of concatenation is simply, so far as I can discover, that "concepts keep discourse on the rails." But concepts are memory dispositions corresponding to single words, so that we seem to need some further account of how a memory of what ϕ things are like, together with a memory of what ψ things are like, can amount to a knowledge of how to set about concatenating 'ψ' and 'ϕ' in discourse. Such an account is not too difficult to give, provided we are prepared to identify the points at which the exit from the verbal maze is made not as words but as sentences. Quine, in *Word and Object*, offers an account of this sort. After suggesting that some of the earliest verbal strings which a child learns are sentences, which may consist of one word—for example, 'Ouch', 'Red', 'Square'; or several—for example, 'My foot hurts', he remarks that:

> It is evident how new sentences may be built from old materials and volunteered on appropriate occasions simply by virtue of the analogies. Having been directly conditioned to the appropriate use of 'Foot' (or

'This is my foot') as a sentence, and 'Hand' likewise, and 'My foot hurts' as a whole, the child might conceivably utter 'My hand hurts' on an appropriate occasion, though unaided by previous experience with that actual sentence.[7]

For Quine, then, a child's earliest lessons in language are lessons both on the interconnection of words and on their connection with the world. Explicit explanations of syntax are not, or not in principle, required, since information about syntactic relationships is built into the fundamental units of language which the child learns to connect with elements of the world, and can be extracted by the child himself from these fundamental units by analogical reflection upon the nature of the circumstances in which he is taught to utter them. The sentences formed in this way resemble the sentences— 'Ouch', 'My hand hurts', etc.—which are explicitly taught to the child, in being linked, like them, to fixed ranges of nonverbal stimuli. Moreover, the set of initially learned sentences of this type and the set of sentences formed from them by analogical substitution together make up a set of sentences any member of which *could* be taught directly to the child by associating it with a fixed range of nonverbal stimuli; it is, in fact, a matter of chance which members of the total set any particular child is explicitly taught and which he constructs himself by analogically guided substitution.

This account does seem to fill the gap between the ability to identify referents and the ability to concatenate, but the relationship between it and Price's bare assertion that "concepts keep discourse on the rails" may not be obvious. What relates them is, it seems to me, the fact that both articulate—Price's in brief and aphoristic form, Quine's in more detail and with some show of scientific (or at least behavioristic) rigor—a very ancient and fundamental empiricist doctrine about the nature of structure in natural languages and its relationship to meaning. Put briefly, this doctrine asserts that there are some questions concerning the concatenation of the elements of a natural language which could, at least in principle, be settled merely by establishing associative linkages between some elements of the language and some extralinguistic existents.

[7] *Ibid.*, p. 9.

Again it may not be immediately obvious what this claim amounts to. Perhaps we can get clearer about its implications if we consider an alternative theory which we have as yet no reason to regard as the true one, but which at any rate might conceivably be true. It might be the case that one could list the rules of a language in their entirety, and that each of the sentences in this list would have the overall form of a prescription or injunction: that is, no indicative sentence would occur in the list unenclosed in a prescriptive matrix. Associations between language elements and world elements might be represented in the list by imperative or prescriptive sentences (thus: "'ϕ' is to be associated with x," "Associate 'ϕ' with x"), but many of the rules of the language would not express associations of this type. We need not suppose the list to be unstructured (that is, to consist of logically discrete items): it might, for example, be ordered into hierarchically arranged subsystems of rules, like certain sorts of computer programs; some of the rules might mention other rules; or still other forms of internal ordering might be exhibited by the list. It might further be possible to show that all questions concerning concatenation (for example, the questions (1) whether 'John frightens sincerity' is a permissible concatenation of the expressions 'John', 'frightens', and 'sincerity' or not; and (2) why 'Sincerity frightens John' is a permissible concatenation of those expressions while 'John frightens sincerity' is not) could in principle be answered by reference to the list. That is, for each phenomenon of concatenation requiring explanation it would be possible to give a perfectly satisfactory explanation which would refer only to the presence of some item or items in the list, or to the structure of the list itself, or both. It is clear that, in the event of these possibilities being realized, we should have shown that no question concerning concatenation in that language depended in any way upon the truth or falsity of any contingent proposition expressible in the language, except for propositions concerning the structure of the list of linguistic rules, or the presence in or absence from the list of certain rules. If we were prepared to accept a version of the Tractarian distinction between *showing* and *saying*, we could, indeed, dispense with the final clause of the previous sentence. We could say that questions concerning concatenation never depend upon the truth or falsity of any contingent proposition expressible in the language, because what such questions depend upon is either expressible only in sentences which do not express propositions (for example, the prescriptive or gerundive items of the list of rules), or does not need to be expressed in words at all, but merely "shows itself" (for example, the structure of the list, which does not consist of further sentences over and above the sentences which comprise the items of the list; or the identity of the items of the list, which is shown by the list itself without the need for a further set of propositions of the form "____ is a member of the list").

It is clear, now, that if anyone claims that some questions about concatenation in a language are settleable merely by establishing associative linkages between some elements of the language and some extralinguistic existents, this commits him to the further claim that *some* questions concerning concatenation *do* depend upon the truth or falsity of contingent propositions other than propositions about the structure or contents of the list of rules of the language. We can see this if we consider a hypothetical language set up by establishing associations between two phonemic strings, 'ϕ' and 'ψ', and two extralinguistic existents, x and y. This language will have, *ex hypothesi*, two rules, which may be stated as

(1) 'ϕ' $\longrightarrow$ x

(2) 'ψ' $\longrightarrow$ y

where $\ulcorner$'a' $\longrightarrow$ $b$$\urcorner$ may be read as $\ulcorner$'a' is to be associated with $b$$\urcorner$ or any other formula of similar intent. We now assume it to be the case, merely in virtue of our stipulation of (1) and (2) as rules of the language, that the concatenation of 'ϕ' and 'ψ' in that order (namely, '$\phi\,\psi$') has a sense, while the reverse concatenation, '$\psi\,\phi$', is senseless. We can now reasonably ask why, given the rules of the language, this should be so. And clearly, whatever answer we give, it cannot merely consist in the assertion that rule (1) occurs in the list of rules of the language, or that rule (2) occurs in the list, for (1) and (2) merely record decisions to associate language elements and world elements and can thus throw no light on the question why the language elements in question should concatenate in one way rather than another. Similarly our answer cannot merely consist of statements about the structure of the list of rules of the language, for the list has no structure: it consists simply of (1) and (2) in juxtaposition. Nor can we suppose that the language contains a further rule forbidding the concatenation '$\psi \phi$': *ex hypothesi*, (1) and (2) are the only rules. It follows that the fact that '$\phi \psi$' has a sense while '$\psi \phi$' has none must depend upon some fact or facts about the empirical nature of x and y, for no other possibility remains open to us. The facts about the concatenation of 'ϕ' and 'ψ' could be explained, that is, only by pointing to certain contingent facts about x and y, and hence it would follow that, for the language defined by (1) and (2), certain questions about concatenation would depend upon the truth or falsity of contingent propositions other than propositions about the rule system constituted by (1) and (2).

We must now justify the claim that Price and Quine are both committed by their views to the doctrine that some questions concerning concatenation are settled the moment we establish associative linkages between some language elements and some world elements, and its rider to the effect that some questions of concatenation depend upon the truth or falsity of contingent propositions other than propositions about the contents or structure of systems of prescriptive rules. Price is pretty clearly committed to this doctrine by his thesis that concepts are what guide the flow of thought and discourse, given his view of what concepts are. To be able to recognize ϕ things as ϕ is to possess a disposition to associate 'ϕ' with ϕ-ness: if this is enough to dismiss certain concatenations of names of basic concepts as senseless—and I think we must assume that it is, since presumably there will exist levels of thought and speech which make use only of basic concepts, and presumably not all concatenations of names of basic concepts will have sense ('red sound', for example, will not, though 'red door' will)—then this must be because ϕ things are, as a contingent matter of fact, the sort of things which it would be for some reason absurd to characterize as ψ, for some values of 'ϕ' and 'ψ'.

What chiefly distinguishes Quine's account of concatenation from Price's is Quine's suggestion that the child can, in effect, be presented with paradigms of correct concatenation through the association of simple sentences, as well as single words, with fixed ranges of stimuli. Quine supposes that the child will then be able to construct new sentences "by analogy" with these paradigms. Quine's theory nonetheless manifestly involves the claim that the setting up of associations between linguistic and extralinguistic entities may be sufficient in principle to determine questions of concatenation, since the dispositions to associate 'hand' with hands, 'foot' with feet, and 'My foot hurts' with pains in his feet, which *ex hypothesi*, comprise the child's entire linguistic equipment prior to the point at which he spontaneously volunteers the sentence 'My hand hurts', are, after all, just associations, of a sort which Price would no doubt have to identify as concepts in his sense of the term. We could write the rule of Quine's child's language prior to his first venture into originality as follows:

(1) 'foot' $\longrightarrow$ $\langle s'_1, \ldots, s'_n \rangle$

(2) 'hand' $\longrightarrow$ $\langle s''_1, \ldots, s''_n \rangle$

(3) 'My foot hurts' $\longrightarrow$ $\langle s'''_1, \ldots, s'''_n \rangle$

where the notation to the right of the arrow represents what Quine calls a "fixed range of stimuli." Let us suppose, now, that the child, having assimilated these rules, knows that 'My hand hurts' is a permissible concatenation of 'My', 'hand', and 'hurts', whereas 'hurts hand My' is not. He cannot have derived this information from any of the three rules of his language taken separately, for each of these rules tells him simply to associate a certain utterance with a certain fixed range of stimuli and none of the utterances in question happens to be 'My hand hurts', or for that matter 'hurts hand My'. Nor can he have derived it from the structure of the list of rules, for the list is unstructured. Now I think it is obvious enough that what Quine has in mind when he speaks of the child building a new sentence from old materials "simply by virtue of the analogies" is something like the following. The child sees that each member, s'''_m, of the stimulus range $\langle s'''_1, \ldots, s'''_n \rangle$ includes within itself as a part some member, s'_m, of the stimulus range $\langle s'_1, \ldots, s'_n \rangle$ and that s'_m is always related in a certain way to the other elements of s'''_m. The child sees further that the word associated with the stimulus range $\langle s'_1, \ldots, s'_n \rangle$ is present in the phrase associated with $\langle s'''_1, \ldots, s'''_n \rangle$ and that this word, similarly, stands in a certain relationship to the remaining elements of the phrase. The child now encounters members of a new stimulus range $\langle s_1'''', \ldots, s_n'''' \rangle$, the members of which exactly resemble the members of $\langle s_1''', \ldots, s_n''' \rangle$ except that where each of the latter contains a member of $\langle s_1', \ldots, s_n' \rangle$ standing in a given relation to its remaining elements, each of the former contains a member of $\langle s_1'', \ldots, s_n'' \rangle$ standing in exactly the same relation to *its* remaining elements. The child sees that the relationship between s_m' and s_m''' is represented by the relationship in which 'foot' stands to the remaining elements of 'My foot hurts', and hence he argues that the identical relation obtaining between some s_m'' and the remaining elements of each s_m'''' can, *by analogy*, be represented verbally by allowing 'hand' (that is, the word associated with $\langle s_1'', \ldots, s_n'' \rangle$) to replace 'foot' in 'My foot hurts' so that, in effect, 'hand' stands in the same relationship to 'My' and 'hurts' in which 'foot' stands to them in 'My foot hurts'. The child has now, *by analogy*, arrived at a sentence which he can associate with $\langle s_1'''', \ldots, s_n'''' \rangle$; so the list of rules of his language is now expanded to include

(4) 'My hand hurts' $\longrightarrow$ $\langle s_1'''', \ldots, s_n'''' \rangle$

Now it is evident that, on this view, what brings it about that 'My hand hurts' is a sensible concatenation of elementary signs whereas 'My foot hand' is not, is simply the contingent fact that members of some classes of stimuli, but not others, happen to occur as elements of the members of certain other classes of stimuli, standing in certain relationships, but not in others, to the remaining elements. 'My foot hand' is a senseless concatenation of elementary signs, in other words, simply because stimuli of the range corresponding to 'hand' never, as a matter of fact, stand to stimuli of the range corresponding to 'My foot', in the relationship in which stimuli of the range corresponding to 'hurts' often stand to these latter stimuli. It follows, I think, that we can fairly ascribe to Quine, as to Price, the doctrine that some questions of concatenation depend on the truth or falsity of contingent propositions other than propositions about the contents or structure of systems of prescriptive rules.

In the process of discovering this, we have also uncovered a further implication of the doctrine itself. If some questions of concatenation depend on the truth or falsity of propositions about extralinguistic matters, it follows that the contents of the list of rules of a language must depend not merely upon human convention but upon how the experienced world is actually constituted. That is, we might make an empirical discovery which would, without the need for any stipulation on our part, and as it were, without our volition, *have the effect of altering*—extending—the rules of our language. That this follows is intuitively obvious if we reflect that possibilities of concatenation must in some way be marked by the rules of the language: the rule system cannot simply be *indifferent* on the question whether a certain concatenation is feasible or not, for otherwise it will not be at all obvious that we ought to identify it as a representation of *the rules* of the language in question. If concatenation depends in part on the nature of the world, then, if that nature changes or turns out to be other than we had supposed, this change or discovery will simply appear as a change in our representation of the rules of the language. What *sort* of change depends on what sort of representation of "the rules" one opts for, and on how it represents concatenation. Thus for Quine the change will appear as the addition of a new rule of the same type as (1)–(4). For Price it will appear as a change in the content of the range of entities with which some basic word or words is associated through a memory-disposition. The point is, *whatever* mode of representation we choose, if questions of concatenation are ever dependent upon matters of extralinguistic fact, then it will necessarily prove impossible ever to complete the job of representing within that mode "the rules of a language"; for linguistic inquiry will, after a certain point, fuse with empirical inquiry in general, so that a complete account of the rule structure of language will prove to be available only as a by-product of a complete account of "the world." Such a dependency between concatenation and empirical fact need not be fatal to the autonomy of linguistics or necessarily to the idea that it is possible to complete the description of "the grammar of a language," provided we continue to formulate the program of linguistic science in ways characteristic of the type of descriptive linguistics of which Bloomfield is a leading representative. What such a dependency would entail, in Bloomfield's terms,[8] is

_____

[8] Leonard Bloomfield, "A Set of Postulates for the Science of Language," *Language* (1926), pp. 153–164, def. 2.

that the membership of the class of constructions of a language would be subject to variation contingent upon the state of empirical knowledge of the speech community using that language. But Bloomfield has defined a *language* as "the totality of utterances (that is, acts of speech) which can be made in a speech-community"[9] where "can be made in a speech community" means roughly (my paraphrase) "will elicit a consistent reaction from other members of the speech community when uttered by one of their number." It follows that if the number of constructions in a given language increases, the number of utterances which can be made in the speech community of that language also increases (provided we avoid questions of infinity by requiring utterances to consist of not more than, say, 10^6 words); and we can simply refuse to recognize the resulting totality of utterances as constituting the same language as that constituted by the totality of utterances which could be made in the same speech community prior to the increase in the number of constructions.

Alternatively, one could make it a matter of definition that the grammar of a language is independent of any change in the extra-linguistic world, by refusing to consider as a *grammatical* fact any linguistic fact which is not independent of the world. Thus Martin Joos, in a well-known paper, remarks that

> all phenomena . . . which we find we cannot describe precisely with a finite number of absolute categories, we classify as non linguistic elements of the real world and expel them from linguistic science.[10]

Chomsky and other generative grammarians have, however, a more radical conception of the task of linguistics. They see it as the task of representing and explaining every aspect of a native speaker's linguistic competence in terms of an internalized system of generative rules. Now, clearly, a native speaker's linguistic competence includes his capacity to recognize the correctness or incorrectness of *any* concatenation of the basic signs of a language. It follows that if any

---

[9] *Ibid.*, def. 4.

[10] Martin Joos, "Description of Language Design," in Martin Joos, ed., *Readings in Linguistics*, vol. 1 (Chicago: University of Chicago Press, 1966), p. 351.

questions concerning the correctness or incorrectness of concatenations depend upon the truth or falsity of propositions about matters of extralinguistic fact, then the program of generative-transformational linguistics must be incompletable, since the content of a speaker's linguistic competence (that is, which expressions he recognizes as well-formed expressions of his language) will depend, not—or not entirely—upon a system of internalized rules, but in part upon the, in principle, indefinitely variable content of his experience. Hence, although it would not be fatal to some programs for linguistic science if the ETL were true, it would be fatal to the program of generative grammar.

1.4 The two doctrines about concatenation which we have been considering must, it seems to me, be held in some form by anyone who accepts that "meaning," in the full-blooded sense of that term in which to know a word's meaning is to know how to deploy it in discourse, is introduced into a language through the association of basic utterances with elements of the world. For if one accepts this view, then either one must simply say, with Price, that we know how to deploy words in discourse because we know what they *mean* (that is, refer to) or else, with Quine, that the child is presented with paradigm examples of correct concatenation in association with fixed ranges of stimuli and that he determines what further sentences can and cannot be constructed on the model of these paradigms, by reference to the composition of the members of the ranges of stimuli with which the paradigms are associated (which, after all, is as much as to say: by reference to *his memory of what the realities associated with particular utterances are like*).

It might appear that there is a third alternative: that of treating all questions of *meaning* in the sense of *what names stand for* as determined by a basic level of associative conventions, and all questions of *use*—or how names can be concatenated in sentences— as determined by a second level of "rules of use" superimposed upon the primary associative level and containing stipulative rules of various sorts. It might then be possible to show that all questions of concatenation depend simply upon the fact that we (or "the linguistic community") have legislated in certain ways with regard to the uses of words, although the actual *meanings* of words—the *content* of our discourse, as distinct from its syntactic *form* or *structure*—depend purely on association. But, as we shall see in Chapter 5, this alternative turns out to be thoroughly incoherent.

The theory of concatenation characteristic of the ETL contains a third component which we have not so far touched upon. We can best introduce it through the consideration of a possible objection to what I have said so far. It might be urged that I have no grounds for supposing that Quine is committed to the belief that the rules of a language are things of the type designated by (1)–(4), for no one can believe what is manifestly absurd, and it is manifestly absurd to call such things "rules," for they are not *rules* at all, but at best schematic representations of stimulus-response connections. Moreover, Quine would never wish to say that the rules of a language comprise only, or for that matter any, "rules" such as (1)–(4). For obviously Quine would not deny that any natural language exhibits a highly complex implicit structure of syntactic, morphological, and phonological rules. Indeed, Quine's position might perhaps be better expressed by the formula: "There are rules of language, but there are no semantic rules."[11]

Now, part of this objection is merely terminological, and part of it is not. There is a certain license both in philosophical usage and in everyday English for calling the sort of things designated by (1)–(4) *rules*. They are somewhat similar in form to Carnapian "semantic rules," for example, and they also rather resemble some of the more trivial rules—we might call them "ground rules" of a board game such as chess: for example, the rule that the expression 'Queen' designates an object of a certain conventional shape. Moreover, I would not think there could be much doubt that the existence of the relationships schematically represented by (1)–(4) is important to Quine's theory of semantics in the ways we have so far suggested. However, if one thought that, on Quine's view, one could describe the syntactic, morphological, and phonological rules of a language without referring in any way to such relationships, and if one thought that all of these undoubted "rules of language" were of a quite different logical form from (1)–(4), then one might well want to

---

[11] I am indebted for this formulation, which I think is quite accurate, to Professor J. M. E. Moravcsik.

reserve the term "rule of language" for the rules of syntax, morphology, and phonology, and to deny its application to the conventional associations which introduce meaning into a language. This is
the substantial part of our hypothetical objector's point, and this
part of his point is well taken. Quine could claim that it is possible
to make an absolutely clear-cut distinction between on the one hand
the syntactic, or morphological, or phonological rule systems of a
language, and on the other hand its semantics. For on his view, all
that one can say about the semantics of a language is that certain
utterances are as a matter of fact conditioned to nonverbal stimuli
and certain utterances to verbal stimuli. And certainly it would seem
possible in principle to discuss syntax and morphology, for example,
without mentioning relationships of conditioning, or associations,
at all, for the rules of syntax and morphology are not concerned
with associations, but with relationships holding between structurally
defined classes of expressions.

In the same way, any upholder of the ETL can, and most do,
uphold a rigid distinction between syntax and semantics, and it is
the upholding of such a distinction which constitutes the third element of the ETL, considered now as a theory of concatenation, to
which we referred earlier. It is important to see that what is at issue
in this distinction, as it is usually maintained, is merely the question
of whether the form and content of an adequate syntactic description
of a language can be clearly distinguished from the form and content
of an adequate semantic description of the same language, and not
the deeper question of what relationship, if any, there is between
the contents of one type of description of a given language and those
of a description of the other type. What the ETL theorist holds, in
other words, is that, since the semantics of a language has to do only
with associations between words and things, or between sentences
and things, or between sentences and sentences, whereas what
syntax has to do with is, roughly, the ways in which the members
of certain structurally defined classes of words or morphemes can and
cannot stand in relationship to one another in sentential contexts,
syntactic description can proceed without ever mentioning any point
of semantics, and vice versa.

So much, then, for the substantial part of our critic's objection.
On the verbal question of the application of the term "rule" I shall

conclude against him, for the following reason. The fundamental question which will concern us is that of the nature of linguistic convention, including the conventions which introduce meaning into a language. We need some general term to designate everything which is, or could be regarded as, a conventional stipulation accounting for any feature of a natural language, and "rule of language," although slightly tendentious, has no obvious alternatives. Later on we shall distinguish various kinds of "rule" more precisely. Using this terminology we can say that the empiricist theorist of language holds that the fundamental conventions which introduce meaning into a language (semantic rules) are all of the same type as (1)–(4), but holds that there exist also, for example, syntactic rules, which are of a radically different type, and that, hence, the syntax of a language can be described fully without saying anything about its semantics. And this seems to express his position well enough.

<h1 style="text-align:center">1.5</h1> Let us return now to Price's version of the ETL. To possess a basic concept 'ϕ' is, according to Price, to possess the ability to recognize ϕ's as ϕ's—an ability which the learner acquires by being made acquainted with a range of ϕ things which are designated as 'ϕ' by his teachers. The model of the fundamental moves in language learning with which Price is here presenting us is the familiar one of ostensive definition. According to this model in its simplest form, we are to picture a parent taking the first step in teaching his child the use of language as directing the child's attention, by pointing or some other device, to a paradigm series of red things—tomatoes, roses, Cardinals' hats—and solemnly pronouncing the word 'red'. The ritual elements of this picture are not essential to the model. We need not suppose that parents utter the first words their children learn with the explicit intention of teaching the children their meaning or that any stereotyped gesture is made. All that we need to suppose is that objects are somehow brought to the attention of the child at the approximate moments when their names are uttered. Thus a child who is frequently handed a spoon, which he needs to begin his dinner, at the moment when the word 'spoon' is uttered in his hearing, may be having the word 'spoon' ostensively defined for him.

This account of language learning raises at least the following three obvious questions:

(1) How does the child know that a given noise uttered by its parents is a *name*, rather than an expression of emotion (like a cluck of disapproval or a friendly babble) or a sign of some impending event (dinner, a walk)?

(2) How does the child know that the way to discover what a name names is to look for that property or combination of properties common to all objects in the paradigm series?

(3) How does the child know that the word 'red' uttered in association with a presented paradigm series means 'red' and not 'object', 'colored', 'pretty', 'surface', and so on, since the objects in the paradigm series, though certainly all red, are equally all objects with pretty colored surfaces?

I do not think that any of these questions as they stand would necessarily put a determined supporter of ostensive definition at a loss for an answer, and I introduce them here mainly as a means of directing the discussion toward getting clearer about what is involved in the theory of ostensive definition. The least useful question to consider for this purpose is (3); accordingly I shall defer it to Chapter 3 and occupy myself here with (2) and (1). An answer to (2) would, I think, have to run roughly as follows. Much human thinking, so far as it is concerned with the interpretation of our environment, is inductive in character. Coming to know, for example, that a certain sort of cloud presages rain is a matter of inductively abstracting from a range of situations in which such clouds have appeared the one circumstance—rain—which has invariably, or almost invariably, accompanied their appearance. The learning of language is a further exercise of the innate human capacity to perform this sort of inductive abstraction. Thus Price:

> The ground, and not merely the origin, of taking 'cat' to mean objects like Pussy and Tabitha and not objects like Fido or Tray, is the ostensive process of noticing the objects in whose presence this sound is commonly uttered by our neighbours, and generalizing inductively from what we have noticed; it is the observation of constant conjunctions, as it is also the observation of constant conjunctions which is our ground for thinking that ice floats in water.[12]

[12] Price, p. 223.

The answer to question (2) is, then, that the child does not have to learn or be told that the way to discover the meaning of a word is to abstract what is common to all the situations in which it is uttered. The capacity and the tendency to do this are both part of his innate behavioral–mental equipment—part of what constitutes his "intelligence."[13] Similarly, to turn to question (1), the child does not need to be told (and indeed, how could he be "told," prior to the acquisition of any understanding of language?) that 'cat' is a *name* or that the performance of ostensive definition is a conventional procedure for establishing the meaning of a word. Learning which elements of a range of complex environmental situations which include the utterance of the word 'cat' are constant and which are variable *is* learning the use of the word 'cat' as a name for the constant elements in such situations. And just because it is a natural function of the child's mind to deal with its experience in this way, it is not wholly true to say that ostensive definition is a "conventional procedure." We may indeed conventionalize ostensive definition by reducing it to a stereotyped ritual. Thus, a teacher may point ceremoniously to a series of geometrical figures and say with appropriate gravity "These are all *triangles*." But such conventions rest on the foundation of the naturally inductive bent of the human mind; hence it is not necessary for a small child to understand the significance of the pointing gesture, or the conventional emphasis in the schoolmaster's intonation, for him to come to know by experience what 'dinner', 'walk' and suchlike words mean.

It is important, in view of the arguments which will be presented in later chapters, to notice how Price's account of the ostensive acquisition of the basic words of a language depends for its explanatory force on an appeal to innate capacities of the human mind. For Price, the most fundamental rules of a language are not conventional but "innate" and "natural" in this sense: that the performances by which we teach a child his first words (for example, saying 'bottle' while giving him his bottle) require no conventional rules by reference to which the child is to interpret the significance of such performances; rather such performances, as it were, implicitly

---

[13] For an elaborate development of this sort of account of the relationship between language and intelligence, see John Holloway, *Language and Intelligence* (New York: The Macmillan Co., 1951).

contain their own rules of interpretation, given the innately inductive character of the child's mind.

We shall find that, almost without exception, the explanations of linguistic phenomena offered by theorists within the empiricist tradition explain what they are supposed to explain only if we take it for granted that the faculty of inductive abstraction is all that a child requires in order to extract knowledge of linguistic relationships from the observed linguistic behavior of his elders. Consider, for example, Quine's remarks on analogical substitution, quoted earlier. It is "evident" to Quine that a child who has been "directly conditioned to the appropriate use of 'Foot' (or 'This is my foot') as a sentence and 'Hand' likewise, and 'My foot hurts' as a whole," may "simply by virtue of the analogies"[14] volunteer 'My hand hurts' on an appropriate occasion, even though the child has never been conditioned to utter that particular sentence. But it is surely not, on the face of it, evident that this must happen or is even likely to happen. We can perhaps see what Quine might reply to this, if we abandon for the moment the language of behaviorism and think of the child as if he were, *per impossible*, a small anthropologist consciously reflecting on the language of the curious large beings among whom he finds himself. The process of reflection through which a child will have to go in order to arrive at 'My hand hurts' as an utterance appropriate to a pain in his hand will presumably be roughly as follows: (1) utterances of 'foot' are rewarded only in situations which include his foot as an element; (2) 'foot' plus 'hurts' is rewarded only when there is a pain in his foot; (3) the hypothesis that 'foot hurts' denotes his foot can thus be eliminated, and the hypothesis that 'hurts' denotes the pain can be adopted; (4) by elimination, 'foot' must denote his foot. By a similar process of reasoning the child can also conclude (5) that 'hand' denotes his hand and (6) that he can therefore tentatively conjoin 'hand' and 'hurts' to produce an utterance appropriate to the situation in which his hand hurts.

We need not, of course, seriously adopt the absurd theory that the child consciously reasons along these lines. No doubt what we have been doing is only to write out, *as if* they were steps in a conscious

---

[14] Quine, p. 9.

process of reflection, the stages in the complex process of inductive abstraction which a child naturally and instinctively carries out at the subconscious or behavioral levels. But it is only if we add some such gloss as this to Quine's account of the genesis of sentence construction that Quine's account becomes in any sense an *explanation* of the ability to construct sentences which one has not been specifically conditioned to utter. If we can assume that a child will instinctively perform some such complex act of inductive abstraction, or its behavioral analogue, then we can give some concrete meaning to the thesis that he sees the appropriateness of 'My hand hurts', given his grasp of 'foot', 'hand', and 'My foot hurts', "simply by virtue of the analogies." And if not, not: for if we cannot put this sort of construction on the phrase "by virtue of the analogies," then this phrase becomes simply a tendentious way of stating the puzzling facts about the genesis of the ability to construct original and appropriate sentences, without contributing anything to the explanation of those facts.

It is worth noticing that such appeals to the capacity to perform inductive abstractions generally serve more than one theoretical purpose, or, to put it another way, block more than one awkward question which might otherwise be put to the theorist. We can see this if we reflect that we might construct an alternative to Price's account of how a child comes to learn the meanings of names. In this alternative account we would have two postulated innate capacities where Price has one (since we are in any case constructing purely speculative theories, postulates may be inserted at will). These postulates would be: (1) an innate grasp of 'the concept of a name'; and (2) Price's capacity to abstract inductively. We would refer to postulate (1) when we wanted to explain *how the child knows what the outcome of a given piece of inductive abstraction is to be*: for example, the establishing of the meaning of a name, rather than the establishing of the status of one type of natural event as a sign of—that is, as presaging, or indicating the simultaneous occurrence of—another. And we would refer to postulate (2) when we wanted to explain how the child knows how to set about establishing the meaning of a name, given that that is a goal which—thanks to postulate (1)—the child can envisage.

In Price's account, now, a single postulate, roughly equivalent to

(2), performs both the theoretical functions performed separately by (1) and (2) in the above account. And similarly, in Quine's account of how a child gets his first understanding of syntactic relationships (assuming that Quine would accept our gloss on his words), an appeal to abstraction—to the noticing of common properties of various stimulus ranges which constitute the circumstances of utterance of various phonemic strings—answers both members of the pair of questions: (1) How does the child know that his parents' speech exhibits any syntactic relationships at all? and (2) How does he discover what they are?—the answer to (1) being, presumably, that to notice relationships of the sort to which Quine's account implicitly refers just *is* to notice syntactic relationships.

In the construction of speculative theories, postulates may be introduced at will; but it is nonetheless important to inquire whether a given postulate can really bear the burdens placed upon it by the theory. In what follows I shall try to show at length that the postulate of an innate tendency for the child to process his experience in inductive or abstractive ways is incapable of bearing any of the various theoretical burdens which the ETL places upon it.

1.6   The concern of ETL theorists with inductive abstraction may, I think, help to render intelligible their recurrent interest in the idea that it may be possible to understand meaning and reference in terms of mental imagery. The theory that, to put it crudely, "the meaning of a word is a mental image" is thought to be refuted by the observation that we often talk intelligently without entertaining any imagery at all. But this objection is only conclusive against one form of the theory: the form in which it states, in effect, that the difference between words spoken with understanding and words merely parroted, is that the former are the verbal expression of a stream of images which accompany the words and constitute the "thought" to which the words give voice. Locke, no doubt, held some such theory as this, but it is not necessary for the image theory to be held as a theory of intelligent utterance. It can equally well be held as a theory about the nature of language. In this form it tries to explain what sort of device language is, and the answer which it gives to this question is that language is a system of noises arbitrarily assigned to stand as token substitutes for images.[15] The whole point of tokens is that they can be used in the absence of the currency that they represent: thus, as we become more facile in using words, the laborious passage from image to image and from image to words tends in both discourse and thought to become telescoped so that we pass directly from word to word. This does not mean, however, that language is independent of imagery, for if we never cashed our words against images we would never come to use them in uncashed "purely verbal" thinking and talking. As we have seen, according to the ETL a noise acquires the status of a basic symbol by being associated with a series of paradigm objects and situations. The process of definition is complete when the learner can apply the newly defined word correctly: that is, to objects and situations which resemble the members of the paradigm series in just the respects and degrees in which they resemble each other. And, again as we have seen, it would be a mistake to look for a *learned* rule of use by reference to which the learner interprets the series of paradigms: a rule, that is, which guides him in the passage from applying the noise to specifically designated members of the paradigm series to applying it to other objects or situations of the same general sort. If we ask what enables the learner to make this passage, we can only point to the innately inductive character of human intelligence. As Price remarks in another context:

> We shall have to suppose . . . that the human mind has an innate (un-acquired, unlearned) tendency to notice and remember . . . this special sort of likeness-situation, where there is one likeness in the midst of many unlikenesses. This situation is not so alarming as it looks. It only amounts to saying that intelligence itself is an innate or unlearned capacity. For the noticing and remembering of likeness-situations of this sort is the indispensable first step in conceptual cognition.[16]

Suppose, now, that the learner is shown a paradigm series of actual objects and situations ("the object series"), but that no noise is associated with the series. Instead, the learner is able to produce at

[15] This, it seems to me, is the theory of image thinking to be found in Price's *Thinking and Experience*.

[16] Price, p. 71.

any time a series of mental (or, for that matter, physical) pictures ("the image series") representing the objects or situations in the object series and having the same internal resemblance-relations as it. There seems, now, to be no reason why the image series should not fulfill in the learner's thinking all of the functions normally fulfilled by an ostensively defined noise. Admittedly the mechanism of symbolization would differ in the two cases. The noise would symbolize by serving as an associative substitute for the object series whereas the image series would symbolize by picturing the object series. But the process of interpreting the image series in applying it to new perceptual situations would be an inductive process exactly paralleling the process of interpreting the object series in learning to apply a basic word correctly and, like it, would be dependent not on a learned rule of use but simply upon the fundamentally inductive character of human thinking. In a sense, that is, the image series by its nature prescribes its own use. Someone who can produce such sets of images to order is able, in effect, to recapitulate the process of ostensive definition whenever he pleases; and it is difficult to see why a process of thought in which the function of basic symbols is fulfilled by such pictorial recapitulations of ostensive procedures should not be as efficient as one in which the link between basic symbol and ostensive procedure is a merely associative one.

In short, the image theory of meaning is not, as many philosophers nowadays seem to think, an isolated curiosity of thought, but a natural and inevitable outgrowth of the ETL.

1.7 We are now in a position to list the main doctrines composing the ETL. I have tried to exhibit in the foregoing sections some of the theoretical connections which unite these doctrines into a single theory of language, but at this point it seems desirable to get a clear view of what it is that the theory asserts. This—the essential skeleton of the theory—seems to me to be comprised in the following tenets.

Tenet 1: The utterances of a language can be divided into basic and nonbasic utterances. (Different empiricist philosophers differ about the
basis of this distinction, but not its feasibility. Thus for Locke
some concepts (ideas) are inherently basic (simple); for Quine the

basic–nonbasic distinction is one which is settled *de facto* for each language learner by the nature of his particular history of language learning: any utterance *might* be 'basic' for me but in fact only some are.)

Tenet 2: It is only through the basic utterances that meaning enters a language, which would otherwise amount merely to a system of inter-verbal relationships.

Tenet 3: The form of the conventional stipulation in virtue of which meaning attaches to a given basic utterance of a language is exactly the same as that of the stipulation which attaches meaning to any other such utterance. Every such stipulation stipulates simply that a given language element shall henceforth be associated with a given world element. It follows that differences of meaning can never arise as the result of differences in the form of the rules attaching meaning to different utterances but only as a result of differences in their content: that is, differences in the identity of the terminal points of the associations involved.

Tenet 4: At least some questions concerning the ways in which the basic utterances can and cannot be concatenated to form compound utterances are settled merely by virtue of the fact that we have established conventions of the type described in tenet (3) to the effect that the basic utterances in question are to be associated with given elements of the extralinguistic world. Tenet (4) is crucial to the ETL, since it justifies the claim that what the learner learns when he acquires a disposition to associate a given word or utterence with a given set of stimuli is "the meaning of a word (utterance)" in a sense of that phrase strong enough to include the ability to use the word or utterance, and to understand its use, in discourse.

Tenet 5: What is included in the list of rules of a natural language depends not merely upon what conventional stipulations language users choose to make, but also in part upon how the world is, as a matter of empirical fact, constituted. Thus, one could never complete the task of listing the "rules of a language" in the liberal, but not, I think, overliberal, sense of "rule" explained earlier.

Tenet 6: A sharp and clear distinction between the syntactic rules of a language and its semantic rules can be drawn as follows. A semantic rule is simply a conventional association between some element of language and some element of the world. A syntactic rule is concerned solely with "relationships between signs": that is, it instructs the learner to combine, or to refrain from combining, certain signs with certain other signs. Presumably, though conventional formulations of the distinction seldom make this clear, syntactic rules must have some such form as the following:

(1) "Always combine *a* with *b* according to schema *s*."
(2) "Never combine *a* with *b* according to schema *s*."
(3) "Combine (Refrain from combining) *a* with *b* according to schema *s if you wish to construct a grammatical sentence* (phrase, utterance)."

Tenet (6) enables the holder of the ETL to concur with the descriptive linguists' view that the *grammatical* rules of a given language can be studied without reference to semantic intuition.

Tenet 7: The conventional stipulations which introduce meaning into a language make up an unstructured list: that is, a list of logically discrete items. 'Semantic rules' of the type envisaged by the ETL cannot logically conflict with or be logically entailed by each other; nor, for that matter, can they exhibit the weaker relationships of mutual reference and presupposition exhibited by the rules which go to make up cooking recipes, computer programs, or the instructions for playing card games. The fact that I have already chosen to set up one or more associations between basic utterances of a language and elements of the world places no restrictions whatever on the setting up of further associative linkages. It follows that, just as differences of meaning never depend upon the form of semantic rules (if the latter are conceived in the manner suggested by the ETL), but only by their content, so concatenation remains unaffected by the form of these rules, although it may, as we have seen, depend in part upon their content (that is, upon the empirical nature of the termini in the world of language–world linkages).

Tenet 8: The information which a learner acquires in learning a language, including both (1) the information that certain very general types of linguistic relationship (syntactic relationships, the relationship between a name and its denotation) exist; and (2) specific information concerning what relationships of these types exist in a given language, essentially *amounts to* a set of inductive generalizations. It is important to see here that what ETL theorists maintain is not merely that, *as a matter of fact*, language acquisition can take place solely through the agency of an innate faculty of inductive abstraction. They certainly do maintain this, but their ground for maintaining it is precisely that *what* is learned in learning languages is essentially a set of inductive relationships.

A child in learning its native language must pass in some way from merely hearing blocks of sound to hearing the same blocks of sound as semantically and syntactically interpreted; that is, as a piece of discourse. The ETL theorist holds, now, that the process of arriving at such an interpretation is an inductive process and holds, moreover, that what the learner acquires as the outcome of this process is not merely a habit of performance or a disposition to take one event as a sign of another (which are the sort of things that one might reasonably, *prima facie*, expect him to acquire as a result of such a process), but something more mysterious and intrinsically linguistic in nature: namely, a grasp of *the meaning of a word*, or *the syntactic role of an expression*, or *the syntactic structure of a sentence*. That the ETL theorist sees nothing odd, or demanding explanation, in the supposition that a grasp of meaning and syntax issues from an essentially inductive process of interpretation, is a consequence of the fact that his theory elsewhere represents a knowledge of both meaning and syntax as *amounting to* a knowledge of inductively ascertainable relationships between linguistic signs and their circumstances of utterance. This assimilation is primarily what we shall be questioning in the succeeding chapters.

2 Signs and images

2.1 In Section 1.5 we distinguished between knowledge that a given noise is a name (or, more generally, an utterance in a language) and knowledge that just such a noise is an inductive sign.[1] It is not, of course, obvious that any such distinction can be made, and many philosophers have in fact held that verbal utterances are signs and that natural languages are systems of signs. This thesis, if correct, would tend to support tenet (8) of the ETL by diminishing the number of theoretical burdens which the postulate of an innate capacity to perform inductive abstractions must bear. For if utterances are signs, then learning *what* a particular utterance signifies—learning its "meaning"—just is learning what function it has in the language as a whole (that is, the function of signifying what it signifies), so that there remains no gap between coming to understand the *possibility* of utterances having *types* of function in language and coming to understand that a particular utterance

[1] In the sense of 'sign' employed by Price (*Thinking and Experience*) or, with considerably more technical apparatus, by Charles Morris in "Foundations of the Theory of Signs," in *International Encyclopedia of Unified Science* (Chicago: University of Chicago Press, 1955), *Signification and Significance* (Cambridge, Mass.: The M.I.T. Press, 1964), and elsewhere.

possesses a particular function of one or another of these types. And of course both types of understanding can, if the sign theorist is correct, be very plausibly represented as flowing from the performance of acts of inductive abstraction.

There are, it seems to me, three main objections to be brought against the inductive sign theory. These are that the theory fails to offer a satisfactory account of

(1) the element of originality and creativeness in our use of language;
(2) what takes place when a linguistically competent adult recognizes as ill-formed a grammatically or otherwise ill-formed sentence; and
(3) the distinction between understanding what it is that an event portends and understanding what it is that a sentence asserts.

I shall briefly summarize these objections in that order.

2.2 Learning that something, x, is a *sign*, is a matter of learning, through repeated experience, that there is a standard correlation of some sort between the occurrence of x and that of some feature of the world not identical with x. It is obvious that this process will be involved equally in learning that x is a sign *of* something (for example, that daffodils are a sign of spring) and in learning that the occurrence of x serves as a sign *to* some organism.

For example, suppose a man buys cheap off a tramp a dog which happens to be a stolen sheepdog. This dog, unbeknown to its new owner, has been trained to respond to a fairly complex system of whistle signals. To his surprise the owner discovers that the dog will always come to heel in response to a whistle of a certain sort, and from then on he discovers, by trial and error, a range of other signals to which the dog responds in various ways. It will be worth looking at some features of this situation. First of all, the owner clearly cannot know beforehand that a given whistle will have a given effect, or any effect, on the dog. Before he can use a given whistle to signal to the dog he must find out, by a process of trial and error, whether, and how, the dog will respond to that particular whistle. Second, even when he has discovered several signals to which the dog is disposed to respond, he cannot add a further signal to the list without a further period of trial and error.

We may contrast the situation of the owner of the stolen sheepdog with that of an anthropologist who is investigating a previously unknown human language. After a certain period spent acquiring the elements of the language, the anthropologist can begin, at first hesitantly and then with greater confidence, to construct, *without any period of trial and error*, utterances which are designed to have certain effects on his native hearers, and which do in fact have those effects. He says, perhaps, "Bring me the machete from the rafters of the house," even though he has never heard or uttered this particular string of phonemes before, knowing that it will elicit from his hearers the response which it does elicit. It might be objected that this is only true if one makes certain very naive assumptions about human intercourse. The natives may not bring the machete on demand, for they may consider it demeaning to do so, or fear that they may be attacked if they do, or consider a direct request impolite. Surely the anthropologist will have to use trial-and-error methods to discover the best way of obtaining the machete (which may not be the obvious one of asking, straight out, for it) just as the sheepdog's owner has to use trial-and-error methods to discover the best way of getting the dog to come to heel.

This argument rather supports than rebuts my point. There is an obvious distinction between *telling* someone to do something and *getting* him to do it. What the anthropologist must discover by trial and error is how to *get* the native to bring the machete. This is an inquiry into the native's outlook, manners, and social conventions; it is not an inquiry into the rules of his language. Discovering how to *tell* (instruct, beg, wheedle, suggest, and so on) a native to bring a machete *does* involve conducting an inquiry into the rules of his language, but this inquiry, as we have seen, is not one which proceeds, at least beyond a certain point, by trial-and-error methods. In the case of the stolen sheepdog, of course, no distinction between *telling to do* and *getting to do* can be drawn. This is because the possibility of making such a distinction depends on our being able to establish the meanings of utterances in other ways than by considering how those to whom the utterances are addressed respond to them. In the case of human languages this is possible: even though none of the natives respond appropriately to the anthropologist's innocent request for the machete (because, for example, they are bitterly

offended by a stranger's *making requests*), the anthropologist may
be in no doubt as to the *meaning*, given the rules of the language, of
what he has just said—he may indeed say later, "It was my asking
for a machete that made them throw me out of the tribe." But in the
sheepdog example, if the dog fails to do anything in response to a
given whistle, all we can conclude is that this particular whistle was
not, after all, an item in the unknown trainer's repertoire of signals.
Again, if the dog growls or shows anger in response to a given whistle,
we must conclude simply that this is the signal for getting the dog to
bark or show anger. In short, we can assign "meanings" to the
whistles that the owner tries out on the dog only by reference to what
the dog does in response to those whistles: hence, the distinction
between *telling to do* and *getting to do* has no application to situations
of this sort. It is clear, also, that in no sign situation, if we understand
this term in any of the strict technical senses which it bears in the
writings of sign theorists, can there be any criteria for regarding
something, x, as a sign having a certain significance, except the fact
that certain organisms behave in certain ways in response to occurrences of x. I conclude that the distinction between *telling to do* and
getting to do cannot have any application to any system of signs, if we
define *sign* as sign theorists do define it. And this seems to me to
amount to strong *prima facie* grounds for doubting whether a natural
human language can possibly be, in that sense, a system of signs.

2.3   A fluent speaker of a language is
able not only to construct grammatically correct and appropriate
utterances in that language, but to recognize as ill-formed those
utterances which are grammatically or in other ways incorrect. The
resources of a theory of signs, it seems to me, will allow us to formulate only one sort of explanation of this fact: namely, an explanation
in terms of the disappointment of conditioned expectations. The
sign theorist must make the claim, to put it in its crudest form, that
what is recognized by the speaker who recognizes a grammatically or
otherwise incorrect expression *as* incorrect, is that the expression is
unusual, or unexpected, or unconventional. But put thus crudely,
his explanation explains too much, for a great many perfectly well-
formed expressions may be unusual or unexpected or unconventional.
The sign theorist must thus look for a tighter formulation of his

point. It is not difficult to see how this next formulation will run. It will consist of the claims (1) that grammatical rules are conventional, and (2) that learning the grammatical conventions of a language involves learning that certain expressions cannot follow certain other expressions, where "cannot" is to be construed as equivalent to "do not, in the speech of native speakers." But (1) and (2) together entail the view that knowing AB to be a grammatically or otherwise well-formed expression is a matter of knowing that AB has occurred in the speech of some native speaker or other. Hence, on the sign theorist's present view, knowing that AX is an ill-formed expression (grammatically or otherwise) is a matter of knowing that AX does *not* occur in some very long disjunction of expressions $AB \lor AC \lor AD \lor \ldots$, whose disjuncts include among their number every expression which can be formed by the operation of adding to A any other (grammatically and otherwise) well-formed expression capable of being formulated in the language wherever this operation yields a product which a native speaker will admit as (grammatically and otherwise) well-formed.

There are at least two considerations which count against this theory. The first, most obvious, objection is that such a theory entails the view that in order to accurately distinguish against improper sequentia of A, the speaker must have been conditioned to admit as well-formed expressions beginning with A all, and only, the contents of the disjunction $AB \lor AC \lor AD \ldots$. But it is surely obvious that even if we put some arbitrary limit on the length of the expressions which we can combine with A to compose disjuncts, the length of the disjunction $AB \lor AC \lor AD \ldots$ will for any natural language be for all practical purposes infinite (imagine, for example, that A is "a" and the language English). No native speaker could possibly have been conditioned to expect all, and only, the contents of such a disjunction, since any given native speaker would in actuality never have heard most of them. I can tell that "a whereas" is wrong (unless "whereas" is, or is intended to be construed as, in quotes), although I have never become acquainted with more than a small minority of the vast number of correct English expressions beginning with "a."

The sign theorist might try to evade this conclusion by elaborating a version of his theory constructed in terms of grammatical categories. All the fluent speaker needs to know, he may contend, is that the indefinite article must be followed by either a noun or noun phrase, and so on. This gives us a comparatively short disjunction. We can quite easily, perhaps, imagine a child abstracting disjunctive rules of this type from a fairly limited array of examples of correct utterances; and they need only be combined with a set of criteria for assigning expressions to grammatical categories in order to be sufficient to guide him in all future linguistic contingencies.

But this line of argument will not work, for a quite simple reason. Any set of *general* criteria for assigning expressions to grammatical categories must refer to the fact that certain expressions can or cannot be combined in certain ways. What we mean to convey, for example, by grouping certain expressions as noun phrases is (among other things) that native speakers do as a matter of fact consider it incorrect to combine any of them in certain ways with certain other expressions. It is quite unhelpful, therefore, to attempt to explain the native speaker's ability to see at first sight that a given combination of this sort would be incorrect by reference to his (putative) knowledge that it involves a noun phrase, for it is *because* he sees (among other things) that that combination would be incorrect, that the expression involved *is* a noun phrase.

The sign theorist can still, of course, claim that his hypothetical set of disjunctive rules framed in terms of grammatical categories is to be conceived as supplemented, not by a set of general criteria for assigning any given expression to a grammatical category, but by a straightforward list arbitrarily stating the grammatical category of each and every expression capable of being formulated in the language. But this move, as well as bringing into the open certain difficulties conncected with ambiguity and context dependency of grammatical category, renders the sign theorist's position open once more, because of the enormous length to which such a list would have to run, to our original objection to the disjunctive-rule thesis.

A second objection to the disjunctive-rule thesis is, it seems to me, that if it were true, all judgments about the correctness or incorrectness (grammatical or otherwise) of utterances would be in the nature of, and would possess all the tentativeness and uncertainty commonly (and no doubt rightly) attributed to, inductive generalizations of the 'All swans are white' variety; whereas it seems plain that some, at least, are not inductive generalizations of that sort at all but possess a kind of certainty and finality which such generalizations lack. Occasionally we do reach conclusions about correct usage in the way which the disjunctive-rule model describes: I may doubt, for example, whether I ought to say "the committee believe" or "the committee believes" and I may decide the issue in ways (for example, looking up what old Jones put in the last lot of minutes) which amount to inquiring what is the customary usage of other native speakers. And where my experience of the usage of other native speakers in this respect is limited or fragmentary, or where I have reason to doubt whether they are any less illiterate or incapable of speaking standard English than I am, I may be in serious doubt about the outcome. But cases like this are exceptional. I know straight off, for example, that

(1) Tomorrow will be a sufficient day to do the shopping

(2) Look, a balloon proceeding in the direction of up

(3) I rapidly saw him getting out of the taxi

are wrong and are not to be accepted on the analogy of

(4) Tomorrow will be a good day to do the shopping

(5) Look, a balloon proceeding in the direction of Manchester

(6) I distinctly saw him getting out of the taxi

despite the fact that in two of these pairs the words substituted might be thought to have the same grammatical function. I know this, moreover, simply by reflection on the proposed sentences themselves (I don't propose to discuss until Chapter 11 what sort of reflection this is) without asking myself whether any of them has actually been used by a native speaker of English and without casting anxiously about in my memories of talk about balloons, shopping, and taxis to see if I can recall anything of the sort having been said by anyone of my acquaintance. If I were to ask questions of this sort as a means of coming to a decision about the wrongness of such utterances, my judgments of wrongness would *always* take some such form as "I'm pretty sure people never say ..." or "I don't think one would say ..." But in the case of (1)–(3), for example, what we would normally say is "This *just isn't* an English sentence." Moreover, if we were to find (1)–(3) printed in some eminently respectable work on the English language, put out by the Oxford University Press under the aegis of a glittering body of scholars and linguists, we would not, I think, be cowed into accepting them but would take them for misprints or errors in the proofreading. And, in our letter pointing them out to the editors, I think we would either claim or take it for granted as obvious to any intelligent native speaker that the English words *sufficient, up,* and *rapidly cannot* occur in the contexts in which they are placed in (1)–(3) and not just that they never do. What the force of this sort of "cannot" is we shall have to examine later.

2.4   There is, it seems to me, an important distinction to be drawn, which the sign theory obscures, between an event's being a *portent* and its being the vehicle of an affirmation. I can perhaps explain this distinction as follows.

Suppose I am taken to a bad Ruritanian operetta, in Serbian or some such language. It is very dull, and the only thing that sticks in my mind is that whenever one or other of the characters calls out "Zhivio!", a white-haired gentleman in a preposterous uniform comes on stage with a little retinue and harangues the crowd. I conjecture, reasonably enough, that "Zhivio!" means something like "Here comes the mayor," but I find out after the performance that "Zhivio!" is really Serbian for "Down with the aristocrats." It seems that we can make a distinction between what *zhivio* means to a Serbian speaker, and what it "means" (in the inductive sign sense) to me. It might be argued, however, that the distinction is only possible because of the limited nature of the situation. The Serbian speaker, it may be said, differs from me only in that he has been exposed to the full range of events which tend to follow utterances of "Zhivio!" while I have been exposed only to a very limited segment of this range. The difference in our understanding of the meaning of "Zhivio!" does not represent two different senses of meaning but only a difference of extent in our experience of using utterances of "Zhivio!" as bases for inductive inference.

But at this point, it seems to me, the sign theorist goes too far. The difference between the Serbian speaker and me *can't* be that the Serbian speaker is aware of *more* things that might be inferred or expected on the basis of hearing the utterance "Zhivio!" than I am, for it is just in the relative poverty of the inferences which they permit that verbal utterances differ from inductive signs. When Jones says to me "There is an alligator in the bath," there are a number of things that I can infer from this string of sounds *taken as a physical occurrence*. I can infer that Jones is frightened, that he is adenoidal, and astonished, that he comes from Newcastle, that he has been taking elocution lessons, that he will appear round the bend of the stairs in thirty seconds, and so on. On the other hand if I take the same sounds *as constituting the vehicle of an affirmation*, then only one thing follows; namely, that unless Jones is lying there is an alligator in the bath. Jones has told me only that there is an alligator in the bath, but the peculiar properties of his utterance, considered as a physical event, have revealed to me a number of other things.

I can see no way in which one could, within the resources of a theory of signs, distinguish between what I shall call the *content* of an utterance and the *embarras de richesse* constituted by the multitude of inductive inferences which it may be possible to draw from the fact of its occurrence. A consistent sign theorist could have no reason, that is, for saying that "There is an alligator in the bath" *means There is an alligator in the bath* any more than it means *Jones has adenoids* or *Jones will round the bend in the stairs in thirty seconds*. But this is plainly absurd. Signs *reveal* or *indicate* or *show*. Sentences *assert*, or *state*. Hence I can distinguish between what I infer from a person's behavior, or from *the fact that* he says something, and what he (*by* saying something) *tells* me. Any adequate theory of language must explain the ground of this distinction; but sign theory plainly cannot.

2.5   It will be worth concluding this chapter of preliminary criticisms of the ETL with some remarks on the version of the image theory of meaning which we formulated in Section 1.6. It will be recalled that this version of the theory claims that the functions of ostensively defined basic symbols in a language could equally well be served by sets of pictures, and it is immaterial whether the pictures in question are mental images, paintings, photographs, or any form of physical representation or replica.

Some types of image are, however, uninteresting to an image theorist of this sort, because their meaning can be understood only in the context of a pre-existing linguistic culture. Ideographs are an extreme case; here, more or less highly stylized pictures serve simply as conventional marks for utterances in a spoken language; but there are many other situations in which we make use of pictures which require interpretation in the light of specific and often involved conventions and which serve in effect as shorthand devices for avoiding long and elaborate verbal explanations. Let us call pictures of this kind *schematic pictures*: examples of schematic pictures include the use of contour lines and crossed swords to represent hills and the sites of battles on maps; the diagrams which accompany chess problems or instructions for assembling electrical circuits; the pictures on seed packets (the convention here is that the picture is not merely decorative, like the pictures on matchboxes, though like them it does not represent the actual contents of the packet). With schematic pictures we may contrast pictures whose function is simply to simulate visual experience: for example, a Canaletto or a good photograph of the temples at Abu Simbel. Pictures of this kind, which I shall call *portrayals*, do not need to be interpreted by reference to a conventional rule: if I can recognize men in real life, then I can recognize them when they are depicted in good photographs, drawings, or paintings, whereas the ability to recognize the slopes of the hills above Ullswater may be no help at all if I am presented for the first time with a contour map of the area and asked to identify a certain spot on it.

The image theorist claims, in effect, that (1) the role of basic symbols in our private thinking could in principle be played by sets of portrayals. Claim (1) commits the image theorist to the further claim that (2) it is only by an accident—the contingent fact that the only portrayals which human beings can produce at will are private ones—that the presentation of protrayals does not occur as a form of communication between men, paralleling the more basic forms of communication by language. Here, it seems to me, the theory is vulnerable. When we consider actual cases which involve the interpretation of presented portrayals we find, I think, either that the portrayals in question have no *meaning* in any sense which is not trivial or irrelevant to the understanding of language, or else that they have a meaning only through being involved in contexts of social and linguistic convention to such an extent that we must regard them as schematic pictures.

If we are to take claims (1) and (2) seriously, we must imagine two people showing each other sets of portrayals but having no other intercourse of any kind with each other, since the thesis of (1) and (2) is precisely that there might in principle exist some very basic form of communication—corresponding to those forms of verbal communication which make use only of basic verbal symbols—involving only such showings.

Such situations, though rare, sometimes occur. We can, for example, imagine a road sign which simply portrays a tree. What are we to say is the meaning of such a sign? It might mean that one is in a managed forest where fires are forbidden ("Keep Our Forests Green"); or it might mean that saplings are for sale nearby; or, like a bush over the door, that the new wine is in. We can only interpret such a sign by postulating something about the man who put it there: that he is a forester, an innkeeper, a nurseryman, or something of the sort. Once we have made such an assumption we can assign a meaning to the pictured tree: it means "Don't light fires" or "New wine here." But we can only discover whether our interpretation is correct by exploring the situation further: if we come across a band of foresters roasting an ox, then evidently the picture did not mean what we thought it meant; perhaps after all it meant "recreation area." One may contrast this situation with the interpretation of a sign written in English. We do not need to guess at the intentions of the painter of the sign to know that it says, for example, "Beware of the bull"; in fact the meaning of the sign itself gives us a strong clue to the painter's intentions. Moreover, if inspection discovers no bull in the vicinity we may suspect on this ground that the sign may be obsolete, but never that it says anything other than what is does say.

I don't think these remarks need to be modified to meet the case of a man exhibiting a series of protrayals resembling each other in one and only one respect. Here again, interpretation depends on what intention we take the exhibitor to have in showing the pictures. Are they intended to form a narrative? Is he simply showing us pictures of the nine cats of different breeds that he has at home, depicted in a variety of attractive postures? Are these plates from a work on the domestic cat? Is he advertising a pet shop where all these breeds can be bought? Are the pictures ideographs, and if so, does each picture, or some set of pictures, stand for a single idea?

Two points need to be made here: (1) the exhibitor cannot make his intentions clear by showing more pictures, because the more pictures he shows the greater becomes the range of possible motives that we can impute to him; and (2) it is not at all probable that someone unfamiliar with empiricist theories of language would interpret the exhibitor's performance as an attempt to utter the general term *cat*. Perhaps indeed the performance is an attempt to comment on the presence of a cat or cats which the exhibitor can see but which are invisible to the person to whom he shows his pictures; but is there just one cat or as many cats as there are pictures? Once again, we can only tell whether we have interpreted the exhibitor's intention correctly by exploring the situation further in ways which go beyond the showing of more pictures. It is important to see that (1) these explorations would be undertaken not only to establish the *truth* of the exhibitor's pictorial "utterance," but to establish its *sense*, and that this sharply distinguishes the situation from one in which someone uses the general term "cat" to draw attention to a cat invisible to his hearers; and that (2) although such explorations might enable us to tag each picture or set of pictures with a verbal equivalent, such a tagging would amount only to treating the pictures as ideographs, that is, as schematic pictures. What is wrong with the image theory, it appears, is not just that some rule of use is necessary to determine the purport of an image, but that the rule in question cannot be identified with the innate and unlearned tendency of the human mind to interpret its experience inductively.

If showing a set of pictures just does not amount to uttering a general word (except where prior convention has established the pictures as an odd kind of ideograph), let alone to asserting something about the objects pictured, then it is hard to see why philosophers should have imagined that thinking might, even in principle, be *simply* a matter of contemplating an inward show of pictures. The temptation to say this stems in part from puzzlement about the relationship between thought and its objects, together with the persistent feeling that it might be possible to understand this relationship in terms of the relationship between pictures and thing pictured.

Pictures are not just dead objects: they do have *reference*, in a sense, to something beyond themselves. Surely the fact that we are shown, for example, a picture of a tree tells us quite a lot about the intentions of the person who shows it: such a picture *naturally suggests* certain things—forestry, timber, recreation—and it is precisely this element of natural suggestion which leads people to choose it as a sign of these things. The plausibility of this argument rests, it seems to me, on a covert transition from talking about the relationship between a picture and what it portrays to talking about the relation between objects and the situations which experience has taught us to associate with them. A tree to us means timber or picnics in forest glades; to a nomadic tribe which, for example, disposed of its dead by putting them in trees, it might mean something very different. Two points should be noticed: (1) one does not have to know sociological facts of this kind to understand an utterance in the language of such a tribe, though ignorance of them may well lead to puzzlement about the implications of certain utterances; and (2) a picture of a tree which "signifies," in the sense that we have been discussing, a recreation area or a graveyard, could be replaced, with no loss of symbolic function, by a real tree. (A real or a pictured wagon wheel does equally well, for example, as a sign of a wheelwright's shop.) In other words, the process of inductive generalization and inference operates on perceived objects, and it is simply irrelevant whether these are real or pictured ones. It cannot (except by a special and highly artificial convention) operate through the " picturing relationship " as a rule for increasing the specificity of the reference supposedly involved in that relationship. In fact, once we disentangle picturing from inductive signification it becomes difficult to see how we are to take the assertion that a picture *qua* picture " has a reference beyond itself," except as a highly tendentious way of saying that a pictured object is not a real object. Pictures are not unusually ambiguous symbols whose denotation just needs to be made more specific: they have no denotation and they are no more (if no less) symbolic than the objects which they picture.

3 Ostensive definition

3.1 The arguments of Chapter 2 suggest that there is something radically wrong with the traditional theory of ostensive definition. If showing pictures of a series of paradigm objects, or, for that matter, exhibiting a series of actual physical paradigm objects, does not amount (in the absence of a special convention established by the parties who thus choose to communicate in this way) to uttering a general word, then it is hard to see what is gained, from a theoretical point of view, by representing general words as associative substitutes for series of paradigm objects or by representing all our linguistic capacities as expressions or by-products of a supposedly fundamental, but seemingly wholly mysterious, process of establishing "associative linkages" between noises and series of such paradigms. We have now to pursue this suggestion.

What is involved in ostensively defining a word? There is a celebrated passage from St. Augustine, which opens Wittgenstein's *Philosophical Investigations*. Here Augustine says that a child is taught language *ab initio*—that is, from the stage at which he has no grasp of any language whatsoever—in the following way: adults point to an object, direct the child's attention to it, and pronounce a word; in this way the child learns the name of the object.

Part of Wittgenstein's argument against this account of language learning has become a philosophical commonplace. It is the objection that in order to understand such a definition the child must know what aspect of the designated object he is supposed to attend to. If I point to a red football and say "red," am I to be understood as meaning "This *color* is red," "This *shape* is red," "This *object* is called 'a red'," "*The manner of joining the segments of this object* is called 'red'," or what? (The list is virtually endless; compare the cases where *red* is taken to mean "new," "fun to play with," "a present from Daddy," "standing on the hearthrug," and so on.) In order to understand such a definition, in other words, the learner needs to know which *logical type* the word *red* belongs to: whether the noise being defined is to function as a color word, or a name of a kind of physical object, or a commendation, and so on.

This argument seems to show that the successful practice of Augustinian ostensive definition will only be possible if the learner already has some grasp of language, and thus to disqualify Augustine's theory as an account of *ab initio* language learning.

At *Investigations* I.33 Wittgenstein argues against an obvious and tempting objection to this conclusion:

Suppose, however, someone were to object: "It is not true that you must already be master of a language in order to understand an ostensive definition: all you need—of course—is to know or guess what the person giving the explanation is pointing to. That is, whether for example to the shape of the object, or to its colour, or to its number, and so on."——And what does 'pointing to the shape', 'pointing to the colour' consist in? Point to a piece of paper.—And now point to its shape—now to its colour—now to its number (that sounds queer).—How did you do it?— You will say that you 'meant' a different thing each time you pointed. And if I ask how that is done, you will say you concentrated your attention on the colour, the shape, etc. But I ask again: how is *that* done?[1]

[1] Ludwig Wittgenstein, *Philosophical Investigations*, 3rd ed., trans. G. E. M. Anscombe (New York: The Macmillan Co., 1953; Oxford: Basil Blackwell & Mott, Ltd., 1958).

We are tempted, perhaps, to give various forlorn-hope replies to this last question: "I do it by screwing up my eyes . . . by following the outline with my eyes . . . with my finger . . . by sedulously *not* looking at the outline but trying instead to see the object *just* as a colored surface." But Wittgenstein can counter with a variety of other embarrassing questions ('How can one point to a piece in a game *as a piece in a game*'—*Investigations* I.35, for example), the tendency of which is to suggest that (1) there is no single performance of any given kind which characteristically accompanies all "acts of attending," and that (2) even if there were a peculiar sort of performance, say, running one's finger round an imaginary outline in the air, which invariably accompanied the act of attending to the shape of an object, and even if both the teacher issuing an ostensive definition of a word such as *square* and the pupil to whom he was attempting to teach the meaning of this word, normally and characteristically exhibited this performance when performing such an act of attention, this would still not necessarily prevent the pupil from misunderstanding the definition. "Cannot the hearer still interpret the definition differently, even though he sees the other's eyes following the outline, and even though he feels all that the other feels?"—*Investigations* I.34.

3.2 I find this train of argument inconclusive. Someone who accepts the theory of ostensive definition, although perhaps not Augustine's version of it, can reasonably object that no teaching process can be logically immune from being misunderstood. All that we can demand is that, in practice, most of the pupils will sooner or later grasp what the teacher intends them to grasp. In the case of ostensive definition there are a number of ways in which we can mimimize misunderstandings even if we never wholly eradicate them or make them logically impossible. For example, the problem of how the child is to know *what* is being singled out as an object of reference[2] can be reduced by the nature of the particular situation in which the word is uttered. For example, when a small baby is preoccupied with a bottle or a doll, it is not likely that it will

[2] Here I am following Price (*Thinking and Experience*).

associate the words *doll* or *bottle* with the meniscus of the fluid in the bottle, or the color of the doll's eyes, or with anything but the doll and bottle as *objects*, even though these are logically possible misunderstandings. Other ways of reducing the possibility of misunderstanding are (1) increasing the number of ostensive definitions and the range of nonessential characteristics in which the paradigm objects differ from one another; and (2) supplying what information theorists call "negative feedback," either by explicitly saying to the child, for example, "This is not a cat"; or by implicitly criticizing (for example, by errors in response, failure to understand) the child's attempts to make use of the word in simple conversational situations.

All these refinements of ostensive technique require us to make certain assumptions about the child's general intelligence and his ability to grasp various sorts of relationship, but any theory of *ab initio* language learning must involve similar assumptions. The demand that we go on elaborating our account of the rules and procedure involved in the initial teaching of language to the point at which we can see the *logical* necessity of a child's learning to use language, provided he is exposed to a teaching process that embodies just *these* rules and procedures, is at root an absurd one. Every teaching procedure can be misunderstood, and if we attempt to exclude any given theoretically possible misunderstanding by elaborating a further procedure, we shall find that it is logically possible for this procedure also to be misunderstood. Thus, we shall be led by way of a vicious regress to the absurd conclusion that the learning of language can never get started at all.

There seems, then, to be nothing to be gained by attempting in this sort of way to go beyond the traditional empiricist account of the initial learning of language; and indeed, it is very difficult to see how one could go beyond it: if the connection between language and the world is not established by some form of ostensive definition, then how conceivably could it be established?

3.3 Let us try to get clearer about the character and assumptions of the account of ostensive definition which we have just elaborated. We seem to be faced at least with a distinction between what Price calls *ceremonious ostension*, where the burden of directing the learner's attention falls upon an actual pointing gesture of some kind, and what I shall call *circumstantial ostension*, where this burden is borne by whatever can be assumed about the natural instincts, concerns, or intentions of the learner in the particular set of circumstances surrounding the issuing of the definition (see the baby-and-bottle example). It is implausible to suppose that the learner acquires an understanding of any word from a single ostensive definition of either sort. What is more likely is that his understanding of the meaning of the word will gradually develop through a series of such definitions. During this process what will happen is that the learner will inductively abstract from the very different circumstances of the various definitions just what is common to all of them. What the learner acquires by this means—or rather, what he gradually comes to approximate more and more closely to—is a grasp of the sufficient and necessary conditions for application of the word to new objects: that is, to objects which have not explicitly been pointed out during the defining process as objects to which the word properly applies. The conditions for correct application of a word so defined can thus always be stated in terms of similarity; for example, for an object to merit the application of the term "red" it is necessary (and sufficient) that it should be similar to those objects $O_1, O_2, \ldots, O_n$, by reference to which the word *red* has been adequately defined, in just those respects in which $O_1, O_2, \ldots, O_n$ are similar to one another. An "adequate" ostensive definition will of course be one which results in the learner acquiring habits of using the word *red* which exactly parallel those of the other members of his linguistic community. And, of course, negative feedback of the kinds mentioned in the last section can be introduced to make a process of ostensive definition more adequate: that is, to help the learner to approximate more rapidly to a complete grasp of the necessary and sufficient conditions for the correct application of the word by expressly ruling out his first fumbling and mistaken hypotheses about the character of the similarities holding between $O_1, O_2, \ldots, O_n$, and by rendering his later and better-founded hypotheses more precise.

At this point, I think, it will be clear that ostensive definition as we have defined it could proceed without anyone consciously occupying the role of teacher. Price is of the same opinion.

The truth seems to be that certain recognisable sounds gradually sort themselves out from the different complex utterances in which they are constituents. And the common factor, e.g. 'cat', in these otherwise unlike utterances is gradually correlated with a common factor in observed environmental situations which are otherwise unlike. Similarly 'black' gradually sorts itself out from another range of utterances which are otherwise unlike, and is correlated with a visible quality experienced in otherwise unlike situations.[3]

3.4 Augustine's theory of ostensive definition is more or less of a straw man. The theory which we have developed (with much assistance from Price) in the preceding two sections is to my mind a much more formidable one, which evades the conventional objections to accounts of initial language learning in terms of ostension. Its intrinsic connections—which I hope are by now sufficiently obvious—with the main body of the ETL make it part of a larger, and not unimpressive, structure of theory. We must now examine its defects.

In general, what seems to me to be wrong with the theory is not that it fails to explain how an ostensive definition of the meaning of a word can be made sufficiently unambiguous for practical purposes, even when dealing with a learner who knows no language whatsoever; but that it fails to explain why a learner who knows no language whatsoever should ever come to take any ostensive procedure as constituting a *definition of the meaning of a word*. There is, for example, a gap, which the theory fails to fill, between, on the one hand, *attending to an event and drawing inferences from the fact of its occurrence*, and on the other, interpreting it *as an utterance of a name*. If it in fact happens that a child hears the word 'bottle' uttered at all and only those times when a bottle is present or when one is just about to appear, one can see why the child should come to take the noise 'bottle' as a sign that it is about to be fed. One would expect, that is, some sort of reflex response connected with the expectation of food to become conditioned to the noise " bottle " as stimulus. But why should the child take the noise " bottle " as a word meaning "bottle"? To say that it is because the child is *attending* to the bottle merely

[3] Price, p. 215.

deepens the mystery: what is there about the mental act of attending which is capable of turning a noise into a word, like the blow of a sword turning a man into a knight? Perhaps it is the element of inductive abstraction that is important, and not the element of attending. But now we are in difficulty again, for if this is so, then the theory of ostensive definition can explain only the acquisition of a system of inductive signs; and we have already shown, in Chapter 2, that a system of inductive signs is not a language. Theorists of ostensive definition generally fail to see this because they blur the distinction between inferring from a given event that another given event is occurring or about to occur, and inferring the identity of the referent of a name from various executions of a naming process. Before a learner can perform inferences of the latter kind, he must have grasped that what he is witnessing *is* a naming process, and, to understand this, he must somehow have grasped the essentially linguistic ideas of *naming* and of *reference*. The theory of ostensive definition throws no light whatsoever on the acquisition of these ideas.

If we try to describe what must happen in the process of ceremonious ostensive definition without illicitly assuming that the learner innately or by some inexplicable means already possesses the concepts of naming and reference, we shall arrive at something like this: the learner observes that the people about him indulge in a ritual of extending the arm from the shoulder (one may substitute any other deictic gesture here). Why, one may ask, should the learner take any notice of these performances at all, and more particularly, why should he ever begin, himself, to utter such noises? It will not help here to say that it is because the learner has an innate capacity to perform inductive abstractions; all that this will explain (if it explains anything at all) is why the learner begins to take the noises as inductive signs, or how, once he has already begun to imitate his teacher's performance, he discovers which noises are appropriate to which perceptual situations. The obvious answer to our second question is that the teacher praises and otherwise rewards the learner for making noises. Given this additional piece of explanatory machinery (which is, it is worth noticing, foreign to the theory of ostensive definition *per se*), one can see how the child may learn to do various things. He may begin to make the arm-extending gesture himself, uttering a noise as he makes it. At first his utterance of noises may be haphazard, but differential reinforcement after the manner of Skinner will no doubt gradually bring him to utter each given word only when certain given perceptual conditions are satisfied. In the same way he will pick up from his teachers new noises-to-utter-while-extending-one's-arm.

We must now look closely at the limitations of what the learner has acquired by these means. He has acquired the habit of making a certain gesture while making a noise drawn from a repertoire of noises, the choice of noise being governed by rules which make reference to the occurrence or nonoccurrence of perceptible events. Let us label this the *pointing ritual*.

Obviously, much more is involved in the ability to use and understand a language than the ability to perform the pointing ritual. But we cannot, by examining the pointing ritual, get any clue as to how someone who had acquired the ability to perform it might go on to acquire any wider linguistic capacities. In explaining the acquisition of the pointing ritual we have explained *only* the acquisition of the pointing ritual. We have contributed nothing whatsoever to the understanding of the acquisition of language. The pointing ritual is in this sense *circumscribed*.

It might be that with a little ingenuity, without extending our stock of explanatory principles, we might succeed in showing how the pointing ritual could be developed into something with wider implications for language. But a moment's thought will show us that this is not the case. The pointing ritual is capable of development in one direction only—towards a larger and larger repertoire of noises. But the size of the repertoire of noises does not alter the essentially circumscribed character of the ritual. Hence the pointing ritual is, in the sense established by these remarks, *sterile*.

The theory of circumstantial ostension has parallel defects. It asks us to suppose that the child regularly, or fairly regularly, hears the word *bottle* uttered while his attention is fixed firmly on his bottle. Once again the theory so far stated provides us with no explanation of why the child should take the slightest notice of this odd concomitance, let alone why he should begin to say "bottle" himself. But by adding explanatory apparatus as we did in the case of ceremonious ostension we can see, perhaps, how the child might become disposed to say "bottle" whenever his attention was caught by his bottle; but this, again, is a sterile and circumscribed ritual.

It is presumably the case that before anyone grasps a given concept (the use of a given word) that concept (the use of that word) must at some time or other and by some definite process, verbal or otherwise, be explained to him. We are at present puzzled by the question of how a child, when he is learning for the first time to use language, comes to grasp the concepts of a *name* and of *reference*: how are these explained to him? Philosophers who believe in ostensive definition have to say that these concepts are explained simply by pointing to an object and saying its name—that the concept of naming is explained by the pointing gesture itself. We can see, I think, that this must be wrong, if we reflect that the pointing gesture can only function as a means of singling something out for the purpose of naming it if the learner already understands the use of the gesture as a means of *directing attention*, while he can only come to realize *this* if he already knows a few names, and hence, *a fortiori*, has grasped the concept of a name. If the learner does not know that, when the teacher extends his arm and forefinger in a straight line from his shoulder, he intends the learner to pay attention to the object intersected by the line from shoulder to fingertip, he lacks a piece of information which it is essential for him to have grasped before he can take the further step of realizing that the noise which accompanies the teacher's pointing is intended to be taken as the name (or *a* name) of the object which the line of his point intersects. But the learner can only be taught the function of the pointing gesture in drawing attention to an object if the teacher has some other means of singling out the object in question. This cannot be some other deictic gesture, for the same difficulty would arise for it as arises for pointing. The only remaining possibility is language: to teach me the significance of pointing, the pointer must at first be able to tell me what he is pointing at. Thus, he may say "Look, a squirrel," and if I know what 'squirrel' means I shall look around for one, and on finding it I shall probably realize that its position is intersected by the line of his point. Now everything becomes clear and when he next points to something and says, for example, "There's an oriole," I shall look first of all where his pointing directs me to look. But what I have acquired by this whole process of teaching is not the concept of a name, or of meaning, but simply an understanding of a certain shorthand device for communicating knowledge of the referents of names.

3.5   The theory of ostensive definition is supposed to explain at least two different things: (1) how we come to take the noises other human beings make as (very often) *names* of things; and (2) how we learn to *apply* names correctly to their proper objects. We have argued so far that the theory gives a very inadequate answer to the first of these questions, and I am inclined to think that it gives a scarcely more adequate one to the second.

The answer which the theory gives to question (2) is that, as the learner begins to get the hang of ostensive definition, he acquires a grasp of a single procedural rule (R_1) which, when applied to any adequately constituted ostensive procedure, will enable him to decide by reference to the series of paradigm objects displayed in the course of that procedure whether any object subsequently presented him is one to which the word defined can properly be applied. We can state R_1 as follows (where W is any basic word, and S is the series of paradigm objects by reference to which it is defined): " W is to be applied to any object which resembles the members of S in all, and only, those respects in which they resemble one another." The claim of the ostensive theory is that R_1 *alone* is sufficient to determine for the learner the correct application of any basic word.

I think this claim is false. Most writers on ostensive definition if asked for an example of a basic word, would offer the name of a color: since Locke, color words have been accepted as palmary examples of words whose referents admit of no description, but only of the bestowal of names upon them by ostensive definition. But in the case of color words we can see very clearly that the application of a word cannot be determined *simply* by the consideration of similarities among members of a paradigm series. Suppose the teacher defines 'blue' by reference to a series of objects which resemble one another only in being colored in shades of blue (the shades will include royal blue, navy blue, eggshell blue, prussian blue, and so on.) If the learner applies R_1 to the members of this paradigm series he will be led to apply the word 'blue' not only to the things that most of us call 'blue' but also to certain shades of turquoise, mauve, violet, and purple, since these shades resemble the shades displayed by the members of the blue paradigm series quite as much as the latter resemble one another. If the learner is to learn to apply 'blue' as it is usually applied, then R_1 requires supplementation by some further rule or rules. Some obvious examples of rules which would do the trick are "The word 'blue' is not to be applied to objects colored mauve" (R_2), "The word 'blue' is not to be applied to objects colored turquoise" (R_3), and so on, the number of rules of this sort we use depending on the fineness of the distinctions between segments of the color wheel which we wish to take note of in our language.

It is to be noticed first that these negative, or restrictive, rules, R_2 and R_3, are of a quite different logical type from R_1, and also, that their function is *not* to make more precise the learner's perception of the similarity holding between members of the blue paradigm series (to show him, for example, that he should have taken their crucial point of resemblance to be not just *blueness*, but, perhaps, *really blue blueness*). If R_2, R_3, and so on, functioned in this way, the same result could be achieved without their help by making the blue paradigm series more discriminating. But how could this be done? The way to make a paradigm series discriminate between two properties a and b, in favor of a, is, presumably, to add to the series (1) a member which resembles all the other members in possessing a, but also possesses b; and (2) a member which resembles all the other members in possessing a, but differs from (1) in not possessing b. Thus, if I want to define 'crocodile' but not 'walking crocodile' by ostensive means I must insure that my paradigm series contains at least one crocodile which is walking and at least one which is not. Clearly this will not work with 'mauve' and 'blue'. The blue paradigm series already contains numerous members which are blue but not mauve. But I cannot, for obvious reasons, add to the series a member which is *both* blue and mauve,[4] and if I add a mauve member I shall do the opposite of what I want to do by, in effect, adding mauve to the range of shades which, according to my definition, count as blue.

It might be argued that R_2, R_3, and so on, only appear necessary because we are considering the ostensive definition of only one color,

---

[4] This is, of course, on the assumption that the members of the blue paradigm series are uniform and homogeneous colored surfaces. The ostensive theory must assume this in order to avoid obvious problems of ambiguity.

blue, in isolation from the remainder. In reality, the teacher would also define mauve, turquoise, and the rest by reference to paradigm series, which the learner would interpret simply by reference to R_1, but the learner would be prevented from misapplying any given color name by the fact that any given shade to which he felt tempted to apply it would already have been given a different name. The trouble with this, however, is that R_1 does not specify that each shade can have only one color name applied to it. Hence, if we wanted our color vocabulary to possess this characteristic, it would have to be introduced by means of a further rule (R_4) to that effect, and we should probably, in practice, inculcate R_4 by restricting the learner's use of color names at certain points (that is, by teaching him through examples to obey R_2, R_3, and so on). In fact, however, our color vocabulary is a good deal less rigid than R_4 would make it. There are, for example, certain shades, such as yellow-green, to which we habitually apply two color names, and others, such as certain particularly indeterminate blue-greens, to which we may be honestly uncertain which of two color names to apply. The ability to tread surely in this curious linguistic maze is partly, I think, governed by rules of the type of R_2 and R_3, but clearly, I think—and this is all I am concerned to establish at this point—it cannot be the outcome of the application of R_1 alone.

My general point, then, is this: the fundamental natural similarities which basic words pick out do not have by nature clearly defined limits; hence, noting such similarities among the members of a set of paradigms cannot be equivalent to establishing the limits of application of a basic word.

3.3 The theory of ostensive definition is usually presented as a theory about the learning of logically basic and unanalyzable terms such as 'red', 'sweet', 'painful', and so on. It now looks as though we have argued ourselves round to the view that the theory is inadequate as a theory of the learning of basic terms but may still give a perfectly adequate account of the learning of nonbasic general terms such as 'crocodile', 'table', 'book', and so on. The criteria of something's being a crocodile are, surely, that it should possess certain distinct properties—that it should have scales of a certain sort, four stubby legs, yellow eyes, a long snout with raised nostrils on the end, and so on—and surely a paradigm series can be so arranged that the application of R_1 to it will single out just these properties.

This, unfortunately, is one of those neat but simple-minded theories which are equipped for survival only in the filtered air of the philosophical gedankenexperiment. The application of R_1 to a paradigm series singles out *all* these properties in which all the members of the series resemble each other. But it is simply false, as anyone with a beginning student's acquaintance with biological taxonomy knows, that for an organism to be counted a member of a given species it must exhibit *every* property common to all the members of any finite set of paradigm specimens of that species. There is a good deal of minor variation (that is, variation insignificant at the level of species differentiation) between different populations of the same species, and one cannot know in advance which characteristics of a given set of paradigm specimens, out of those which happen to be constant within the population from which these particular specimens were taken, will turn out on examination of other populations to be insignificantly variable in this way. Someone who learns the use of the word 'crocodile' by strict adherence to the procedures laid down by the ostensive theory will end, therefore, by using the word 'crocodile' far too narrowly: insisting on taking as species-determining minor variations which merely happened to be constant in the specimens which figured in the paradigm series by reference to which the word was defined for him. The ostensive theorist may suggest that we select the specimens in our paradigm series from all populations, but this will not do, since we can never be finally certain that we have discovered every population of a given species which exhibits minor variations from the norms of other populations. We want to teach our learner (or rather, to explain how learners are taught) to recognize that the members of a new trivially variant population of species A do in fact belong to species A: it is this that the ostensive theory fails to explain.

Suppose, now, that we relax the provisions of R_1 so that it requires, as a precondition for the application of a name to a given specimen, only a rough general resemblance between that specimen and each of the specimens of the paradigm series (which is perhaps more psychologically probable than the obsessive attention to detail required of the learner by R_1 in its previous formulation). We now run into the opposite difficulty. The word 'crocodile' is presumably to be explained to the learner by showing him a series of crocodiles. How, given our present formulation of R_1, is he to tell that an alligator or a gavial are not crocodiles? Admittedly, they are rather unlike the specimens in the crocodile paradigm series, but there is still a very strong general resemblance between them. How is the learner to know whether the differences are species-determining or not? Lacking this knowledge he will use the word 'crocodile' too widely, applying it equally to crocodiles, alligators, and gavials. Once again, we cannot correct his usage simply by supplementing our definition of 'crocodile' by reference to paradigm crocodiles, our definitions of 'alligator' by reference to paradigm alligators, of 'gavial' by reference to paradigm gavials, and so on. For this will not stop the learner treating either 'gavial' or 'alligator' or 'crocodile' as a general term covering all three animals or using all three words interchangeably (compare 'sofa', 'settee' and 'divan', which *may* be defined by reference to markedly different paradigms but are in practice interchangeable), or any two words interchangeably, and so on. We can only correct the learner's usage in these respects by telling him that the word 'crocodile' is *not* properly applied to alligators or gavials; and telling him this is not the same thing as modifying the list of characteristics which go to make up "crocodileness" or "gavialness."

3.7　The theory of naming characteristic of the ETL would work only if we were confronted in our experience with an array of intrinsically clearly differentiated nameables, as enumerable and logically discrete as the pebbles on a shingle beach are enumerable and spatially discrete. Russell's "objects of acquaintance" (particulars and 1 and n-termed predicates ($n > 1$)) are nameables of the requisite sort, as are the objects (*Dingen*) of the *Tractatus*, and Quine's "fixed ranges of stimuli" (*stimuli* and *fixed* are the niggers in this particular woodpile).[5] Were we provided with such an array of nameables we could define the basic utterances in

----

[5] *Cf.* Tullio de Mauro, *Une Introduction a la Sémantique* (Paris: Payot, 1969), p. 167: "Une longue tradition de pensée, du Théétète de Platon jusqu'à Russell et jusqu'au premier Wittgenstein, a affirmé et a cru qu'il y avait dans la réalité des «éléments premiers» (les *individuals* de Russell, les «objets» du *Tractatus*), qui seraient les parties constitutives les plus simples du réél. Ce point de vue, sa permanence ou sa soumission aux critiques et sa dissolution, est d'une importance décisive pour la linguistique."

our language *one by one*, specifying in the case of each a single nameable to which it is to be applied, and then, having thus fully specified a meaning (in the sense of necessary and sufficient conditions of application) for that basic utterance taken in isolation from all the rest, going on to similarly specify a sense for the next, and so on. This is the model which the theorist of ostensive definition has in mind. On such a view, the process of ostensive definition merely serves to single out for the learner's attention, by an appropriate choice of paradigm instances, the particular nameable with which a basic utterance is to be associated on a particular occasion. But we have seen that in order to teach someone the meanings of some quite common nouns (including one which is a basic utterance if any utterances are basic) we would have to go beyond simply rearranging the contents of a paradigm series so as to single out a specific nameable more accurately and unambiguously. We could confine ourselves to the making of such rearrangements only if the limits (that is, the identity) of nameables were to be somehow "given" in nature. But they are not; hence, we must teach the learner rules of a quite distinct type from R_1: rules which refer to basic utterances other than the one which is the ostensible subject of the ostensive definition in question. The rules which determine the application of, for example, 'red', that is, will if we are correct necessarily not be self-contained as they would be if the ostensive theorist's model were adequate; for the limits of application of 'red' will have to be conventionally established by means of rules which refer to the colors and shades peripheral to the red segment of the color wheel.

It appears, then, that naming must be a process involving, not single utterances taken in isolation from all others, but classes of utterances. The fundamental concept which we have to elucidate is not that of a *name* but that of a *taxonomy*. We can perhaps better understand what might be involved in learning a taxonomy by considering the structure of a botanical flora.[6] A flora contains a set of taxonomic descriptions of all the plant species found in a given geographical region, together with a set of directions which, if followed carefully, enables a competent naturalist to assign the correct species name to any

---

[6] See, for example, J. D. Hooker, *The Student's Flora of the British Isles* (London: Macmillan & Co., Ltd., 1950); A. R. Pryor, *A Flora of Hertfordshire* (Edinburgh and London: Oliver & Boyd, Ltd., 1887).

species found within that region. This is, of course, assuming that the flora is exhaustive for its chosen region. We will assume for the moment that it is exhaustive. It is the structure of this set of directions, now, which I find interesting. Normally, this part of a flora begins by posing the user a series of questions concerning "taxonomic characters" which the specimen in hand may or may not possess. (For example, a flower's having a superior, or an inferior, ovary; the arrangement of the flower parts in groups of a certain number— threes, or fives, or sixes; or the parallel or reticulate veining of leaves, are all taxonomic characters for angiosperms although for gymnosperms or bryophytes the taxonomically important characteristics are rather different.) Each question inquires of the user whether the specimen possesses a particular taxonomic character and requires him to answer "yes" or "no." In either case he is then either immediately provided with a species name for the specimen or else directed to another section of the flora, where he will be asked further questions about the specimen, the process then continuing until, sooner or later, assuming that there are no flaws either in his botanical competence or in the completeness of the flora, his answer to some question or other results in the assignment of a species name to the specimen.

We shall henceforth use the term "flora" for this set of directions alone. A flora, now, can be regarded either as a way of codifying all the taxonomically interesting facts about its subject matter—the plants of a given region—or as a device for generating all, and only, the members of a certain class of English expressions; namely, the species names of those plants. The sense of "generate" here is not quite the same as that current among generative-transformational linguists. What they usually have in mind when they use the term is the generation of expressions from other expressions: for example, the generation of transforms from base strings or the generation of words from phonemes. The sense in which a flora is a generative system is this: that no matter what plant from the flora's region the botanist is presented with, he can in a finite time (assuming the completeness of the flora), by following the rules of the flora, arrive at the species name of that plant. It is important to notice what is, I take it, trivially obvious: that a botanist producing species names in this way is not drawing on any previous training in "associating" species names with plants. Provided he can recognize all the relevant taxonomic characters (of which more anon), no one need ever have provided him with an ostensive definition of any species name, for, given the flora, he can determine the species name of any (British, Hertford-shire) plant for himself. Thirdly, and finally, the flora can be regarded not merely as a codification of taxonomically important facts, or as a device for generating all, and only, the members of a certain class of names, but as a set of rules for determining the application of the names belonging to this class. That is, given the flora and a plant specimen from the region it covers and a putative name for that specimen, the botanist can always discover, subject to the usual provisos about completeness and competence, whether that name properly applies to that specimen or not.

The setting-up of a taxonomy (the writing of a flora, that is) is not attended with the difficulties which dog the footsteps of the construc-tor of paradigm series for ostensive definition. We can see why if we consider the following simple schematic flora. The term ' a ' indicates a specimen; ' x ' and ' y ' refer to taxonomic characters; " ' ϕ '," " ' ψ '," and " ' θ '" are species names.

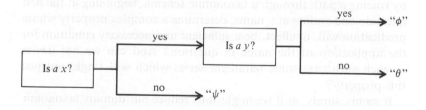

We shall assume for the moment that the class of a's is antecedently well-defined, deferring for a page or two the question of how it is to be defined—which is obviously one which must be answered. The class of a's may comprise the plants of a given region, or the set of all aquatic reptiles, or anything else you please. A flora may have any subject matter: hence it will be as well to introduce a term to refer to floras in general, irrespective of their subject matter. I suggest "taxonomic schema." I shall refer to diagrams like the one above as "dummy taxonomic schemata."

The difficulties which confront us when we attempt to define a single word by associating it with a simple or complex property singled out by a paradigm series are, we may remember, (1) in the case of simple properties—that of establishing the limits of semantically relevant resemblances, or similarities; and (2) in the case of complex properties—that of setting up a paradigm series which can account in advance for unforeseen taxonomically insignificant variation.

Neither problem arises for our dummy taxonomic schema, for all that the user of it has to do is to decide whether or not a specimen possessses certain well-defined taxonomic characters: for any case of the possession or nonpossession of these characters the schema yields (determines) a name. It might be objected that problem (1) fails to arise only because 'ϕ', 'θ', and 'ψ' are clearly not names of simple properties, and we shall return to this objection in a moment. But equally, problem (2) does not arise either. The only criteria which determine the applicability of 'ϕ', 'ψ', and 'θ' are the possession or nonpossession of x and y: we can therefore discount all other properties of a's, foreseen and unforeseen, as taxonomically insignificant.

The reader may wish to press the following objection. Can we not, by tracing a path through a taxonomic schema, beginning at the first question and ending at a name, determine a complex property whose predication will, in effect, be a sufficient and necessary condition for the application of the name in question? And can we not devise in each such case some paradigm series which will single out just this property?

It seems, surely, as if we might thus reduce our dummy taxonomic schema to three complex properties associated, as sufficient and necessary conditions of application, with three names, thus:

$$a\,x\,y \longrightarrow \text{``}\phi\text{''}$$

$$a\,x\,\text{not-}y \longrightarrow \text{``}\theta\text{''}$$

$$a\,\text{not-}x \longrightarrow \text{``}\psi\text{''}$$

This, however, merely leads us back into our original difficulties. For how can one distinguish a paradigm series of not-x a's from a paradigm series of a's? The members of a series of not-x's will have in common, beside the property of not being x, at least the property of being an a. What is to stop the learner, then, from applying 'ψ' to every a, including a's which are x y and a's which are x and not y. Why should the learner suppose that it is the *absence* of some element from the paradigm series—some property which all its members *lack*—which is critical for the application of 'ψ'? And if he is somehow or other aware of this, why should he fix on x as the crucial lack, rather than on one of the infinitely many other properties which all members of the paradigm series resemble each other in lacking?

It will not help to introduce a definition of a further term, 'ϕ' as applying to a's, which *are* x, for this will not make the application of 'ψ' any more precise, and it is over the application of 'ψ' that we are in trouble. And it will do no good either to say that the learner will apply R_1 with the utmost rigor, refusing to apply the term 'ψ' to anything possessing *any property at all* which was not possessed by all the members of the paradigm series by reference to which 'ψ' was introduced into his language; for any a will exhibit *some* property not possessed by the members of the paradigm series of a's, starting with the property of not belonging to the paradigm series.

The only way out of our difficulty is an obvious enough one. Simply specify that if an a is not an x it is to be called a ψ, whereas if it is an x it is to be called a ϕ or a θ, depending on whether it is or is not a y. But this is to make negative rules of the type R_2 and R_3 irreducible components of our system of rules for applying 'ψ' and, at the same time, to reconstitute our dummy taxonomic schema. We see, in fact, that it is precisely because a taxonomic schema essentially incorporates irreducible negative rules of the same type as R_2 and R_3 that a theory of naming based on the concept of a taxonomic schema evades problem (2); and we see, moreover, that it is because rules of this type are an irreducible component of any workable naming procedure that we cannot dissolve a taxonomic schema into a set of Carnapian " semantic rules " associating individual words with sets of sufficient and necessary conditions of correct application.

3.8

We must now return to the objection that our dummy taxonomic schema is not, and perhaps could not be, a representation of a possible set of rules determining the application of names of simple qualities, such as colors or tastes. It is an ancient and hallowed empiricist doctrine that simple qualities cannot be described but only named, and this doctrine has given credence to the view that language is linked to the world only through names of simple qualities (basic utterances on one interpretation) and through them only by association. It seems to me that this supposed connection between these two theses is simply a *non sequitur*. It rests in turn upon the supposition that there are only two possible ways of bestowing meaning upon a word: namely, associating it with a verbal definition and associating it with some element of the extralinguistic world. But if this were true then it would be impossible to define names of simple qualities at all, since, as we have seen, the limits of the natural resemblances to which names of simple qualities refer are not given to us in experience but must be defined by linguistic convention. We might construct a somewhat fanciful taxonomic schema for colors as follows:

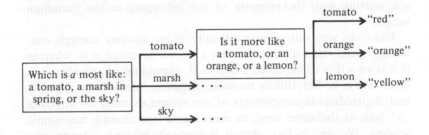

The effect of such a schema is to divide the spectrum exhaustively into segments by a series of qualitative comparisons. It is evident that we can divide up the spectrum as finely as we please by such methods, and that we could write a schema which would represent, for example, the Hopi color vocabulary, as easily as we could write one to represent the color vocabulary of everyday English or that of the slightly more precise English used by painters, couturiers, or chromatographers. Clearly, also, we could not dissolve such a schema into a set of definitions of individual colors by reference to paradigms, because then we should lose the process of proceeding to one or other further question contingently upon the outcome of a comparison: that is, precisely that feature of the schema which embodies the function of the negative rules R_2 and R_3 canvassed earlier and which enables us to assign names to precise regions of the color solid and to divide the color solid *exhaustively* into such regions.[7]

3.9 A taxonomic schema can be regarded as a device for exhaustively subdividing an antecedently defined class of a's. How are such classes defined for the learner of taxonomic schemata? We can put the same question in a slightly different form. The instructions of taxonomic schemata, which mention, among other things, a's and taxonomic characters of a's, are presumably to be regarded as written in some language or other. What language? There is an obvious temptation to solve this awkward problem by reconstructing the ETL distinction between basic and nonbasic utterances in terms of taxonomic schemata. We might say, that is, that the extension of the class of a's (a_n's) for any taxonomic schema T_n is defined by the rules of a further taxonomic schema T_{n-1}, whose rules enable a user to determine whether the appellation "a_n" is applicable to any given a_{n-1}; that the extension of the class of a_{n-1}'s is similarly determined by yet another taxonomic schema T_{n-2}, and so on. In effect this merely pushes the problem back step by step through the levels of a type hierarchy, for we are assuming at each stage that there is some well-defined class of a_m's from which a class of a_{m+1}'s can be carved out by the operations of a taxonomic schema. This regress cannot be supposed to be infinite if the thesis which requires it is to have the least psychological plausibility: there must exist, then, some class of a's which are simply given as well-defined in experience and which therefore do not require any arbitrary definition by linguistic convention. This demand for an ultimate (that is, a naturally well-defined) class of a's is, of course, equivalent to a demand for an ultimate class of taxonomic characters, since the expression 'a' is obviously merely shorthand for some complex of taxonomic characters, and since all that our projected type hierarchy of taxonomic schemata would do, in effect,

---

[7] This account of the logic of color words is carried further in my article, "On Describing Colours," *Inquiry* (1967), and in my book *Form and Content* (forthcoming).

would be to assign names to increasingly complex clusters, or compounds, of ultimate taxonomic characters. What we seem to need, then, in order to prevent our hierarchy of taxonomic schemata from turning into an infinite regress, is a class of taxonomic characters which can be named in isolation—that is, outside the context of a taxonomic schema—simply by the association of a word with each such character.

We have already seen, however, that this is a blind alley, because, among other reasons which we shall examine later, experience does not provide us with nameables-in-isolation. One naming procedure must always be relative to others because the semantically significant limits of resemblance are not defined for us in nature. But, happily, there is no need to enter this particular alley. We can see this if we return to the consideration of the logic of color words. What we are given in experience is a spectrum of continuously related qualities within which we can (and must, if we wish to have a color vocabulary) make arbitrary boundaries for linguistic purposes. We make these boundaries by means of a device of a certain sort—a taxonomic schema of the type suggested earlier—which employs criteria of a certain kind: namely, qualitative comparisons of color samples. This is a taxonomic schema for exhaustively assigning names to colors: in its instructions, therefore, 'this a' presumably means 'this color.' If, like our opponents, we wished to arrange taxonomic schemata in a type-hierarchy we should presumably, then, now have to begin looking for a further taxonomic schema to distinguish 'colors' from other sorts of entity, which schema would then in turn exhibit a more fundamental class of a's requiring to be distinguished from others by a further schema, and so on. We can see intuitively that this is nonsense. If there were entities called colors, they could not (logically) be colored: the color 'red' is not red. But if colors do not possess color qualities, then what qualities do they possess? And how, if they lack qualities altogether, can we distinguish them from other sorts of entity?

We can evade these absurdities as follows. We shall define 'is a color' in terms of the taxonomic schema for assigning names to colors itself: or rather, in terms of the peculiar character of the structure of rules which the schema comprises. We shall say that anything is a color which can be assigned a name by the operation of a taxonomic schema of that type: that is, one which employs qualitative comparisons of samples of a certain sort, and so on.

We can easily show that this move is neither trivial, nor circular, nor an evasion of the problem. The taxonomic schema for color words is not an arbitrary or *merely* conventional construction. It has the character which it has because our experience of colors is what it is. It is therefore neither trivial nor circular to define our experience of colors as that part of our experience which can be handled taxonomically by a certain sort of schema: that is, one which relies on certain procedures of comparison. To say that something is a color is to say that it is part of our experience of colors, and to say this is in turn to say that it could be assigned a name either by the operations of our taxonomic schema for color words, or by some more complex schema of the same sort: that is, one developed from our existing schema merely by specifying one or more further qualitative comparisons (with appropriate exits) at one or more nodes of the schema, these qualitative comparisons being of essentially the same type as those already provided for in the schema. But here the accusation of evasiveness should be heard. "Of essentially *what* type?" "Well, of the same type as other comparisons of *colors*." Doesn't this reply make the whole theory vacuous by resurrecting the original question of the meaning of "is a color"; and isn't it necessary, in order to remedy the vacuity, to give some nontrivial account of what differentiates making color comparisons from making other sorts of comparison—perhaps a psychological account?

The answer to all these questions is "no." It is simply a fact of nature that our experience is in part an experience of colors and that colored surfaces can be arranged in a sequence of continuously related shades. And it is also a fact that because our experience is like this, we can introduce color words into our language by means of a taxonomy which works essentially by imposing arbitrary divisions on this sequence by reference to semantically criterial qualitative comparisons. Now clearly, it is not psychologically necessary to define the expression 'is a color' before teaching someone the names of colors: children do not, as a rule, grasp the use of 'is a color' before that of 'red'. We can get the business of applying color names off the ground simply by showing the child a few color samples and establishing a few semantically criterial limits of resemblance. Let us assume for the moment that the child is aware of colors and that he is aware that we are trying to set up a device for naming *colors*, and not, say, shapes or textures. If these assumptions are mistaken, this fact will appear in the child's later usage, for he will just not learn the taxonomy which we are trying to teach him, but a different one: that is, one which works by reference to different taxonomic characters. He may then say 'red' whenever we point at anything and ask "What is that called?" or (perhaps on account of our having made an unfortunate choice of objects as color samples) he may with perfect consistency apply 'red' to furry surfaces, 'blue' to smooth surfaces, and so on. The point is that for the purpose of inquiring into the nature of the conventions which set up a language, we can, and must, take for granted the cognitive universe of the learner. We have agreed that this universe does not contain ready-made discrete nameables—nameables-in-isolation—but to say this is very far from saying that everything in our experience blends by insensible grada-tions into everything else: for if this were so we could not establish any systems of taxonomy at all. But at the same time, this is not to say that experience comes marked out, as it were, into ready-made "sites" for taxonomic division: the "realm" of colors, the "realm" of material objects, and so on; as if, as it were, the forest of primeval Ohio had grown in neat rectangular plots ready to be further sub-divided by the Federal surveyors. What does seem to be the case is rather that our experience is such that it is often practically possible for us to separate off from our experience a well-defined area for taxonomic division by specifying what one might call a *mode of perceptual attention*. We do precisely this, in fact, when we construct a taxonomy for colors. For the learner of the taxonomy must single out some range of characteristics (of the sample objects with which he is presented) which are linked by a continuous system of relation-ships but which can be separated artificially into recurrent nameables by comparisons of relative similarity. These requirements are purely conventional: we specify them. But it happens to be the case that something in nature (namely, color) answers to these specifications; and the learner is directed to pay attention to this aspect of nature by the formal character of the taxonomy itself.

Similarly, if I say, "Look at the *outline* of these objects (imagine them as flat surfaces and run your glance around the perceived edge) and say . . . ," I shall introduce him to another mode of perceptual attention which, in combination with a certain kind of taxonomy, serves to define another, and quite different, taxonomic realm. The problem of erecting the taxonomies of a natural language is that of hitting upon modes of perceptual attention which will in fact yield taxonomic realms which can be fairly easily exhausted by a taxonomy.[8] A taxonomy is, in fact, a kind of template, which, when applied to the world by means of the mode of perceptual attention which it determines, both specifies and exhaustively subdivides a class of nameables. There is thus no problem concerning the legitimacy of writing the instructions of our model taxonomies in ordinary English, and *a fortiori* no problem which requires to be solved by arranging taxonomies in a type hierarchy. The English formulations in such a model merely indicate perceptual discriminations which the learner would be able to make even if he had never learned the taxonomy in question—or any taxonomy—but which he has been taught to treat as criterial in distinguishing, for naming purposes, individual nameables of some general type specified by the form of the taxonomy as a whole, with its related mode of perceptual attention.

3.10 If this account of the general form of the rules determining the application of names is correct, several interesting consequences follow. The first is that we can now evade certain arguments for assigning epistemological or metaphysical primacy to certain sorts of statements: statements about sense-data, *protokolsätze*, statements involving reference only to 'objects of acquaintance', and so on. The arguments which we evade are all those which rest upon the thesis that if we are to give utterances meaning we must do so either by defining them verbally in terms of other utterances or by associating them with elements of the world. This thesis collapses because to construct a taxonomy which specifies conditions of application for a certain class of words

---

[8] In the case of biological taxonomy, this problem is complicated by the requirement that the resulting taxonomic divisions should represent, so far as possible, the actual evolutionary relations of species. Hence, taxonomy is a substantial empirical subject and not, as some positivist philosophers have supposed, merely a matter of "verbal definition."

does not involve either offering verbal definitions of those words or associating them with elements of the world (nameables-in-isolation). And because a taxonomy both marks out a taxonomic category and subdivides it, we can begin constructing taxonomies at any level of the empiricist's epistemological or ontological hierarchies, without reference to taxonomies constructed at what the empiricist would consider other levels. Thus, given that the learner can discriminate objects within his environment, we can construct a taxonomy of objects: 'tree', 'table', and so on, as easily as one for colors. Indeed, it is rather hard to see how a taxonomy of objects could be constructed "out of" or "on the basis of" a taxonomy of colors: this is no doubt one among many reasons for the invention of the celebrated visual sensum or *colored patch* of empiricist mythology, which is neither wholly a color nor wholly a material object but a bit of both.

The second consequence of our account of the application of names is that, if we are correct, the rules for applying a word are rules relative to a finite universe: the universe constituted by the experience of the inventors and users of the taxonomy to which the word belongs. Thus the taxonomy of living reptiles is adequate— that is, invariably produces consistent applications of names, provided its rules are carefully followed—for the contemporary reptile population of the earth and only for that population. But by the same token, if it is adequate for this finite universe it is adequate *toute courte*. A word has a clear and definite meaning, that is, if we know how to distinguish those entities to which it applies within the finite class of entities which constitutes the universe defined by the taxonomy to which it belongs. It is not necessary, for it to have a clear and definite meaning, that is, that its rules of application should be adequate for the universe of *all possible*—including merely logically possible—*entities*. If that were the case, then *every* characteristic of a named entity would be a taxonomic character—a thesis sometimes expressed by saying that the meanings of most words are *theory-laden*. If we are correct, then this thesis is false; and I think that this is what intuition would lead us to expect, for clearly not every fact about living reptiles figures, as a taxonomic character, in the taxonomy of living reptilia. The study of that taxonomy is complete: the study of reptile physiology, on the other hand, is no doubt far from complete. We shall carry this discussion further, bringing out some of its consequences for the theory of vagueness in Chapter 8. The problem of vagueness is that of showing how a system of linguistic rules which is in itself quite clear and definite can, when operating as a system governing a speaker's linguistic practice, yield a usage which is "vague" at the edges, in Waismann's phrase, or "incompletely bounded by rules" in Wittgenstein's, in just the same ways as our actual everyday language. Wittgenstein's dictum that "language is not everywhere bounded by rules" is sometimes stated as if its purport were that language is bounded by unclear or imprecise rules—rules which are so diaphanous and vague that they can only be apprehended by an unanalyzable act of intuition—that is, as if the exercise of linguistic capacity were akin to the exercise of mediumship or second sight. The implications of this view are that nothing definite can be said about the nature of the rules governing our use of language and that philosophy must proceed by appeal to the linguistic intuition of the reader. But if I am right, this is a groundless view: we can hope to show, at least in the case of the application of general terms, that a usage at once definite and flexible, unambiguous and yet open-textured, may be governed by a set of rules which are in themselves prosaic, concrete, and quite straightforwardly stateable.

Finally, it is perhaps worth emphasizing once again that a taxonomy is essentially a template which we apply to the world: a device for creating nameables, not a device for recording the empirical discovery of nameables. Wittgenstein in the *Tractatus Logico-Philosophicus* puts forward a very general argument for supposing that nameables (in his terms 'objects,' or *dingen*) cannot be objects of empirical discovery, and I am inclined to think that this argument is sound. Wittgenstein says that objects, together with all their possible modes of combination into states of affairs, must be 'given' in advance of any possible use of language to assert anything. If this were not so, Wittgenstein argues, the sense of expressions would not be determinate, since what one proposition meant would depend on whether another proposition were true. This is a notoriously dark saying, which I interpret—perhaps quite wrongly—as follows. Wittgenstein's 'objects' are, it seems to me, essentially entities capable of being named in isolation. The account of a proposition which he gives in the *Tractatus* entails that a proposition can only have a definite meaning if we can asssociate the names in it with such entities.

Until such an association has been made we do not know what a proposition means. If it were an empirical question what entities of the sort required for the execution of such acts of association actually existed in the world, then to discover a new class of these entities would be to establish the meaningfulness of a new class of propositions not hitherto known to be meaningful. But what would it be like to know of the existence of a proposition without knowing whether that proposition was meaningful or what it meant? A proposition is simply an assertion: to entertain a proposition is to entertain the possibility of asserting something. Unless we know what a proposition asserts there is no sense in which we can be said to be entertaining a proposition. But if nameables were empirically discoverable our knowledge of the meaning of any given empirical proposition would have to depend on our knowing the truth of another empirical proposition to the effect that certain nameables exist, and presumably the meaning of this proposition would depend upon the truth of a third, and so on. The only place to break this chain is at the beginning: we must know the meaning (the sense) of every empirical proposition before we assert any, for what is asserted by a proposition is precisely its sense.

This problem of the relationship between truth, meaning, and reference is to my mind a real and important one. Wittgenstein solves it in the *Tractatus* in a way which most philosophers would find unacceptable, by means of his theory of objects, taken in conjunction with the picture theory of meaning. We evade it in a different way by means of our theory of taxonomies. We know that nature will supply exactly as many nameables as are required to give our propositions meaning, for taxonomies are, in effect, machines for generating just that many nameables, by arbitrary partitioning of our field of experience, as and when they are required. Hence all the nameables required for all discourse in a natural language are, in a sense, 'given' in advance by the taxonomies of that language. This is the explanation of the puzzling fact, noted by the Tractarian Wittgenstein, that men can construct languages in which "everything that is true of the world can be expressed," without at all knowing everything that is to be known about the world which is the subject of their discourse.

We have now elaborated in some detail a positive account of the rules which govern the application of names. We have, however, said nothing positive about what it is for something to be a name, although we have criticized the ETL on the grounds that its theory of naming explains, not naming, but only a class of logical parodies of naming: what we have called sterile and circumscribed rituals. But of course, all that the learning of a taxonomy would confer upon a learner is the capacity to execute a relatively sterile and circumscribed performance: the gap between proffering noises in the presence of appropriate stimuli on demand, and using words in discourse, remains as wide as ever. We shall return to deal directly with this problem in Chapter 5. In Chapter 4 we shall approach it indirectly, by way of a discussion of the theory of concatenation offered by the ETL.

4 Abstraction and grammar

It is evident how new sentences may be built from old materials and volunteered on appropriate occasions simply by virtue of the analogies. Having been directly conditioned to the appropriate use of 'Foot' (or 'This is my foot') as a sentence, and 'Hand' likewise, and 'My foot hurts' as a whole, the child might conceivably utter 'My hand hurts' on an appropriate occasion, though unaided by previous experience with that actual sentence.

W. V. Quine, *Word and Object*, p. 9.

4.1 Quine here states, with exemplary clarity and brevity, the theory of grammar which is characteristically suggested by the ETL.[1] I think it can be shown that despite its air of robust common sense it is a vacuous and obscurantist theory. As we have seen, it argues, in effect, that the way in which we first become aware of the existence of grammatical and syntactic relationships is through noticing analogies between the circumstances in which noises are uttered by other human beings. First we notice that the same noise recurs again and again in speech, either on its own ('foot') or in combination with other noises ('Foot hurts'). Then we notice that whenever 'foot' is used, either alone or in combination with other noises, the same bit of the world—namely, a foot—invariably happens to be obtruding itself upon our attention. Something similar has been happening with 'hurts', so that when we hurt our foot and are induced to cry 'Foot hurts' we easily jump to the conclusion that 'foot' refers to the foot and 'hurts' to the hurt. In the

---

[1] Longer expositions of more or less the same theory can be found in (to name only two sources) Price, *Thinking and Experience*, pp. 215–216, and Roger Brown, *Words and Things* (New York: Free Press, 1958), p. 108.

same way we have grasped the reference of 'hand': hence, when our hand hurts, we naturally combine 'hand' with 'hurts' on the analogy of 'Foot hurts'. At this point we can be said to have fully grasped the idea of constructing new simple sentences from bits of ones which we have already learned. This, or some variant of it, is the answer which the empiricist theory of language gives to the question of what is involved in the ability of someone who can speak a language to construct an indefinite number of original and appropriate utterances in that language.

This account is not as logically seamless as it looks. It contains a number of points at which we can reasonably ask for further explanation or clarification.

To begin with, the child is to be taught "the appropriate use" of 'foot' by being trained, through a process of operant conditioning (Quine here, in effect, adopts Skinner's analysis of the tact), to say 'foot' whenever a foot is presented to him. But we have already seen that what can be explained by appeal to this sort of learning procedure is not the learning of "the appropriate use of a word" (if this implies the ability to apply the word correctly in a variety of unforeseen contexts, in the full consciousness that it is a *name*), but the learning of a sterile and circumscribed ritual.

Even if we were to waive this point, we would still be no nearer to seeing why the child should take 'Foot hurts' as a compound utterance, rather than simply as a longish name—'foothurts'. What he is being taught, after all, is a repertoire of noises-to-say-when-certain-environmental-conditions-recur. If we must describe this process in the language of naming and reference, it would seem simplest and least tendentious to say that he is being taught that 'foot' is the name for (I would prefer to say, "the cry with which to greet") a foot, and 'foothurts' the name for a hurting foot. It may be objected that 'foothurts' is clearly complex because it contains 'foot' as a part. But this is only to say that the phonemic string 'foot', which has been assigned one linguistic function, occurs as a portion of the phonemic string 'foothurts', which has been assigned a different linguistic function. The same is true of innumerable other phonemic strings when the relationship is not correlated with any of the machinery of grammar or syntax: for example, 'duck'/'duckboard'; 'say'/'sail', and so on. Our difficulty is (1) to see why the child should be interested in—take any notice of—such phonemic coincidences; (2) to see why he should come to take them as potentially revelatory of grammatical relationships; and (3) to understand how he manages to sort out those cases in which the coincidence of sound has some relationship to grammar or syntax from those in which it has none.

An answer, on Quinean lines, to the third of these questions might be that the child sorts out grammatically revelatory phonemic coincidences by reference to the circumstances in which utterances occur. Thus, 'foot' characteristically occurs when a foot is in plain view, and 'foothurts' when to the foot is superadded a hurt, whereas no such relationship holds between utterances of 'duck', 'board', and 'duckboard', and sightings of duckboards, boards, and ducks. In short, the natural articulations of the child's experience give him clues to the nature of the articulations of grammar and syntax.

This presupposes that the child is actively examining his experience for—is on the lookout for—such clues. But why should he be? How does the child know that certain forms of articulation of his experience are likely to be critical with respect to morphological or syntactic relationships between utterances or parts of utterances. We can say if we like that the child just *does* 'know' this; that it is part of the innate fabric of linguistic dispositions ("linguistic universals") which he brings with him to the learning of language that he tends to look for such concomitances between utterance and circumstances of utterance; that explanations must stop somewhere; and that we cannot hope to explain the learning of language, or of anything else, unless we are prepared to assume that the learner possesses some simple capacity or other which we then take as primitive for the purposes of the inquiry. But this will not do. The problem of concatenation is precisely that of explaining how a child learns how to recombine words in ways which depend, in part at least, upon their application: upon what they mean. We would have arrived at the beginnings of a nontrivial solution to this problem if we could show, for example, that the ability to perform such recombinations could be explained as resulting from the application of systems of rules of a certain type; and we could then perhaps go on to inquire whether the facts about children's learning of language are compatible with the supposition that they in fact learn such systems of rules;

what capacities must be presupposed in organisms capable of such learning; and so on. But to say that a child *just is* predisposed to hunt for concomitances between utterance and circumstances of utterance is to say no more than that it *just does* possess an innate ability to recombine words in ways which depend in part upon their meanings; since this hunt for concomitances is precisely a hunt for word–referent associations by reference to which he can determine which apparently grammatically complex utterances are really grammatically complex, and what are their points of cleavage into simple utterances. As we shall argue later, it requires some vigilance to prevent the concept of a linguistic universal from degenerating from an empirical concept into a device for producing trivial "explanations" of linguistic phenomena on *virtus dormitiva* lines. The trouble with such "explanations" is that they often prevent us from seeing the need for real explanations.

To return to the argument: even if we can assume that the child somehow realizes that 'foothurts' is a compound sign composed of 'foot' and 'hurts', it is still not explained why he should not take this as a piece of information about the etymology of one particular utterance, 'foothurts,' rather than as an implicit rule for constructing utterances. How, in fact, does he come to realize (1) that he can produce an appropriate vocal response to the stimulus of a pain in his hand *by modifying an utterance which he has already learned to produce in other circumstances*; and (2) that he can produce such a response by modifying 'foothurts'? We know *ex hypothesi* that he has been taught to respond to at least one recurring pain (the one in his foot) with the utterance "foothurts': hence the principle of generalization familiar to learning theorists would lead us to expect him to say 'foothurts' when his hand begins to hurt. This is clearly not a pattern of response which we wish to encourage: hence we shall probably punish ("negatively reinforce") or at any rate fail to reward utterances of 'foothurts' in response to hurting hands. But all we shall produce by this procedure is a child who makes no vocal response at all to pains in his hands but remains silent. We could, of course, train the child to say 'handhurts' when his hand hurts, but then we would simply be mechanically extending his repertoire of utterances for it, whereas what we want to know is the process by which we teach him to extend his own repertoire of utterances.

4.2 Quine says that the child sees *by analogy* that 'handhurts' must be an appropriate response to a pain in his hand. This presumably means that the child takes 'foothurts' *as a model for* the construction of the expression 'handhurts'. In general, it seems to me, the relationship between a model and performance based on it is defined in terms of some set of rules for mapping the relevant features of the model on to the performance; these rules determine how the model is to be used to generate the performance, and also establish which features of the model are relevant from the point of view of its status as a model. If, for example, I model my knot-tying on yours, this relationship can be defined as a set of rules connecting certain features of the motion of my fingers performing the same operation. These rules define which aspects of your performance are relevant to its status as a model of knot-tying: they exclude, for example, the grimaces you make and the way you hunch your shoulders, though these things might be relevant if I were using your performance as a model of comic preoccupation.

Suppose now, that the child has grasped, by some unexplained means, that he is supposed to respond to a pain in his hand by producing an utterance modeled on, but not identical with, an utterance which he already knows how to produce and that the model utterance in question is 'foothurts'. How is he to know what rules are to connect his performance with this model: which elements of the model utterance are to be retained in the new utterance; which are to be discarded; and what, if anything, is to replace the discarded elements? The important thing to see here is that, on Quine's account, the child must be supposed to arrive at a grasp of certain *prescriptions*, which are to govern his performance, as a result of contemplating certain *facts* about other people's performances. This gap between observed regularity and prescriptive rule is, I think, the crucial point at which Quine's account fails as an explanation of the rule-governed originality which is the characteristic and most puzzling feature of linguistic performance; for unless we can explain how the learner translates an array of circumstantial observations about the behavior of others into a set of rules for his own performances, we have explained nothing.

It is obvious that there will be no observation–rule translation problem if the child knows *what his elders are doing*: if he knows that when similar phonemic strings crop up again and again as components of longer strings in the discourse of his elders, *what is going on is that names are being transposed within different syntactic schemata.* If he already knows this, he already knows the general character of the rules which he must derive from his observations of his elders' performance in order to guide his own. The problem confronting him now is simply one of filling in details. He must thus, for example, establish the phonemic identity of the names his elders are transposing; locate their referents; determine the limits of recurring syntactic schemata; and determine their grammatical functions. All of this (formidable task though it might seem) presents no obvious *theoretical* difficulty. It is the sort of thing which we can imagine the child doing by the exercise of the sort of inductive methods recommended in elementary logic textbooks. He would have to form hypotheses about the referents of words, and the limits and functions of syntactic schemata, and test these by reference to what he can discover of the actual regularities discernible in his elders' linguistic behavior. He would have, in other words, to apply that useful faculty of inductive abstraction which we have already found ubiquitously playing the role of central explanatory principle in other parts of the ETL. Quine's example of the hurting foot is clearly framed on the assumption that the learner will proceed in some such way: the child is presented with just enough information to enable him by a series of inductive abstractions, to arrive at the conclusion that if anything is to be substituted into the schema '____ hurts' to yield an appropriate response to a hurting hand, it must be 'hand'. Quine treats his hypothetical child, in fact, as if he were a small anthropologist, already familiar with a language of his own and thus equipped with a general knowledge of what grammar and syntax are, attempting by methods of inductive inference and elimination to elucidate the vocabulary and syntax of a strange native language from what he hears of it as spoken around him by the tribesmen among whom he lives. But a real child is not a small anthropologist, and has, as we have begun to see, rather different problems. The anthropologist's problem is to locate the structural elements of the natives' language by framing and testing hypotheses which must be in the first instance based on the structure of his own language. The child has no language; hence he lacks the anthropologist's acquaintance with a familiar syntax, on the basis of which he might frame hypotheses about the syntax of the language he hears spoken about him; hence he can frame no hypotheses; hence he can test no hypotheses; and hence he cannot use the procedures of inductive inference and abstraction as devices for extracting information about syntactic relationships from what he observes of the linguistic usage of his elders. The child's problem is quite different from the anthropologist's. It is to locate the utterances which he is to use as models for generating new utterances appropriate to new situations of various sorts and to acquire a grasp of systems of rules for selectively mapping the relevant features of the models onto the new utterances to be derived from them. Inductive abstraction cannot locate the right model utterances for him (for inductive methods can establish syntactic points of reference in an unfamiliar language only insofar as they can be used in conjunction with definite syntactic hypotheses, which *ex hypothesi* the child cannot frame), and by the same token it cannot reveal to him the nature of the rules for deriving new utterances of a given sort from a given model.

It is worth asking why the theory that children might come to see syntactic relationships " by virtue of the analogies " should have imposed upon so many astute philosophers and psychologists. A clue is to be found, I think, in Quine's use of the phrase, " Having been directly conditioned to the appropriate use of 'foot'.... " Other philosophers (Price, for example), would want to say that what is learned, by what Quine calls conditioning and they would call ostensive definition, is the reference of 'foot': what 'foot' names. We have noticed already that one central doctrine of the ETL is that reference determines use: that to know what a word refers to is automatically to know something, at least, about how to use it in discourse. There is thus a very natural tendency for philosophers within this particular empiricist tradition to slide between thinking of the procedures which establish the basic associative linkages between language and the world: on the one hand as if what is taught by means of them are the referents of words, and on the other hand as if what is taught by them are the uses of words in discourse. The business of initiating a child into the grammar and syntax of his language thus ceases to be thought of as something requiring explanation in its own right but shrinks to the status of a sort of aura surrounding the process of naming (which thus necessarily becomes, as Wittgenstein complains, a very mysterious process indeed)—sufficiently understood if we understand the nature of naming.

It seems to me that an implicit conceptual slide is at the heart of Quine's thinking about analogy. Thus, for Quine, when the child is conditioned to say 'foot' on being shown a foot, what he is being conditioned to is "the appropriate use of 'foot'." This phrase carries with it the assumption that, as a result of this conditioning, the child will know how to deploy the word 'foot', at least in elementary ways, in discourse: he will know something at least of the syntax of sentences containing 'foot', and thus it is possible to imagine him discovering the remainder by the judicious application of the method of framing syntactic hypotheses and checking them by inductive abstractions performed upon the body of linguistic data provided by the discourse of those about it. But once we realize that all that can be explained by theories of conditioning or ostensive definition is the acquisition of the ability to perform a sterile and circumscribed ritual, naming and syntax fall apart, and we are freed from the temptation to make this particular mistake.

4.3 How are we to explain the origination of an understanding of grammar if not in the traditional way? According to the traditional account, an understanding of grammar develops when the learner begins to reflect upon phonemic coincidences in the speech of those about him in the light of the circumstances in which the utterances in question occur. The traditional view holds that the machinery of inductive abstraction is enough to enable the learner to locate clues to grammatical structure in the circumstances of utterance of the discourse of those about him and to bring these clues to bear on the pattern of phonemic coincidences that he discerns in their discourse, in such a way as (eventually) to make the grammatical and syntactic structure of that discourse plain to him. We have argued that the machinery of inductive abstraction is *not* enough to explain how the learner does this. He can do it only if he has at his command not only the machinery of inductive abstraction, but also a grasp of the fundamental concepts of grammar and syntax themselves: these being, however, the very concepts whose acquisition the traditional theory attempts to explain.

If we wish to replace this trivial traditional theory with a genuinely explanatory one we must, I think, lower our sights a little. We must leave on one side for the moment the question of the psychological mechanism of acquisition and concentrate instead on the question of *what is acquired*. It seems clear that what the learner learns to do is (1) to identify some utterance which he already produces as a model for the production of an original utterance, or a class of original utterances; and (2) to modify this utterance in certain definite ways which result in the generation from it of original utterances which are appropriate to the circumstances in which they are uttered. And whatever system of rules it is by the application of which he does these things must, of course, be such that we do not have to postulate that the learner has already mastered—or innately possesses— linguistic capacities equivalent to (1) and (2) in order to explain how he is able to learn the system of rules in question.

The following account seems to me to meet these requirements. For the sake of simplicity of exposition we shall use Quine's example.

Let us suppose that the learner has mastered a taxonomy of parts of the human body. The taxonomic characters in this taxonomy will perhaps be specified in terms of imaginary lines drawn on a schematic body, dividing for example, foot from ankle, ankle from calf, calf from shin; much as the taxonomy of colors arbitrarily divides the spectrum or the color wheel. The procedure of drawing such distinctions will no doubt be part of what defines a thing as a human body, for if I attempt to perform it upon, say, a satyr, I shall find myself in grave difficulties in the vicinity of his hocks and pasterns. But the mechanism of the taxonomy is immaterial: the learner, we suppose, has mastered *some* taxonomy which both effectively singles out human bodies *qua* assemblages of bodily parts as a field for taxonomic division and imposes some such division on that field. Let us label this taxonomy T_A.

By following the rules of T_A the learner can carry out various linguistic tasks. For example, if someone else points to a part of some human body and asks "What's this called?" or merely makes some conventional interrogative noise or gesture, the learner can, by using T_A, derive, or work out, a verbal response. He can, for example, by dividing the body exhaustively into labeled (named) segments by reference to the rules of T_A, find the smallest segment containing the area pointed to or otherwise indicated by his questioner, and utter its name ("smallest" here means "incapable of being further divided into named segments by using the actual rules of T_A"). And one could devise other similar tasks involving the use of T_A to work out an appropriate response: for example, the task of pointing to the appropriate part of someone's body when one of the names defined by T_A is uttered. Such a task is obviously a conventional ritual, defined by a set of procedural rules known to all who are party to the ritual or game in question. We could write the rules of the first task above as follows:

[L_1] When another points to some part of a human body and says "What's this called?" (or utters some other conventional interrogative which, by stipulation, inaugurates an enactment of the ritual [L_1]), generate a response by carrying out the following instructions:

Instruction (1) By following the instructions of T_A, find the smallest named segment of the body which contains the area indicated by the pointing gesture.

Instruction (2) Utter the name of that segment.

I shall call systems of rules like [L_1] *linguistic devices*. They might equally well be called language games; but the game metaphor has not proved an unqualified boon to the philosophy of language, and is now in any case so laden with unhelpful associations that I prefer to use a more neutral term. T_A is not a linguistic device, but were we to write out the rules of [L_2] in full they would embody the rules of T_A in a form appropriate to this particular linguistic device. We can regard T_A, when written out as a taxonomy, as an abstraction from the various forms it takes in all the linguistic devices in which it occurs: as, in fact, a "standard normal form" of T_A.

We now assume that the learner experiences *local* pains: pains which, like a toothache or a headache and unlike a feeling of general muscular exhaustion or of nausea, have a definite site in his body. The ability to locate local pains is not, it seems to me, a linguistic ability. A child can clutch a cut knee or put his hand on a bump on his head, before he can use any language at all. We are not, therefore, assuming any innate or acquired linguistic capacity if we assume that the learner can locate local pains.

We can now introduce another linguistic device.

[L_2] When you experience a local pain,[2] and another asks "Where does it hurt?", generate a response by carrying out the following instructions.

Instruction (1) Locate the pain by putting your finger on the spot which hurts, or by rubbing it, or by imagining yourself rubbing it, or simply by paying attention to its location.

Instruction (2) By following the rules of T_A, generate a name for the smallest area which includes the area affected by the located pain.

Instruction (3) Utter the name which results from carrying out instruction (1).

Instruction (4) Utter the word 'hurts'.

It is worth noticing for future reference that instruction (2) of [L_2] is merely instruction (1) of [L_1] applied in a new way: to areas of the body located by a local pain, rather than by an act of pointing, or in some other way.

The learning of such rule systems as [L_1] and [L_2] can, it seems to me, be understood without presupposing that the learner has any prior grasp of any grammatical concept, or for that matter, that he has any grasp of the conception of a language. All that we have to presuppose is that he can be taught to perform actions of specific types in a regular sequence, in response to standardized cues, and that he can interpolate one such sequence of actions into another without fatally disrupting his conduct of the latter sequence. It is extremely common in nonlinguistic contexts, for organisms (and computers) to learn to do this sort of thing.

Picking up a telephone and dialing is one stylized string of actions, looking up an item in an alphabetical list is another. Sometimes I perform these strings separately; sometimes I interpolate one into the other: I pick up the telephone, look up a number, and dial. There are problems which this sort of performance raises for the psychology of learning,[3] but there is no doubt but that it exists.

---

[2] A "local pain" being in part defined, of course, as the sort of pain with respect to which you can play the linguistic game [L_2], and others.

[3] A good discussion of some of these is to be found in George A. Miller, Eugene Galanter, and Karl H. Pribam, *Plans and the Structure of Behavior* (New York: Holt, Rinehart and Winston, 1960).

We must notice also that $[L_1]$ is merely another sterile and circumscribed ritual. $[L_2]$, however, is not. The rules of $[L_2]$ allow the learner to generate as many utterances as there are names (terminal branches) in the taxonomy T_A. Therefore, once the learner has learned $[L_2]$ he can generate original and appropriate utterances which he has not been explicitly trained to utter. He may, for example, never have heard anyone say 'Ear hurts', until he finds himself uttering this phrase because it happens on some occasion to be generated as a result of carrying out instructions (1)–(4) of $[L_2]$. What he can do, *in effect*, then, is to instantiate the syntactic schema[4] '____ hurts' in such a way as to produce a range of English phrases of that form; and we could, if we wished, rewrite $[L_2]$ so that its rules would appear in part as rules for filling in the schema '____ hurts', although this would obscure their fundamental character as rules governing sequences of operations. As a result of learning $[L_2]$, then, the learner is in much the same position as he would be in if he *had* somehow, simply by reflecting inductively on his elder's discourse and its circumstances of utterance, managed to locate 'foothurts' and other similar utterances as the correct models for his performance in commenting on his hurting hand, and by similar methods to derive a rule connecting these utterances, considered as models, with his own utterance. But because he has not reached this position by the (impossible) Quinean route, the problem of the transition from observation to prescription simply does not arise for him.

We thus have a model of language learning which offers, admittedly in the context of a thoroughly crude and stylized example, the first glimmerings of an understanding of how a finite process of language learning might produce the ability to produce a practically infinite range of appropriate and original utterances. But it is important to see that when the child has mastered $[L_1]$ and $[L_2]$ his linguistic capabilities will still be extremely limited. He will only be

---

[4] In an article, "Categories" (*Proceedings of the Aristotelian Society*, 1939; reprinted in A. G. N. Flew, ed., *Essays on Logic and Language*, 2nd series, London: Blackwell, 1955), Gilbert Ryle introduced the term "sentence-frame" to label such entities as 'Socrates is ____', '____ is wise', and so on; and it has since acquired a certain currency. I propose to add the term "phrase schema" (to avoid the infelicitous "phrase frame"), and I shall refer to both sentence frames and phrase schemata as "syntactic schemata."

able to produce utterances formed by instantiating the schema '____ hurts', and the number of different utterances of this kind which he can produce will depend on the number of terminal branches of T_A. If we are to explain any linguistic capacity more involved than this, then obviously we shall need a great deal more expanatory machinery. To have realized how much more explanatory machinery we may need is, however, perhaps not such a bad result to begin with. One feature of the traditional account in terms of analogy and abstraction is that it suggests that the whole of a child's learning of the syntax of his language can be understood in terms of one simple process—abstraction—which is brought to bear by the child again and again on differently patterned sensory material: the difference in the patterning accounting for the differences in the syntactic information which the child acquires from each application of the process. Thus, the example of Quine's with which we began suggests how the child might get the idea of (roughly) conjoining names to describe a complex situation; and, provided one agreed with the assumptions of this sort of procedure, one could easily formulate other similar examples which would suggest in the same way how the child might learn the use of, say, the *either-or* construction (for example, offering the child a sweet in one hand or the other but not both), the use of quantifiers, and so on. Implicit in this mode of procedure is the idea that there is some one teaching process which will once and for all " give the child the idea of " transposing words according to syntactic and grammatical rules to produce new utterances. If we are right, then this idea is mistaken. The child does not " learn how to transpose " by the repeated application of some one simple rule or habit of mind: he learns how to make specific types of transposition and his achievement on each occasion must be understood in terms of a different and fairly complex set of rules or instructions. When at the start of this chapter I chose to call the traditional theory " obscurantist " I did so because it seems to me that the chief defect of that theory is that by its very plausibility it tends to obscure from us the possibility of the sort of complexities that we have begun to envisage.

5 Names and uses

5.1   We have argued so far that inductive abstraction applied to paradigm series cannot determine either the application of a word or its use in discourse. And we have argued also (Section 3.4) that it offers no account of what it is for something to be a name. But we have as yet given no positive account of what it is for something to be a name.

It is still open to an empiricist, therefore (even one who, *mirabile dictu*, accepts the arguments of Chapter 3), to claim that naming is the association of words with elements of the world, even though such associations cannot be performed separately and one by one.

Holding this, he could adhere to a very popular theory about language, which I shall label the " two-tier theory." This is the theory that a language rests on two main sorts of conventional stipulation. The first sort associates phonemic strings with elements of the world and so creates a stratum of *names*. The second sort specifies the ways in which the items in the first stratum are to be deployed in discourse and so creates a second stratum of *uses*.

The trouble with this theory, it seems to me, is that to call something a name is certainly in part to say that it has some sort of linguistic function. And it is not clear how just *associating* something with another thing can confer any linguistic function or significance on either. What, after all, does 'association' consist in? Does it, for example, consist in the learner's knitting his brows, staring fixedly at the thing named, and murmuring the name under his breath? Unless we assent to some such behavioral explication of association, we shall presumably have to adopt a mentalist explication: that is, we shall have to say that association is a mysterious "connection set up in the learner's mind ..."—but connections set up *there* are by their location effectively insulated from further analysis or empirical study. On the other hand, suppose we accept a behavioral explication of the brow-knitting, breath-holding variety; still, where does this get us? Even if we actually observed that such phenomena invariably occurred when a learner was in the act of grasping the meaning of a word, we would still be utterly at a loss to explain such a curious natural concomitance. We would have to ask ourselves such questions as "Why does brow-knitting always accompany grasping the reference of a name?" "What is the connection between the fact that the learner has knitted his brows and the fact that later on he knows how to *use* the word in question?" and so on. The difficulty about these questions, I think, is not just that it seems as if they would be very hard to answer, but that in order to set about answering them we would first have to solve the very (conceptual) questions about the nature of naming and the relationship between naming and use which the theory (that naming is associating) was intended to solve.

We might attempt to evade these difficulties by recourse to a dispositional account of naming: what we associate with the element of the world is a disposition to do something (utter a certain word when in its presence, for example). But often such dispositions have nothing to do with language. If a child is taught to cross himself whenever he sees a church, or if a man fumbles in his change pocket whenever he sees a bus he proposes to take, the crossing and the fumbling are not *names* denoting, respectively, a church and the bus that the fumbler intends to take. Unless we can show that something, in being given some status or other, thereby acquires some minimal linguistic function, we simply have no grounds for saying that what it has become by virtue of being given that status is a name. And the trouble is, as we have seen, that it is impossible to say how associating a word with something can amount to knowing anything about how to use it. The contrary view is only plausible if we suppose that a knowledge of the empirical character of what is named can be processed by means of the mechanism of inductive abstraction in such a way as to yield grammatical information. But we have seen already that this is a vacuous suggestion, plausible in its turn only because we covertly assume the prior possession of certain elementary grammatical concepts as a background for the supposed inductive processing.

5.2 The view which I *do* wish to put forward can be summarized as follows. To give a meaning to a vocal noise—to involve it in language—is to give it a place in a system of prescriptive rules. Examples of the sort of systems of rules I have in mind have been given already in the linguistic devices $[L_1]$ and $[L_2]$ and their associated taxonomy T_A. It should be clear from these examples that I am not thinking of systems of rules which prescribe particular *utterances* as correct responses to particular occurrences or states of affairs, for this would yield only a repertoire of stereotyped signals, and we have already seen that a language cannot be regarded as such a repertoire. Rather, what I want to suggest is that the production by a learner of utterances of a given sort (statements about the presence and bodily locations of pains, say) is governed by a sequentially ordered set of rules such that by following the rules in their correct sequence the learner can, when he finds himself in a situation to which this particular set of rules is applicable (that is, when he has a pain), generate an utterance appropriate to that situation, even though the utterance which is generated by following the rules on this occasion may not be one that he has ever heard uttered before and certainly is not one that he has been explicitly trained to utter as a response to the particular event to which it relates. The teaching of such a system of rules is a single process, the outcome of which is *both* that the learner acquires the capacity to put certain noises to certain uses *and* that some of the noises in question begin to function in certain ways like names. One cannot divide the learning of such a system into two stages: one in which the *referents* of names are learned, and one in which the *uses* of the same names are learned. One could roughly sum up the difference between the two-tier theory and the view that I am now putting forward, by saying that whereas the two-tier theorist wishes to maintain a radical distinction between name learning and use learning, I hold that name learning is a special case of use learning, in the sense that a learner can *only* learn that a given noise is a name and what it names, in the course of learning some set of rules which enables him to utilize that noise, among others, in constructing utterances capable of serving certain given purposes in a certain given range of situations.

But what is the relationship between language and the world, or more particularly between names and the world, if it is not the relationship of association? I think an answer can be given as follows. We can regard the rules of $[L_1]$ and $[L_2]$ and of the taxonomy T_A as defining a number of *places* which can be filled by phonemic strings. Thus, T_A has a structure which can be schematically represented by a diagram of the following type:

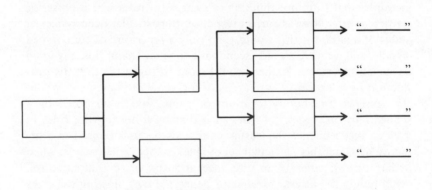

Here the boxes represent questions concerning taxonomic characters, the answers to which determine a path for the user through the taxonomy. The blanks enclosed by quotation marks accept phonemic strings. They are places[1] in the sense which I have in mind, and they can be arbitrarily filled by any phonemic string we choose;

---

[1] *Cf.* Wittgenstein, *Philosophical Investigations*, I.29:

Perhaps you say: two can only be ostensively defined in *this* way: "This *number* is called 'two'". For the word "number" here shews what place in language, in grammar, we assign to the word. . . .—The word "number" [shows] the post at which we station the word.

for no matter what string we assign to a given place it will, given the rules of the taxonomy which govern that place, acquire by virtue of that assignment exactly the same meaning as would be acquired by any other phonemic string which we might choose to assign to the same place. In the same way the rules of $[L_2]$ define a place which in our example is filled by 'hurts' but which could equally be filled by any other phonemic string. If we were to systematically refill the places defined by the linguistic devices of a language we would produce a "different" language only in the sense that its phonetics would be different: its grammar and semantics would remain unaltered.

We can distinguish, then, between the *place-defining rules* of a language (which include, for example, everything that we have so far described as a "rule" of $[L_1]$, $[L_2]$ and T_A) and its *place-filling conventions*. The latter merely assign phonemic strings to the places defined by the former. Giving a word a meaning is not a matter of associating it with some element of the world. There *are* merely associative conventions which operate upon words, but they operate on them not *qua* words but *qua* phonemic strings, and they associate them not with elements of the world but with places defined by the rules of linguistic devices. Linguistic devices in their turn are, as we shall see, "connected with the world" in a very large variety of ways, but the connection never takes the form of an associative linkage operating upon a phonemic string. Names, now, are simply one class of meaningful expressions: namely, those created by assigning a phonemic string to fill one of the places defined by a taxonomic schema.

5.3 We must now consider an objection to the thesis which I have been putting forward. It might be thought that the objection to ostensive procedures, that they open up no possibilities of use, could be overcome by regarding them as procedures for establishing tacts, in Skinner's sense.[2] Here, the learner does learn to make some *use* of a noise; he learns to utter it in the presence of a given object in appropriate conditions of stimulation, response-strength, etc.

---

[2] B. F. Skinner, *Verbal Behavior* (New York: Appleton-Century-Crofts, 1957).

It seems to me, however, that coming to see that some noises are names involves more than coming to see that they can be put to uses, in this Skinnerian sense of 'use'. The arguments which lead me to this view are as follows.

Grasping the concept of naming involves grasping at least the following two principles:

(1) Anything whatsoever has, or can, for special purposes, be given, a name; and anyone can introduce a new name into discourse by means of a conventional stipulation.
(2) It is in principle possible to make any system of nomenclature more precise by further specifying the applications of the names it contains, or by doing this in coordination with the introduction of further names.

That is, someone who does not understand that anything can be the subject matter of a nomenclature, or who does not understand that it is always (logically) possible to specify more fully and accurately the subject matter of a nomenclature, or who does not understand that he can introduce a new name into language whenever he wishes simply by stipulating sufficient criteria of correct application and by arbitrarily designating a phonemic string to which these criteria are to be attached, does not yet fully understand the concept of a name.

Any system of *linguistic* rules (rules establishing a "use of language") is such that the learner, by learning to generate utterances by means of these rules, learns a technique for achieving certain purposes.

Thus, a learner who can operate the rules of $[L_1]$ and $[L_2]$, including those of T_A, has mastered a device for drawing attention to the location of his bodily pains and directing the efforts of other people to cure or reduce them. It follows that, for him, *which* noise he inserts into the schema '____ hurts' on a given occasion will depend, not on an arbitrary convention, but on what he wishes to achieve by uttering the result of that insertion. What he achieves by uttering the result of instantiating '____ hurts' with 'ear' (namely, that he attracts the attention of others and sets them about applying remedies to his ear) could not, for obvious reasons, be equally well achieved by instantiating '____ hurts' with any other noise (for example, 'foot' or 'hand').

In terms of $[L_1]$ and $[L_2]$ we can begin to see how the learner might come to grasp the concept of naming.

The learner in our example can generate an utterance which will serve to draw attention to a pain in a particular part of his body only if, in the course of learning $[L_1]$ he has been taught a sufficiently rich version of T_A, for otherwise his attempt to carry out instructions (1) and (2) may yield either no body-part name at all (if his version of T_A is a taxonomy only of the lower half of the body, for example) or a very misleading one (if, for example, it covers some areas of the body in great detail and others only sketchily). To be inarticulate is frustrating; therefore, the learner has a reason for becoming interested in *what the parts of his body are called*. Moreover, he possesses, in $[L_1]$, a definite procedure for increasing his stock of names of bodily locations: he can point to any part of his body and ask someone else " What's this called? " He grasps, in fact, that any item of a particular sort (any part of his body) either has or can be given a name, because he sees how, if he wished, he could give any such item a name; and he sees *this*—his attention is drawn to this—because he can see what would be the *point*, for him, of bestowing names in such a way (it would make possible a richer array of pain avowals and hence a more precise direction of other people's attempts at succor). What he is grasping here, of course, is also the idea of making a nomenclature more detailed and precise: the idea that one can have, for example, a noise which goes with touching a joint of one's finger as well as one which goes with touching a finger. He has at this point, I think, got hold of the concept of naming, at least as far as the naming of parts of his body goes. To explain how he grasps the idea of naming other sorts of thing (for example, colors; objects with different uses, or with no use—'ornament', 'toy'; states of mind; meals; days of the week; conditions of antiques—'broken', 'restored', 'incomplete', 'imitation'), we should have to discuss in detail the rules of other linguistic devices besides $[L_1]$ and $[L_2]$. This is because grasping the idea that the members of a certain class of objects can be named is a matter, in part, of coming to see some point in naming them (we don't, for example, name the volumes of space which the walls, ceilings, pieces of furniture, and so on, in a room delimit), and this is a matter of coming to understand what purposes can be served by the systems of rules in which such names are to be given a place (a use).

Let us now return to Skinner's model of the learning of tacts.

Here the learner is trained by the methods of operant conditioning to utter a given noise (given certain preconditions of response strength, and so on) when a certain object is present. The association between the object and the noise uttered is one which is established by the trainer to suit his purposes, whatever they may be. All the learner knows is that there are certain objects each of which has this characteristic, that when a certain noise is uttered in its presence, a piece of food (or whatever other standard reinforcer is being used) rolls out of a slot. There is no reason at all (that is, none that is given within the terms of this model situation, so far as we have described it) why the learner should suppose that *every* object of a given sort should have this characteristic (have a name, that is). There is no reason, either, why the learner should come to regard such a characteristic as something capable of being conferred on an object by some conventional procedure; to him, it is just a fact of nature that some objects have reinforcement-evoking noises associated with them, and some don't. For all he knows, of course, some of the latter objects *may* have reinforcement-evoking noises associated with them, but even if they do, he has no means of finding out for himself what these noises might be; and he certainly has no means of *making* a noise of his own devising a reinforcement-evoking noise with respect to a particular object. Moreover, there is no reason why he should come to regard some sorts of objects (pieces of furniture, parts of the body) as more likely to have reinforcement-evoking noises (names) associated with them than other sorts of objects (volumes of space, for example). Finally, because he does not see that names can be conferred by a conventional procedure, and that therefore anything can be given a name if the purpose of discourse makes it desirable to give it one, the learner of tacts will lack the prerequisites for grasping the fact that a system of nomenclature can be made more precise. Hence, since the tact-learning model does not throw any light on how a learner might come to grasp any important feature of the concept of naming, there seems nothing to be gained by identifying tact learning with name learning. The "use" of noises which the tact learner learns is not a *linguistic* use at all.

The reason why the tact-learning situation throws no light on naming is that, from the learner's point of view, the purpose of uttering any tact is identical with the purpose of uttering any other tact: namely, to obtain food or whatever other standard reinforcer is being used in the training process. What the learner needs in order to grasp the concept of a name is (1) that he should be introduced to a class of purposes which can be achieved only by using words (getting accurately directed succor from other people, for example); (2) that there should be some member of this class which he can only achieve by using a particular name which he does not know, although he knows what it would be like to know it (what sort of thing it would be and what he would do with it); and (3) that he should be acquainted with a definite procedure either for discovering what the name in question is or for introducing a new name to fulfill this particular function. The tact-learning situation has nothing in it which corresponds to requirements (2) and (3). There is no purpose which can only be achieved by uttering some tact which the learner does not yet know, for the purpose for which one utters tacts (to obtain reinforcement) can be obtained by uttering any tact (in the right circumstances); hence, the learner need never feel the need for a device for discovering or stipulating new tacts, which in any case he lacks; he will just wait until he has a chance to use a tact which he has already been taught.

But what about the association between the tact and the object or state of affairs with which its utterance is associated? Isn't the existence of this association enough to give the learner the idea of naming? To this we can only reply that we have shown already that there is more to the concept of naming than the mere establishing of associations.

It appears, then, that the two-tier theory of language learning is quite untenable: learning that some words are names and learning how to apply particular names correctly, are precisely examples of use learning, in the sense of 'use' which we have begun tentatively to define.

The two-tier theory is an uneasy compromise between referential and use theories of meaning. It is important, I think, to see (what many people who accept the theory in some form or other seem not to see) that to hold the view that "meaning is use" in such a context is to hold it in a form in which it so bristles with difficulties as to be practically indefensible. For, if we accept that the concept of naming and the application of particular names can be sufficiently explained to a learner by setting up in his mind associations of noises with, say, classes of stimuli and proceed to argue that " rules of use " are then imposed on the array of names so established, so as to convert the whole chimerical structure into a language, we shall find it very difficult to give an intelligible account of the nature of the rules of use in question. Grammatical rules will hardly fill this role. According to one view, they are merely negative and prescribe that certain expressions shall not occur in a sentence if certain other expressions have already occurred (for example, ' He was ' excludes ' convince ' as a possible continuation). Restrictive rules of this description can hardly be the only rules governing sentence construction: a man must have some idea of what he means to say, and how to go about saying it, before it is possible for him to infringe, and by infringing to become conscious of, such rules. What shows him how to begin the tentative construction of sentences? The referential theorist has a ready answer waiting—the nature of the referents of the words which occur in those sentences—but this is an answer which the use theorist cannot accept, although, *faute de mieux*, it seems he must.

Again, the rules of a transformational grammar seem poor candidates for the role of the philosopher's rules of use, since the rules of use of a language must *ex hypothesi* be such as to determine its semantics, while the relationship between transformational grammar and semantics remains obstinately obscure.

But what, then, are we to make of the formula: "The meaning of a word (sentence) is its use"? The use of a name, presumably, is to name something: and if we have accepted the first half of the two-tier theory, then we shall have to grant the adequacy of the usual empiricist accounts of the meaning of names. What about the uses of sentences? It is difficult to know what to say here, and current conventional wisdom seems to suggest only one further possible answer: namely, that sentences are used for performing *illocutionary acts*,[3] such as making statements, delivering verdicts, making promises, and so on. But it will hardly do to say that the

---

[3] See J. L. Austin, *How To Do Things with Words* (Cambridge, Mass.: Harvard University Press, 1962).

meaning of a sentence consists in its being used in performing a certain illocutionary act, for we can still ask what makes the sentence a fit instrument for performing that particular illocutionary act, and now the only possible answer seems to be, *what the sentence means*.[4] And " means " in this latter sense is clearly not to be explicated in terms of how the sentence is used; once again we are forced away from a use theory of meaning, back towards the standard empiricist accounts. Austin, of course, is not guilty of trying to explicate meaning in terms of illocutionary force: in *How to do Things with Words* he distinguishes illocutionary force from meaning "in the sense in which meaning is equivalent to sense and reference."[5] But if we accept the two-tier theory we *are* committed to the attempt to explicate meaning in terms of use at the level of sentences rather than at the level of words; and it is very hard to see how one can explicate the concept of use at this level other than in terms of illocutionary force or some similar concept. In order to avoid these difficulties, it seems to me, we must abandon the vision of language as an array of names enveloped in a superimposed network of rules of use. Instead, we must see language as an array of concrete and limited techniques for communication (of which the technique of issuing pain avowals in Chapter 4 is one). Such a technique will involve vocal noises in various ways, and it will be in various ways "connected with the world"; but the machinery of this connection will differ from one technique to another, depending on the peculiar functions and character of each. The connection between language and the world must thus be conceived as something which comes about in a great many different ways as a result of the character of particular systems of rules of use, not as something which is estabished prior to the establishment of rules of use; or of something which, whenever it is established, is established in the same standard way; or as something which essentially involves words, or names, and not other units of language.

---

[4] I am indebted for this point to Gary Iseminger's "Uses, Regularities and Rules," *Proceedings of the Aristotelian Society* (1966–1967).

[5] Austin, pp. 100, 120.

6 The tasks of a phiolsophical theory of language

6.1 To what discipline, exactly, are the arguments of the preceding chapters intended to contribute? Have we been doing philosophy, or psychology, or linguistics, or some curious and suspect blend of all three? To these straightforward questions we can offer a relatively straightforward answer, though not a very simple one.

It is obvious that children begin by not being able to speak any language at all, and end, barring such accidents as enforced deprivation of social intercourse at maturationally crucial stages of their childhood, by speaking at least one language fairly fluently. One can ask at least two different sorts of question about this phenomenon. One can ask, on the one hand, "How does it come about that a child learns to speak his native language?" or "What is the psychological mechanism by which it comes about that he learns to speak his native language?"

If psychologists made within their subject the same sort of rough and ready distinction that is commonly made between experimental and theoretical physics, then such questions would clearly be questions for the experimental psychologist. They are causal questions, and answering them would mean adding to our store of knowledge by formulating and testing empirical hypotheses rather than merely imposing some sort of conceptual order or systematization upon existing knowledge.

On the other hand, again, one can ask such questions as " What does an adult speaker's ability to speak a language consist in?" or, what amounts to the same question, "What is it that a child learns in learning to speak his native language?" These questions are conceptual questions. That is, they are not demands for more *facts* about language. We know, after all, as plain men and (some of us) as linguists, plenty about language. What we don't know is what to make of all the facts we know. We need in some way to make sense of them, to find some order in them: we require a conceptual model.

The construction of a conceptual model is not a matter of spinning armchair fantasies about the workings of nature, founded upon some viciously *a priori* set of assumptions. To begin with it is necessary to establish criteria of adequacy for the sort of model that one intends to attempt to construct. These criteria of adequacy will require in part of any successful model that it be such that explications of a great many diverse phenomena can be given in terms of the model. And they may also require, for example, that the model explicate the phenomena in such a way as to permit them to be made objects of fruitful and nontrivial empirical investigation. Such requirements place strong empirical constraints upon the construction of a conceptual model.

Associationism and stimulus-response theory in psychology are, it seems to me, conceptual models and are widely regarded as providing an essential theoretical basis for the prosecution of experimental studies in psychology. It is evident that a work like Skinner's *Verbal Behavior* is not written to demonstrate a causal concomitance between observed episodes of operant conditioning and the observed acquisition of linguistic skills. For if it were, then it would consist largely of observational reports and results of surveys and experiments, instead of consisting, as it does, of discursive argument of a generally philosophical character. Moreover, Skinner expressly disavows a concern with observation and experiment and explicitly states his intent in the book as that of showing that the phenomena of verbal behavior can be explicated in terms of the conceptual vocabulary of operant conditioning. We can see, moreover, that if Skinner were trying to establish a causal concomitance of the above type, his work would be, while important, far less important than *Verbal Behavior* would be if it successfully demonstrated the truth of its conclusions. For if experimental work were to establish beyond reasonable doubt that nothing essential happens to a child in the process of learning its mother tongue, which is not strictly analogous to what happens to a rat learning to press the bar in a Skinner box, we would still be no nearer to *explaining* how language is learned. We would have discovered an extremely puzzling natural con-comitance; and we would be in much the same position as the one we would be in were we to discover that a child kept in solitary confinement developed the power to talk, in a quite normal way, provided it was plunged in cold water once a day. In other words, we would have discovered *that* a certain event or set of events E is a sufficient and necessary condition for the development of a capacity C, but we would as yet have no idea *why* E is a sufficient and necessary condition for the development of C. *Verbal Behavior* sets out to do more than barely postulate the existence of a natural concomitance of that sort (that could be done on half a sheet of note paper and would in any case be pointless unless we had some theoretical reason for expecting such a concomitance to exist). It sets out to establish theoretical connections between operant conditioning and language, such that if we discovered *that* exposure to operant conditioning was in fact a sufficient and necessary condition for the acquisition of language we could reasonably claim to know also *why* it was a sufficient and necessary condition (to know, that is, not only certain genetic facts about language learning, but the rationale of language learning). We are engaged on a similar enterprise. Whether one calls this enterprise philosophy, or philosophical psychology, or theoretical psychology is, to my mind, merely a matter of taste.

The ETL, it seems to me, is a mixture of conceptual model and empirical hypothesis. That is, it offers us simultaneously an account of what is learned in learning language *ab initio* and an account of the psychological mechanism by which the learning of language proceeds. The plausibility of the empirical hypothesis depends upon the adequacy of the conceptual model: it is only if the ETL theorist is correct in his claim that all of the phenomena of language can be represented in terms of his favored conceptual vocabulary of associa-tion, inductive abstraction, ostensive definition, and so on, that it becomes plausible to suppose that children learn their native language by being trained to associate phonemic strings with sensory stimulation patterned in ways carefully determined by the linguistic community to which they belong.

What I have tried to show so far is that the conceptual model provided by the ETL is wholly inadequate. It is supposed to offer a nonintuitive explication of a whole range of concepts which are normally explained by appeal to linguistic intuition, of which the concepts of meaning and of concatenation (the central problem here is to explain the ways in which the meanings of sentences depend both on the meanings of their component words and on their syntactic and morphological structure) are the most important and the ones on which the theory concentrates. I have tried to show that the conceptual vocabulary by reference to which the ETL proposes to explicate these linguistic concepts is simply irrelevant to what it is supposed to explicate. For whenever the ETL theorist proposes such an explication (of naming in terms of ostensive definition, for example, or of syntactic function in terms of the patterning of the sensory material associated with differently structured sentences), we find that we must either postulate a purely magical connection between *explicans* and *explicandum*—that is to say, convert the ETL theorist's proposal from a conceptual model to a rather odd empirical hypothesis and interpret him as claiming, for example, that it is just a matter of empirical fact that the practice of ostensive definition with small children leads (somehow or other, in some fashion not explained by the theory) to their coming to grasp the concept of a name—or else, in order to make the connection between *explicans* and *explicandum* intelligible, if only on a trivial level, we must covertly assume that the child in question already grasps, in some form or other, the very concepts which the ETL theorist's account is supposed to be explicating.

The vacuity of the ETL as conceptual model thus vitiates the ETL as empirical hypothesis. For once the illusion of understanding which suggested the empirical hypothesis in question has been dispelled, it is of no more intrinsic interest or plausibility than any quite arbitrary hypothesis that we might frame: for example, the hypothesis that there is a causal connection between learning to talk and eating plenty of fruit.

6.2 So much for the critical and negative portions of the preceding chapters. We have also laid the foundations of a conceptual model different from that offered by the ETL, and we must now ask what sort of model this is, and what are the criteria of adequacy which it must satisfy. As should by now be obvious, we are not in the least concerned to advance *a priori* theories about the psychology of language acquisition. Rather, we wish to discover a mode of representation of what is acquired. We assume that the verbal behavior of an adult speaker of a language L is the result of the application of some set of learned conventional rules—the rules of L—to the infinitely variable combinations of circumstances in which the adult speaker may produce significant and appropriate utterances. We assume that these rules are a finite set since it is possible to master a language in a finite space of time: once fluent in his native language a man may develop stylistically, but he cannot thereby be said to be learning more about the rules of his language, any more than a chess player who improves his endgame may thereby be said to have improved his knowledge of the rules of chess.

We assume, moreover, that the content of the set of rules of L remains virtually constant from speaker to speaker, since otherwise L would not be a single language.

We wish now to represent the general form of the rules of a language L, in such a way that we can see clearly how we might set about filling in the details of this formal outline so as to arrive at the actual rules of a particular natural language.

We are trying to construct a theory of linguistic competence in the sense defined by certain linguists, including Chomsky and others. A theory of competence represents as a system of rules some aspect of an adult speaker's linguistic competence—for example, his syntactic competence or his phonological competence. Such a theory is not to be confused with a theory of performance. A theory of performance would tell us the mechanism by which a speaker produces utterances which are original, significant, and appropriate to their circumstances of utterance. Let us call the neurological mechanism which governs this activity the *language machine*. A theory of competence, now, tells us only that the language machine must contain as a component either some specified set of rules S or some formally different set S_1 which is equivalent to S in that the operations of S_1 produce exactly the same linguistic results as the operations of S. But, even if we have separate theories of competence for syntax, semantics, and phonology, there still remain the problems of how the content of these theories is (1) represented and (2) related in the language machine. Both (1) and (2) are obviously aspects of the same problem: it is a problem which is relatively trivial where it concerns the relationship between syntax and phonology, but extremely difficult where it concerns the relationship between syntax and phonology, on the one hand, and semantics on the other.

The first criterion of adequacy for our model is that it should solve this latter problem. We are concerned, that is, with elaborating a theory of the form and content of the rules which govern the production of significant and appropriate utterances: thus, with a theory of total linguistic competence, in its semantic as well as its syntactic and phonological aspects. This yields two quite severe empirical constraints upon a successful model of this type: it must prove capable of representing in some form or other the content of an adequate competence theory of syntax, and it must supply convincing interpretations of the known facts about children's learning of syntax.

In connection with the latter requirement we must obviously not elaborate systems of rules of types which are clearly, or even probably, beyond the capacity of children to learn. Preferably our rule systems should presuppose only the capacity to execute general types of performance which human beings are known to execute in extra-linguistic contexts, but it will not be necessary to confine ourselves to types of performance which animals are known to execute, or to types of performance whose psychological or physiological mechanism is well understood.

It would be impossible to fulfill these rather exacting requirements completely without constructing a more detailed model than I am in a position to construct or could be contained within a book of this length; but I shall try to show in Chapters 12 and 13 that a theory of linguistic devices seems at least in principle to be capable of fulfilling them.

A further obvious criterion of adequacy which we must meet is that our model must explicate a number of concepts having to do with language, and normally explained by appeal to linguistic intuition, without itself covertly assuming any understanding of these concepts or making any appeal to intuition. The concepts in question include those of a name, of meaning, of synonymy, of a sentence, and of syntactic relationship (the relationship which unites the component words of a sentence into a sentence), of a word, of semantic vagueness, of metaphor, and of what is sometimes called semantic category by philosophers and semantic anomaly by linguists. We shall not altogether exhaust this list in the succeeding chapters, and it could be lengthened.

6.3 Someone might object as follows: "Is language *really* a system of rules of any type, let alone the type you propose? Are you not really doing armchair empirical psychology, whatever you say to the contrary, since you propose to tell us *what a child learns, in the process of learning language*, but to do so not on the basis of detailed observation of children but rather on the basis of a purely theoretical argument? And isn't the point at which your argument becomes viciously *a priori* precisely the point at which you assume that an adult's linguistic behavior is the result of 'applying' to something (to his experiences, to his circumstances, to the world as it appears to him?) some system of rules?"

I think what we have already said stands in part as an answer to this objection, but something more needs to be said. A model is not an assertion about reality. It is merely a demonstration that reality can be systematically represented according to a certain schematism. The reason why I have been careful to stress the status of the assumption that what different speakers of a language have in common is a grasp of the same system of rules is precisely that I wish to do justice to this distinction. Because of this distinction it is quite inappropriate to ask whether a conceptual model is *true* or whether it offers the *correct representation* of the phenomena to which it applies. For no doubt it may be possible to systematically represent any set of phenomena in terms of several, or perhaps even on occasion many, different conceptual schemata. Thus, we can represent a volume of heated gas as a congeries of particles, as a pattern of convection currents, and in other ways. It is not sensible to ask which of these is the correct way, but it is sensible to ask whether each of them is of interest, and why.

Whether a given conceptual model, *qua* demonstration of the possibility of subjecting a given set of phenomena to a given schematism, is of interest, depends on, among other things, whether it is empirically fruitful. The representation of language as a system of rules has been conspicuously fruitful in linguistics and to some extent also in philosophy; and therefore, it seems worth trying to carry this line of inquiry further in order to see whether it may not be possible to construct a unified theory of linguistic description. And I think it is reasonable to expect that the successful construction of such a theory would make possible a more fruitful intercourse between linguistics, empirical psychology, and perhaps also certain forms of philosophical analysis. Some psychologists have recently turned their attention to the study of children's syntax, proceeding on the assumption that the syntax of children, like that of their elders, can be represented as a system of rules; and it is not unlikely that similar empirical studies could be pursued with semantics, if we could see how to represent the semantics of a language in terms of systems of rules. In this connection it is worth noticing that a linguistic device is a species of *plan*, as that word is defined by Miller, Galanter, and Pribam in their book *Plans and the Structure of Behavior*.

part two
Structure and meaning

7 Linguistic devices

7.1 We must now turn to the detailed formulation of the theory of language whose outlines we sketched in Chapters 3–5.

We can best begin by developing some more examples of linguistic devices, commenting, as we go along, on some of their logical characteristics. As an arbitrary starting point, let us consider the learning of the use of the word 'bring'.

A learner might begin with the following procedure:

[A] The learner is shown an object, for example, a ball, and is taught to bring it to the teacher on the command 'Bring the ball'.

It is worth noticing (1) that this is something which animals, for example, dogs, can be taught to do. If a dog can, for example, fetch a thrown stick and lay it at its master's feet, we are not inclined to say that the dog "knows the meaning of" or "understands" the word 'bring', although we may well say that it "knows how to bring (fetch)." (2) The command 'Bring the ball' is part of a *system of signals*, in the sense in which we defined that phrase in Chapter 2. In [A] the learner is taught what in Chapter 3 we called a *sterile*

and circumscribed ritual. And we can see, in the light of the arguments
of Chapter 4, that it would be misleading to say that in [A] the learner
has learned the *meaning* (reference, relation to the world) of the word
'bring', or that he has learned that 'bring' is a *name* (that is, the
name of the action ' bringing '). Indeed, in [A] 'bring', 'the', and 'ball'
have no separate function. The functional unit is the string ' Bring
the ball', and this is not "associated" with some part of the world
but serves as a cue to initiate a certain response on the part of the
learner.

[B] The learner is taught the application of a set of labels—'book', 'doll',
    'dog', and so on—a primitive taxonomy of everyday medium-sized
    physical objects.

There are several reasons why we should *not* be prepared to say
that [B] involves *naming* in the sense made familiar by the ETL.
To begin with, the learner of [B] is again learning to *execute a
performance.* He is learning to make certain vocal noises (utterances
of 'book', 'doll', 'dog', and so on) when objects of certain sorts
are presented to him in certain standardized ways (perhaps involving
verbal cues; for example, the question "What's this?")
  The main claim of the theory of naming characteristic of the ETL
is that the learner's ability to abstract, to perceive similarities between
objects and between utterances, can function as a rule, and the sole
rule, governing the execution of such performances. But if we accept
this claim, we shall find ourselves committed to the trivializing
assumption that the learner must bring with him to his initial learning
of language a prior grasp of the concept of a name, for it is only if
he already possesses this concept that the principle of inductive
abstraction *on its own* can suggest to him how he should interpret
his teacher's promptings and model his own performance on the
paradigms with which his teacher presents him.
  If we allow ourselves a little less parsimony where rules are concerned, we can avoid this sort of assumption. What the learner has
to do if he is to master [B] is (1) to grasp that on each occasion when
the teacher says "What's this?" and presents an object, he is supposed to respond by uttering *one* member of a series of standardized
vocal noises ('book', 'doll', 'dog', and so on); and (2) to acquire a

set of criteria for determining *which* member of this series to utter on each occasion. We thus arrive at the following schematic representation of the rules of **[B]**.

[B] (1) When someone says, "What's this?" and presents an object in the usual way, utter one, but not more than one, of the following responses: 'book', 'doll', 'dog', 'cat', and so on.

    (2) To determine which response to utter on a given occasion, apply the following criteria.

If this account of the rules of **[B]** is correct, then **[B]** is not a device for setting up associations between elements of the world and recognitional capacities. The ability to detect similarities simply does not function as a *rule* of **[B]** at all, although possibly it may be a *necessary precondition of a learner's coming to grasp the rules of* **[B]** that he should be able to detect similarities.

The rules of **[B]**(2) will have the form of a taxonomic schema of the type discussed in Chapter 3. That is, they will not be associative in character but will approximate in character to a computer program or a set of rules for carrying out a qualitative chemical analysis. They instruct the learner to ask certain questions about the object being presented to him; depending on whether he answers "yes" or "no" they instruct him to produce an utterance or to ask a further question, and so on. A further reason why we should not regard **[B]** as a *naming* procedure in the sense characteristic of the ETL is as follows. For the empiricist theorist of language, to know the reference of a name is to possess a concept; concepts "determine the flow of words";[1] hence to know the reference of a name is to know how to use that name in discourse. But someone who has grasped **[B]** is not able to use 'ball', 'dog', 'cat', and the rest in discourse. All he can do is to produce correct vocal responses when he is presented in a standard way with certain sorts of object. The device **[B]** is, in fact, another sterile and circumscribed ritual. It is still not capable of being put to any useful purpose in communication between the learner and other people, for its rules do not include among their number any which might enable it to be put to any such

---

[1] Price, *Thinking and Experience*, p. 349.

purpose. The words which are given application by the taxonomic schema of **[B]**(**2**) are capable of taking on the character of names through the involvement of that taxonomy in other uses of language, since in relation to these further uses it will be possible to distinguish them functionally from words of other types and to grasp both the nature of the necessity for, and the technique of, introducing further words of the same type into the language. But in relation to **[B]** they are not names but something more rudimentary and shorn of the associations of syntactic function and nomenclature which normally enter into the everyday concept of a name. We may call these proto-names *labels*: **[B]** on its own is not a naming but a labeling device.

If **[B]** is ever to be put to use in communication it can only be because **[B]**, as a subordinate linguistic device, is incorporated in some other device of wider scope.

This is in effect, what happens in **[C]**.

[C] To generate correct responses to utterances of the form 'Bring ____',
    in all cases in which the blank is filled by one of the labels whose application has been learned in **[B]**, apply the following set of rules:
    (**1**) Examine all the objects visible in the vicinity and determine (by means of **[B]**(**2**)) what the correct vocal response would be in each case if the teacher were to ask of that object, "What's this?"—that is, if teacher and learner were operating device **[B]**.
    (**2**) As you determine the correct vocal response for each object, utter it subvocally.
    (**3**) Detach 'bring' from the teacher's utterance, and compare the remainder successively with each of your subvocalizations.
    (**4**) When this comparison produces a match (defined within certain phonological limits), perform on the object which generated the matching subvocal utterance the operation which you learned, in learning device [**A**], to perform on balls in response to the command 'Bring the ball'.

The rules of **[C]**, like those of any other linguistic device, are essentially instructions for executing a certain set of *procedures*. And just as, in learning **[B]**, the learner is not learning *to associate names with their referents*, so, in learning **[C]**, he is not coming *to grasp the syntactic function of bring*. He is not, for instance, learning that 'bring' is a transitive verb, or even that sentences beginning with 'bring' express commands. All he is learning is that in dealing with (generating acceptable responses to) utterances of the form 'Bring ———', one must, at a certain point, detach 'bring' from the remainder of the utterance in order to compare the remainder with a series of other utterances which have resulted from the carrying out of another operation.[2]

It is one of the most puzzling facts about our knowledge of language that someone who "knows" a language, say English, in the sense that he can speak it fluently, may nevertheless be quite unable to state the rules of English grammar as these are understood by a grammarian or a linguist.[3] Our knowledge of language on these occasions seems instinctual rather than conscious: we can do the trick but we don't know how we do it. Indeed, the task of reflecting upon our instinctive linguistic performances, in the effort to see what general rules or conceptual distinctions are implicit in them, is an extraordinarily arduous one: it requires hard work and intelligence to produce even the simplest (decent) bit of conceptual analysis or linguistics.

It is difficult to understand in terms of the ETL why this should be so. If the learner of language *ab initio* is inductively acquiring a grasp of syntactic functions and relationships it should be relatively easy— not perhaps immediately, but at a later stage when the necessary

---

[2] Berkeley, in a famous passage (the Introduction to *Principles of Human Knowledge*, §XIV), objects to Locke's account of general terms on the grounds that, if it were true, children could not "prate together of their sugarplums, and rattles, and the rest of their little trinkets" until they had "first tacked together numberless inconsistencies and so framed in their minds *abstract general ideas.*" People often talk as though Berkeley's target here were not (what in fact, I think, it is) the idea that children must unite *inconsistencies* in framing the ideas which give words meaning for them, but were rather the idea that children are capable of thinking inductively in quite complex ways. It should be clear that this unexceptionable view is not my target any more than it was Berkeley's. My objection here to the ETL is not that if it were true children would be even better at thinking inductively than in fact they are, but that if it were true, children would be conscious and accomplished grammarians, which they manifestly are not.

[3] R. M. Hare, in "Philosophical Discoveries," *Mind* (April, 1960) discusses some aspects of this problem.

words are available to him—for him to say what these functions and relationships are.

In terms of our model, however, the difficulties which we encounter when we try to describe just what it is that we are doing when, flawlessly and confidently, we speak our own language, are exactly what we would expect. The learner whom we have imagined becoming accustomed to detach 'bring' from certain sorts of utterance in order to perform a certain operation on the remainders, will in the course of time acquire a good many other dispositions of similar types in connection with other sorts of utterance involving the word 'bring'. By virtue of possessing all these distinct habits of performance, he will be able to use the word 'bring' in discourse. But his knowledge of English grammar will remain, to borrow Ryle's distinction, "knowledge how" rather than "knowledge that," for he will not as yet have learned any *rules of grammar* in any sense in which grammarians or linguists understand that phrase. He may now, by reflecting carefully upon his own linguistic performances, construct grammatical rules of a kind with which grammarians and linguists are familiar. But these rules, while they may constitute a *description* of certain aspects of his linguistic performances, will not be identical with the rules by adherence to which he *produces* his linguistic performances. Later on we shall examine this difference in more detail.

Let us return to our discussion of [C]. The device [C] is in effect a set of rules for producing appropriate responses to any utterance produced by filling in the blank in 'Bring _____' with any noise which has come to function as a response in [B]. What the learner does in coming to "understand" [A], [B], and [C] is to acquire a certain array of routine habits of performance—of dispositions to initiate certain sequences of operations in response to certain cues—and to continue or terminate them by reference to certain criteria. (I have in mind here such things as the criteria for what constitutes a match between two phonemic strings, or the criteria which determine whether the learner at some given point in a sequence of operations like [B](2) is to produce an utterance or proceed to a further question.) It follows that, if the learner understands [C], then if he is presented with any utterance produced by filling in the blanks in 'Bring _____' with any utterance which has come to function as a response in [B], he will be able to apply to that utterance the sequence of operations prescribed by the rules of [C] and so generate an appropriate response to it. Thus, he will not need to be explicitly taught an appropriate response to every new utterance (that is, any utterance previously unheard by him) in order to produce an appropriate response; for, given the utterance, he will be able to generate for himself an appropriate response to it, by applying the rules of [C].

It thus appears that the system of linguistic devices [A]–[C] possesses just that characteristic of natural languages which we have found most puzzling; that a finite process of teaching can result in the acquisition of capacities of performance which go beyond the limits of what has been explicitly taught.

Let us call this property of a system of linguistic devices its *fertility*. It is worth noticing that the fertility of the system [A]–[C] is introduced into it by [C]. Both [A] and [B] are sterile; [B], for example, contains a repertoire of verbal responses, and new responses can only find their way into the discourse of the [B]-speaker (unless, that is, he learns a new device, such as [C]) if his teacher introduces, by a process of explicit teaching, a new item into this repertoire. The reason why [C], on the other hand, is fertile, is that its rules mention—refer back to—the rules of other devices. It is this element of reference to other devices, also, which introduces into [C] the earliest beginnings of syntax: which makes it possible, that is, for us to regard [C] as a set of rules for generating responses to a variety of fillings-in of a syntactic schema, 'Bring ____'.

What I wish to suggest is that fertility in language is made possible only by the existence of hierarchical relationships of presupposition between different linguistic devices, relationships which are all of essentially the same type of those obtaining between [C] on the one hand, and [A] and [B] on the other, insofar as they all involve the interpolation, into a main sequence of operations, of subsidiary sequences of operations, which the speaker has learned to carry out in other circumstances and for other purposes, in such a way that the outcome of the main sequence is rendered variable within certain limits.

The fertility of the system [A]–[C], however, has its limits. The learner who has mastered [A], [B], and [C] can do just one sort of thing: he can bring objects when he is asked to do so, even when the object is one which he has never been asked to bring before, provided the repertoire of responses which he has learned in [B] contains the appropriate item. We shall need more explanatory machinery if we are to understand how a learner might progress beyond this point to more elaborate linguistic performances. We have, however, reached a minor vantage point from which we can inspect from a new direction one of the central errors of the ETL. By insisting on treating ostensive definition as a procedure capable of teaching the 'meaning' (the whole use in discourse) of a word, what the empiricist theorist of language has done, in effect, is to represent a linguistic device which (because its rules mention no other linguistic device) possesses no fertility whatever, as if it possessed—what no simple device or small set of such devices can possess—a degree of fertility equivalent to that possessed by language (considered as the total collection of linguistic devices) itself.

7.2 It may be argued that someone who has mastered [A]–[C] must surely, at any rate, know *what bringing is*. And indeed it is tempting to suppose that the learner must by now have made the association between the noise 'bring' and a certain action (the action of bringing) and that having made this association he will surely require no further training to enable him (1) to ask for things to be brought to him, and (2) to characterize other people's acts of bringing as acts of bringing.

These plausible claims rest on dubious assumptions. So far, 'bring' for the learner is merely a noise which occurs in certain verbal cues to which he knows how to make appropriate responses. It does not function for him as a name of an action: there are as yet no criteria of application attached to it as there *are*, for example, criteria of application attached to 'book' and 'doll' (as we shall see in a moment, there are special problems about formulating criteria of application for names of actions). Hence, he does not yet know how to name the action of bringing in his discourse with others, and hence he cannot command others by naming the action which he wishes them to perform. Indeed, we have no reason to say that the learner has yet grasped the notion of commanding: he does not know that the cues to which he responds are *commands*, for he does not know what purpose they serve in the life of the person who issues them; hence, nothing in his learning of [A]–[C] as we have described it explains why the learner, having grasped this much, should suddenly know *how to command*.

Learning how to ask others to bring things, then, involves learning a separate linguistic device, the rules of which we can reasonably represent as follows:

[D] To get someone to bring you an object which you wish to have hold of:
   (1) Utter the noise 'bring'.
   (2) Look at the object you wish your hearer to bring, and by using the rules of **[B]**(2), generate the noise which you would utter if you were being shown the desired object in the context of **[B]**.
   (3) Utter this noise.

In order to make this schematic model more closely represent linguistic reality, we would have to add, of course, (at least) rules governing inflection and gesture, so that the learner would produce the utterances generated by **[D]**(1)–(3) with the inflections, and so on, appropriate to *requests*.

It is evident, however, that if the learner executes instructions (1)–(3) in sequence and without mistakes, this will result in his uttering a range of requests: 'Bring . . . book', 'Bring . . . doll', and so on. Which of these requests he makes at a given time will depend on which object he happens to desire at that time. In general, his learning of **[D]** will bring it about that whenever he desires an object he will be able, by applying the rules of **[D]**, to generate for himself an utterance which will function as a request for that object, provided, of course, that the object in question is one which has figured in his learning of **[B]**. We can if we wish, then, regard the rules of **[D]** as rules for filling in, in the context of a certain species of social intercourse, the syntactic schema 'Bring ____'.

It is worth noticing that **[A]**, **[B]**, **[C]**, and **[D]** have, from the learner's point of view, quite different *purposes*. In a sense, **[A]**, **[B]**, and **[C]** have no purpose from the learner's point of view. They are simply games which he plays with his elders, games belonging to the same family as Pat-a-cake and Three little piggies, which have no winners and no point but consist simply of an intriguing pattern of behavior coupled with an intriguing verbal rigmarole. Even so, **[B]** is quite different from **[A]** and **[C]**. The device **[B]** is, we might say, a showing-and-saying game; **[A]** and **[C]** are both saying-and-doing games. The device **[D]** is different again. When he learns **[D]**, the learner discovers that games of utterance and action can have practical functions: you can use one of them, at least, to get other people to bring you things. This is a quite limited and particular discovery, but one which foreshadows a great many other discoveries of the same sort about the multifarious workings of language. What this helps us to see, I think, is that the learner's " coming to see the point of" language may not be a matter of his suddenly tumbling to something—a single great discovery expressible in some such words as " *Now* I see what meaning is!" " *Now* I see that words *refer* . . . that there is such a thing as *grammar* . . . that language is *about* the world!"—but may rather take the form of a very long series of particular discoveries about the functions of linguistic devices, in the course of which the child is gradually " humanized " by being initiated into one after another of the innumerable forms of social intercourse and relationship which language makes possible, and which in turn determine the structure of the linguistic devices which serve them.

7.3 We have not so far discussed the use of the word ' bring' in the giving of information. How, for example, might someone learn to make appropriate use of an expression like ' He is bringing the book'?

B. F. Skinner would no doubt want to say that the emission of tokens of the type ' He is bringing the book' is under the stimulus control of a complex pattern of stimuli consisting of observations of bodily movements on the part of another person.

For Skinner, if I have understood him correctly, a controlling stimulus is a collection of sensory experiences such that the occurrence within some given space of time $t_0 - t_n$ of *all* the members of the collection is a necessary, although not a sufficient, condition for the emission of a certain response. It follows that on Skinner's view one could ostensively define the utterance (the tact) ' He is bringing the book' (place it under the control of the relevant stimuli) by reference to a paradigm series of charades in which an actor performs a sequence of bodily movements involving a book. An appropriate schedule of reinforcements applied in connection with such a sequence of charades should result in the learner's coming to exhibit the required disposition to utter the response ' He is bringing a book' only in circumstances which include someone executing, with the aid of a book, just those bodily movements which are intrinsic to the act of bringing a book.

The trouble with this account of the matter is that it is impossible to exhibit *any* sequence of bodily movements which is intrinsic to the act of bringing a book (consider, for example, the cases of someone (1) walking towards us with a book in his hand; (2) sliding down a rope with the book in his pocket, or (3) clenched between his teeth; (4) pedaling up the drive with a large folio Milton in the basket of his bicycle; (5) leaning from the gondola of his balloon, which is drifting towards us, waving the book energetically above his head to demonstrate its presence.

When we are in a position to use a well-formed taxonomic schema to determine the application of a word W to certain members of a given class of objects O, the following condition will be met: namely, that we shall be able to specify a range of characteristics, C_1, C_2, ..., C_n, possessed by at least some members of O, such that when we are considering whether W is properly applicable to a given member M of O, the discoveries, first that M possesses C_1, then that it possesses C_2, and so on, make it progressively more probable that M is a W (C_1, C_2, ..., C_n being, of course, taxonomic characters for W). Thus, for example, if we discover that a certain animal, besides having a hairless, horny skin, has legs and besides having legs has a long snout of a certain shape, it becomes progressively more probable that we are dealing with a crocodile.

Our real difficulty, now, is that in the case of the putative application of the word 'bringing' to certain members of the class of sequences of bodily movements, this condition is not met. We can see this, perhaps, if we contrast words like 'bringing', 'chopping', 'poisoning', 'mending', 'playing', all of which "designate actions," with words like 'crouching', 'kneeling', 'nodding', which really do designate bodily postures or movements. If I am told that the head of a certain man whom I cannot see has tilted backward and forward several times, then I know that he is nodding, though of course I don't know whether he is consciously indicating assent, is under the influence of a hypnotist, or has some nervous tic. I know that he is nodding simply from what I have been told about the physical movements of his head. On the other hand suppose I am told, of some absent person, whom I have never seen or heard of, before being given this information, that he is walking across a room, opening a drawer, taking out a book, putting it in his pocket, walking to the door, opening it, walking down a corridor. . . . Up to this point I have no inkling of why this man is doing these things: he may be taking the book out for a quiet read in the park, he may be going to throw it away, he may just be putting it in his pocket for future reference (perhaps it is a diary). In a few minutes, however, the same man enters the room where I am sitting: he hands me the book. *Now* I know that (for some purpose yet to be revealed) he has brought the book to me. Presumably then, at least since he took the book from the drawer, he has been *bringing* it to me; yet I could not possibly have known this simply from the description which I was given of his bodily movements while he was in the other room. Equally clearly, no possible amplification of that description could have identified his action as a case of bringing: it would not have helped a bit if, for example, I had been informed, perhaps through the medium of some sort of choreographic notation, of the exact position of his fingers, or his feet, relative to the rest of his body and the objects in the room, at each successive moment. The accumulation of information about a series of bodily movements *never*, in itself, serves to make it any more probable that a particular action word applies to the person who is executing those movements, for a description of bodily movements is invariably compatible with more than one description in terms of actions.

That this (or some such) "logical" distinction between descriptions of actions and descriptions of bodily movements exists is, of course, a philosophical commonplace. It is harder to see what sort of learning process might underlie the distinction (might make the workings of the English language, once learned, such as to force such a distinction upon us). The following (model) sequence of linguistic devices may, I think, suggest a possible answer.

[E] The teacher says to a third party 'Bring *a*' (this being an utterance generated by the rules of [D]. A few moments later he asks the learner, ' Is he bringing *a*?' The rules by reference to which the learner generates an answer to this question are as follows:
   (1) Answer either "yes" or "no."
   (2) Determine which answer to give by reference to the following instructions:

(i) Determine whether the person P to whom the request 'Bring a' was addressed has moved his position.

If he has not, answer "no."

If he has, proceed to (ii).

(ii) Determine whether P has any object visibly in his possession or attached to him.

If he has not, answer "no."

If he has, proceed to (iii).

(iii) Generate the name of each object noted in (ii) using the rules of [B](2).

(iv) Detach the noise 'bring' from the original request ('Bring a', in this example) and compare the remainder successively with the products of (iii).

If no match is discovered, answer "no."

If a match is discovered, proceed to (v).

(v) Observe whether P is moving (a) toward the teacher, or (b) away from him, or (c) is stationary.

In case (b), answer "no."

In case (c), answer "no."

In case (a), answer "yes."

This exposition of the rules of [E] is—in places—too condensed and simplified for it to constitute a plausible account of the functioning of an actual linguistic device. For example, further criteria for the identification of the person P need to be added in (i); while in (ii) further criteria would be required to represent the process by which the learner determines, for example, whether P has or has not some object in his possession. And, of course, provision should be made for the response, "I don't know." However, this sort of elaboration seems to me to present no new theoretical problems, and I have avoided it for the sake of simplicity of exposition.

The rules of [E] make no reference to any specific postures or movements which P may make or adopt while the learner is observing him. Thus for example in (v), the learner is simply required to determine whether P is moving toward or away from the teacher or whether he is stationary. It is quite immaterial whether he is walking or hopping, bicycling or riding a horse towards the teacher; hence, it does not matter, for the purposes of answering the question 'Is P bringing a', that P's posture and movements may be totally different depending on whether he is doing one of these things or another. Similarly, for the purposes of (ii) it is irrelevant whether *a* is in *P*'s pocket, clutched in his hand, tucked under his arm, strapped to his thigh, and so on.

This is not, however, the main reason why a description of a man's postures and bodily movements never by itself suffices to determine whether he is *bringing*. The main reason is that some of the rules of [E] have to do with the social context in which *P*'s movements and postures are executed. Thus in order to carry out instructions (i), (iv), and (v), the learner must first ascertain that someone has in fact issued a request addressed to *P*, identify the person in question, and learn in what words he issued his request. Plainly, no description of *P*'s movements and postures can give the learner these three items of information. Hence, a description of *P*'s movements and postures can never be made to determine whether or not *P* is *bringing* by being made more detailed and specific. For although by making it more detailed we shall soon reach a point at which, in one sense, our descriptions are *too* detailed (more detailed, that is, than is necessary to enable the learner to comply with (ii), or with (i) and (iv), given the other information which he needs to comply with these); in another sense we shall never reach a point at which our descriptions are detailed *enough*, for we shall never reach a point at which they include the contextual information necessary to enable the learner to carry out (i), (iv), and (v).

7.4   At this point an objection may be raised which it will be as well to dispose of before going further. It may be argued that since [A], [C], [D], and [E] are four separate devices, and since we seem to want to maintain some form of the thesis that "meaning is use," and since the words 'bring' and 'bringing', have different uses in these four devices, then these words must have four different meanings—a highly implausible conclusion. The answer to this, I think, is simply that the linguistic devices [A]–[E] are not separate in the required sense, but compose a structure in which the components—the individual devices—are intimately related in various ways. Thus for example, [C] contains essential references to [A] and [B]. Again, once the members of a group of learners have all mastered the devices [A]–[C], they must, if they are to be able to put this mastery to use in bringing things for each other (as well as for the teacher), learn a further device like **[D]**. The rules of **[D]**, in fact, are what they are because the rules of the earlier devices are what they are. The same relationship holds between the rules of **[E]** and those of the earlier devices. If we want to teach one member of the group to say of another member that ' He is bringing' when, and only when, that member is following the rules of **[C]**, then the rules we teach him will necessarily have to be those of **[E]**, as we have represented them, because of the nature of the rules of **[C]** and **[D]**.

Learning "the meaning of" the word 'bring' is learning to operate a series of devices related in these and other ways. It is these (and other) complexities which we obscure from ourselves when we attempt to represent meaning as a simple relationship between a word and some recurrent fragment of experience.

8 Vagueness

8.1 It is worth noticing that only a finite amount of information is necessary to enable the learner to comply with (that is, to decide whether to answer "yes" or "no" or to proceed to the next instruction) each of the instructions (i)–(v) of [E](2); from which it follows that only a finite amount of information is necessary to enable him to decide whether the word *bringing* is or is not applicable to a given sequence of events. This result may occasion some surprise, for it is a common assumption of much current philosophy that no finite amount of information about any particular object of reference, O, can ever suffice to establish *with certainty* whether any given general term would or would not be correctly applied to O. Most current discussion of this supposed phenomenon stems from a paper[1] in which Professor Waismann introduces the linked terms "vagueness" and "open texture." The first of these terms, together with a simpler version of Waismann's thesis, is of much earlier provenence. Thus, we find Russell claiming that

[1] Friedrich Waismann, "Verifiability," in A. G. N. Flew, ed., *Essays on Logic and Language*, 1st series.

the meaning of a word is not absolutely definite: there is always a greater or less degree of vagueness. The meaning is an area, like a target: it may have a bull's eye, but the outlying parts of the target are still more or less within the meaning, in a gradually diminishing degree as we travel further from the bull's eye. As language grows more precise, there is less and less of the target outside the bull's eye, and the bull's eye itself grows smaller and smaller; but the bull's eye itself never shrinks to a point, and there is always a doubtful region, however, small, surrounding it.[2]

The reason why the meaning of any word is vague in this sense is, Russell thinks, that for each and every one of its users the word in question will have been (ostensively) defined by reference only to some subset of the total set of particular objects of reference to which the word is correctly applicable. Thus, in the mouth of any given user, a word will inevitably "mean something slightly different" from what it means in the mouth of any other user. Russell makes this clear in, among other places, Chapter V of *The Problems of Philosophy*: "The word 'German' will, again, have different meanings for different people. To some it will recall travels in Germany, to some the look of Germany on the map, and so on."[3]

Let us, simply for the purposes of the present argument, define an *employment* of a word W as an occurrence of W on a single particular occasion in discourse. We can now distinguish between two theses about vagueness, namely:

Thesis 1: In every employment of any general term, the meaning of that term will be vague.
Thesis 2: The meaning of any general term may be vague in some of the employments of that term.

Let us call thesis (1) the strong thesis and (2) the weak thesis.

It is clear, I think, that Russell, in the above passages, is concerned to argue for the strong thesis. It is obvious too, it seems to me, that if Russell is right in thinking that the meanings of general terms are

[2] Bertrand Russell, *The Analysis of Mind* (New York: The Macmillan Co., 1921), pp. 197–198.

[3] Bertrand Russell, *The Problems of Philosophy* (London: Oxford University Press, 1912), p. 55.

established ostensively, by associating each such term with some range of instances of its correct use, he is right to conclude that, since no one can ever be exposed to every correct employment of such a term, the meaning of any such term will always differ slightly for each different user, and hence that any use of any such term will inevitably be to some extent vague—in one sense of "vague," for here we must exercise caution and distinguish between two senses of this term. In Russell's sense of "vague" (which we shall mark in discourse by the expressions "$vague_1$" and "$vagueness_1$"), the meaning of a term is $vague_1$ in a given employment if, and only if, the pattern of habitual associations which it evokes in the minds of its hearers is not uniform from hearer to hearer. In the second sense of "vague" (which we shall mark in discourse by the expressions "$vague_2$" and "$vagueness_2$"), the meaning of a word is $vague_2$ in a given employment if, and only if, the user is uncertain whether or not the word is applicable to the particular object of reference to which he wishes to apply it. Waismann sometimes uses the word *vagueness* to mean $vagueness_1$ but most often to mean $vagueness_2$, although we shall have occasion to distinguish within his usage two distinct types of $vagueness_2$.

Waismann begins his discussion of vagueness by claiming that most of our empirical concepts are 'open-textured'. The arguments which establish this are drawn essentially from the armory of epistemological scepticism.

What I mean is this: suppose I have to verify a statement such as 'There is a cat next door'; suppose I go over to the next room, open the door, look into it and actually see a cat. Is this enough to prove my statement? Or must I, in addition to it, touch the cat, pat him and induce him to purr? And supposing that I had done all these things, can I then be absolutely certain that my statement was true? Instantly we come up against the well-known battery of sceptical arguments mustered since ancient times. What, for instance, should I say when the creature later on grew to gigantic size? Or if it showed some queer behavior usually not to be found with cats, say if, under certain conditions it could be revived from death whereas normal cats could not? Shall I, in such a case, say that a new species has come into being? Or that it was a cat with extraordinary properties?... Have we rules ready for all imaginable possibilities?[4]

[4] Waismann, p. 119.

According to Waismann, most empirical concepts are insufficiently defined by the "rules of our language" for us to be quite certain whether or not such concepts are applicable to exceptional or unusual cases. And, of course, it is always (logically) possible that the unusual case—the cat which grows to gigantic size, or explodes, or begins to speak Old Norse, or turns into a griffin—may one day turn up. We could, of course, resolve our doubts in any such case by placing arbitrary limits on the applicability of the concept in question. We might decide that a cat which spoke Old Norse was not a cat (but a devil)—or again, we might decide that it *was* a cat (but one which had been surgically interfered with by whimsical Professor B). In either case our decision would be just that: a decision. There would be nothing in the rules governing the employment of words as they existed before we came across the exceptional case which could in any way guide us in making such a decision. This fact about most empirical concepts—that they are not defined "with absolute precision, that is, in such a way that every nook and cranny is blocked against entry of doubt"[5]—is what Waismann labels the open texture of such concepts.

Waismann now defines "vagueness" in terms of open texture in the following sentence: "Open texture, then, is something like *possibility of vagueness*."[6] How are we to interpret this definition? It would be natural, I think, to construe it as follows. We have a case of vagueness when some actual state of affairs (for example, the discovery, under the kitchen table, of a cat which asks for milk in Old Norse) forces us to admit that we are in doubt whether a certain concept applies to this state of affairs or not. To say that a concept is open-textured, on the other hand, is to say that there is a logical possibility of cases arising which would call its applicability in question in the above way.

There are, however, potent reasons why we should not place this construction upon Waismann's words. Waismann wishes to say that an open-textured term may not be vague in many of its ordinary everyday employments, although it is open-textured: "a term like 'gold', although its actual use may not be vague, is nonexhaustive or of an open texture in that we can never fill up all the possible gaps through which a doubt may seep in."[7] And he also wishes to say that

[5] *Ibid.*, p. 120.

[6] *Ibid*.

[7] *Ibid*.

while open texture cannot be remedied by giving more accurate rules for the use of words, vagueness can. But if we interpret Waismann's account of the relationship between vagueness and open texture as we have done above, we shall find that our account conflicts with both these statements of Waismann's.

We may exhibit these conflicts as follows. Let us grant for the sake of argument that the discovery of a cat speaking Old Norse would force me to admit that I simply did not know whether the word 'cat' was properly applicable to such a creature or not. Is it consistent with this thesis to claim that when I am confronted with a perfectly ordinary cat I need feel myself subject to no doubts concerning the applicability of the word 'cat' in this case? Plainly not, for however ordinary the cat now before me may appear, it is nevertheless logically possible that it may at any moment begin speaking Old Norse or turn into a griffin. We may accept, for the sake of argument, Waismann's assumption that the rules governing the application of the word 'cat' *are* such that the word is neither definitely applicable nor definitely inapplicable to animals which are in the habit of speaking a human language. It follows that, unless I can completely exclude the possibility that the animal before me is sometimes in the habit of speaking a human language, I must remain in some doubt as to whether the word 'cat' is definitely applicable to it. But this possibility is one which, by the very nature of epistemological scepticism, it is logically impossible for me ever to completely exclude. It appears, then, that vagueness in one of its Waismannian senses (namely, vagueness which, as it were, comes into being as a by-product of the possibility of epistemological doubt and which we shall henceforward label "vagueness$_{2E}$") must, if it infects any use of a given word, infect every use of that word, even in the most commonplace circumstances. Waismann has in fact inadvertently committed himself to a version of the strong thesis about vagueness. We need feel no surprise at this, for it is precisely the distinguishing characteristic of the doubts canvassed by epistemological scepticism that they are not specific doubts, arising only in special circumstances, but doubts *in principle*, capable of being raised with respect to any situation whatsoever.

Related arguments will show that vagueness$_{2E}$ cannot be remedied by "giving more accurate rules [of language]." Let us suppose that I decide that the word 'cat' is to be definitely not applicable, at least in my usage, to animals which speak a human language. The meaning of 'cat' will still be vague$_{2E}$ for me in every ordinary context, since in every such context I shall be able to raise sceptical doubts concerning the secret (or future) linguistic proclivities of the apparently ordinary animal in front of me. Again, suppose I decide that the word 'cat' shall apply to anything that resembles a cat, even if it does speak a human language. It still remains logically possible that the behavior of an apparently ordinary cat might, in an indefinitely large number of other ways, turn out to be so odd that I should feel obliged to cease speaking of such a creature as a cat; and it remains logically possible that the animal in front of me may exhibit behavior of one or other of these kinds.

8.2 Our first interpretation of Waismann's account of the distinction between vagueness and open texture turns out, then, to be untenable. It collapses under its own weight into a different interpretation, according to which to say that the meaning of a word is vague is to say that we can *never* be quite sure whether or not it is applicable to any particular object of reference. On this interpretation no distinction can be drawn between vagueness and open texture either by claiming that vagueness is a property which words exhibit on particular occasions while open texture is a (dispositional) property which they exhibit at all times (words which are vague are, on our second interpretation, vague in all uses), or by claiming that vagueness can be eliminated—while open texture cannot—by making the rules governing the application of words more precise, since manifestly, on our second interpretation, it cannot be eliminated in any such way. It looks, in fact, as if on our second interpretation, the only difference left to be marked by the vagueness–open texture terminology is a trivial one: we can say, if we like, that to say of a word that its meaning is vague is to say that we can never be certain whether or not to apply that word to any given particular object of reference, while to say that a concept is open-textured is to say that in its case there is a permanent logical possibility of our discovering queer cases which will forcibly remind us of what in the ordinary run of events we may have forgotten—the reality of all-pervading vagueness.

It would seem, then, that what appeared to be a very natural interpretation of Waismann's distinction between vagueness and open texture gives it implications which are possibly counterintuitive and certainly contrary to Waismann's intentions in formulating it. We must ask, therefore, whether Waismann can offer any other way of construing the distinction. In "Verifiability," Waismann offers two examples of words whose meaning is vague: the words 'heap' and 'pink', which he contrasts with 'gold' in a passage which we have already quoted in part and must now quote in full:

> *Vagueness* should be distinguished from *open texture*. A word which is actually used in a fluctuating way (such as 'heap' or 'pink') is said to be vague; a term like 'gold', though its actual use may not be vague is non-exhaustive or of an open texture in that we can never fill up all the possible gaps through which doubt can seep in. Open texture, then, is something like possibility of vagueness. Vagueness can be remedied by giving more accurate rules, open texture cannot.[8]

The trouble with these examples, it seems to me, is that we cannot construe the term " open texture " by reference to them (that is, without applying the definition of open texture as " possibility of vagueness ") without making nonsense of Waismann's primary account of open texture. The " vagueness " of meaning of 'heap' and 'pink' consists in the fact that, as Waismann says, they are used in a *fluctuating* way. What this means in the case of 'heap' is that some people are prepared to apply the term 'heap' to smaller aggregates of material than those to which other people would prefer to restrict the application of the term: this leads to trivial arguments about how large such an aggregate must be in order to be called a heap. (For example, are four grains of sand enough, provided that the fourth is placed on top of the other three arranged in a triangle?) Similarly, some people are prepared to call 'pink' what other people would call 'light red', and so on. It is, I think, crucial to notice that in many uses of 'heap' and 'pink', no doubt arises about the applicability of the word. A stack of coal in a merchant's yard or a shocking-pink scarf provide clear and undoubted cases of a heap and of pinkness. What makes these words vague is simply the fact that surrounding the clear and undubious cases is a penumbra of doubtful ones: the four grains of sand, the light red rose, and so on, It seems to me, now, that the sense of 'vague' in which

[8] *Ibid.*

'heap' and 'pink' are vague cannot be identified with vague$_{2E}$. The vagueness of 'heap' and 'pink' does not stem from the possibility of epistemological scepticism but from linguistic considerations the nature of which we shall discuss in what follows. We are dealing, then, with a further sense of "vague" and "vagueness" which we shall mark in discourse by the expressions "vague$_{2L}$" and "vagueness$_{2L}$."

Now, if open texture is the permanent possibility of vagueness$_{2L}$, then open texture has nothing to do with epistemological scepticism. For consider the case of the four grains of sand arranged tetrahedrally. My doubt as to whether this is a heap is quite different from the doubt which Waismann's investigator of cats feels concerning whether or not the animal in the next room is a cat or not. The cat investigator's doubt is one which involves questions about the conformity of appearance to reality. His worry is over whether this is a *real* cat (or a hallucination, or a devil, or a disguised Venusian spy plotting the conquest of our planet...). Consequently, his doubts can have no final resolution, since they are indefinitely renewable: no sooner has one possibility of mistake or error been excluded by empirical investigation than further possibilities suggest themselves, together with the attendant thought that however many possibilities of error the investigator recognizes and excludes by empirical tests, the logical possibility of unrecognized possibilities of error remains unexcluded; and furthermore, that the techniques of empirical investigation themselves afford a foothold for a further order of indefinitely ramifying possibilities of error. Again, besides being indefinitely renewable, the investigator's doubts are all-pervasive; they can all be raised with respect to any putative cat whatsoever (indeed, to the investigator no cat, however seemingly authentic its empirical credentials, can be more than a putative cat).

In the case of the four grains of sand arranged tetrahedrally, our doubts are not appearance–reality doubts at all. We *may* say to ourselves, "Is this really a heap?" but this does not mean that we are in any doubt about *what* we have before us, for we are not: it is a tetrahedron of sand grains. Our doubts are not epistemological but linguistic: what worries us is not the thought *this might be in reality quite other than what it appears to be*, but the thought *one could equally well argue that this ought to be called a heap or that it ought not to be called a heap*. Accordingly, my doubts are not indefinitely renewable ones: if I find that most English speakers would apply the word (or deny its applicability) to the sand tetrahedron, or if I stipulate (perhaps in connection with some scientific inquiry) that the word is, in certain contexts, to apply to such objects, that settles the matter. For the same reason my doubts are not all-pervasive: the fact that I can raise them in connection with the sand tetrahedron does not mean that I can raise them in connection with a forty-foot stack of anthracite. Epistemological doubts can, of course, be raised here, but this is irrelevant: the linguistic question is, " Given that this *is* a stack of anthracite (and not an hallucination, a shadow cast by the other stacks, and so on), is it the sort of thing that, in English, is called a heap?"

' Pink ' can be treated in similar ways. By building on these examples of vagueness$_{2L}$ Waismann could, it seems to me, have constructed the sort of distinction between open texture and vagueness which, as his remarks in " Verifiability " make clear, he thought he had constructed. For example, Waismann clearly wishes to advance what we have called the weak thesis about vagueness: the " actual use " (that is, the general run of employments) of words like ' gold ' is, he thinks, not at all vague. As we have seen, if we identify vagueness with vagueness$_{2E}$, we are inevitably committed to the strong thesis. The identification of vagueness with vagueness$_{2L}$, on the other hand, commits us to the weak thesis. Thus, there are some employments of the word ' heap' in which it is not vague at all, and these include the vast bulk of its everyday employments. On the other hand, the fact that the word is not vague in these employments offers us no guarantee that we shall not in the future come across cases (like the sand tetrahedron) which place us in doubt about the applicability of the word. But these doubts have no tendency to " overflow " these special cases and to infect everyday cases, as the doubts characteristic of vagueness$_{2E}$ have.

Again, Waismann asserts that vagueness (unlike open texture) can be remedied by the introduction of new rules of language. As we have seen, vagueness$_{2E}$ cannot be remedied in this way. But, clearly, vagueness$_{2L}$ can. Let us suppose, for example, that I am doing a study of the mechanics of sand dunes. It turns out that certain mechanical processes affect sand grains arranged in aggregates, the largest of which is the dune itself and the smallest the sand tetrahedron. Since the dune is a heap of sand, it is natural and useful to extend the term ' heap' to all subordinate aggregates affected by the same mechanical processes including the sand tetrahedron (we can imagine, for example, that the mechanical processes culminating in the formation of the dune only begin to take effect when sand tetrahedra—which we may suppose to be more stable than loose sand grains—are formed by the random shifting of grains). Suppose that this terminology is useful enough to catch on in the literature. The question " Is a sand tetrahedron a heap?" now has an answer: it is "Yes—for the science of dune mechanics." The form of this answer displays the fact that the doubts characteristic of vagueness$_{2L}$ are always doubts relative to a given linguistic system. " Ordinary language " will continue to provide no definite answer to the question, unless ordinary men become so passionately interested in soil mechanics that the usage of soil scientists gradually supplants traditional usage in this sphere. At the same time, however, our hypothetical soil scientist's use of the word ' heap ' is not an arbitrary departure from ordinary usage but a well-grounded extension of it. It was always true that grounds could be found for the view that the word ' heap' ought to apply to a sand tetrahedron (just as it was always true that grounds could be found for the opposite view). What has happened is merely that the soil scientist's discoveries have added to these grounds, in such a way as to make them conclusive, by showing that sand tetrahedra, besides marginally resembling other things that we call heaps, resemble them in other respects which are important enough to make the extension of the application of the term something which is seriously to be desired for the purposes of informative discourse, rather than something to be toyed with in the course of a flight of whimsy.

8.3 If we have argued correctly, the introduction of considerations of epistemological scepticism into Waismann's discussion of vagueness makes his position thoroughly incoherent.[9] The reason for this, it seems to me, is simply that

[9] The exegesis of Waismann's thought on this point is further complicated by the fact that in his discussion of vagueness (in *The Principles of Linguistic Philosophy* (London: Macmillan; New York, St. Martins Press, 1965), chap. 4) vagueness throughout seems to be used as synonymous with vagueness$_1$ (Russell's sense). There is no mention of vagueness$_{2E}$ or vagueness$_{2L}$ or open texture. Moreover, Waismann here seems to assume the truth of the strong thesis (consistently with his identification of vagueness with vagueness$_1$) and speaks, for example, of " the actual use of a word, wavering and fluctuating though it is."

epistemological scepticism has nothing to do with vagueness of meaning in language. To begin with, it follows from Waismann's remarks on the verification of 'There is a cat next door',[10] that *whenever* I discover an *x* which exhibits some unusual property, however trivial, which no *x* hitherto known to me has exhibited, I must of necessity be thrown into doubt as to whether the thing before me is an *x* at all. This seems to be just false. Thus, for instance, if I were to find a cat with bright green fur the color of copper oxide or a pineal eye between its ears, my first thought would probably not be " Can this really be a cat?" but "This is a very curious cat," or "This cat displays what must be a very unusual mutation." Cases of unusual properties displayed by cats (or anything else) seem in fact to fall into three categories, which we shall illustrate with examples drawn, I am afraid, in part from science fiction.

(1) Cases where the oddity does not make me for a moment doubt that the animal which displays it is a cat, even though I have never come across it before (for example, polydactyly; a cast in one eye; growling instead of mewing).

(2) Cases where the oddity at once rules out the possibility of the animal's being a cat. (For example, the skin is found to contain only electronic and hydraulic apparatus mounted upon a stainless steel skeleton.)

(3) Cases where I am in doubt whether to call the animal a cat or not. (For example, the animal is four feet high at the shoulder; has a very large cranium and modified paws and vocal apparatus; and can speak English and use tools. I know, moreover, that it was not born in the ordinary mammalian way but was "grown" in a tank of nutrient fluid by methods of tissue culture—like the Bokanovsky fetuses in *Brave New World*—from a piece of cat epithelium which had been subjected to various sorts of genetic and other modification.)

With reference to the above examples we can distinguish two quite different senses in which it can be said of us that we are in doubt whether to call something a cat or not. On the one hand (doubt type A), we may recognize that the general appearance, behavior, and so on, of the animal are catlike but still wonder whether further acquaintance with it might not reveal that it possessed qualities of the kind

[10] Waismann, "Verifiability," p. 119.

covered by case (2) above, which would rule out the possibility of its being a cat. This is not a *linguistic* doubt, for it does not arise as a result of any ambiguity or incompleteness in the rules governing the application of the word 'cat'; rather, it arises because of the (necessary) incompleteness of our knowledge of the particular animal which is before us now.

On the other hand (doubt type B), what we know about the animal may be such that we can make out an equally good case for saying that it is a cat and for saying that it is not a cat. Thus in our science fiction example of case (3), we might find ourselves arguing that, after all, the original scrap of epithelial tissue from which the animal was grown was *cat* epithelium—its chromosomes are cat chromosomes, even though much modified by the techniques of (say) 21st-century experimental genetics—and that, therefore, we ought to concede that it is a cat; But yet being instantly swayed by opposing arguments (the tissue was not, after all, germ tissue but epithelial tissue; surely, then, it is not a cat at all, but a monstrously transformed bit of cat skin). Our doubts here are not epistemological doubts. They do not arise because our knowledge of the animal is incomplete (or because it is —logically—incompletable). It is what we already know about the animal that puts us in doubt what to call it. No further information about the animal could resolve these doubts; the only thing that could resolve them would be, in fact, a well-grounded decision to add to the rules of our language.

All Waismann's examples of doubt about whether or not things are cats, men, or samples of gold, are examples of type A doubts. And if, as we have suggested, only type B doubts have anything to do with linguistic vagueness, then Waismann's examples are all irrelevant to this topic.

How did Waismann come to miss the distinction between questions about whether things are really *x*'s or not and questions about whether they are the sort of thing to which '*x*' either clearly does or clearly does not apply, and the still more fundamental distinction between doubts of type A and doubts of type B? Part of the answer, I think, is that Waismann's thought, despite his debt to Wittgenstein, still moves within a set of assumptions characteristic of the ETL.

Waismann assumes that the meaning of a word—say, 'gold'— is given by stating a list of characteristic properties of objects to which it refers. Normally we apply the word 'gold' to things which exhibit the complete set of characteristic properties of gold. But suppose we come across something which exhibits an incomplete set:

> What would you say if a substance was discovered which looked like gold, satisfied all the chemical tests for gold, whilst it emitted a new kind of radiation? [11]

Here doubt about the applicability of the word sets in. This view is very closely connected with the idea that one learns the meaning of a word by associating it with paradigm cases of its correct application. The rule whose operation is assumed by this account is, as we have seen, "Apply the word 'x' to anything which resembles the members of the paradigm series of x's in just those respects in which they resemble each other." The application of this rule to samples of gold would give us Waismann's assumed list of characteristic properties of gold. Now, if this is the rule which we must follow in applying any word, then our actual ability to apply words must depend on the extent of our knowledge of the objects to which we propose to apply them, and any uncertainty in our knowledge must thus appear as uncertainty about the applicability of words. Thus, I can only be sure that the animal before me is a cat if I can be certain that it resembles all the paradigm cats with which I have hitherto been made acquainted in just those respects in which they resemble each other. But this is something of which—the resources of philosophical scepticism being what they are—I never can be certain.

This, then, I think, is the crucial point at which considerations of epistemology and considerations of the structure of language as a system of learned conventional rules, become confused, and it is this confusion which vitiates Waismann's views on vagueness. For that matter, Russell's account of vagueness is vitiated by essentially the same confusion: it is because Russell believed at the time of *The Analysis of Mind* that most words get their meaning by being ostensively associated with paradigms of correct application that we find him arguing that the meaning of such words will necessarily differ from user to user, and hence that any use of such a word will inevitably be attended with some uncertainty about its meaning.

[11] *Ibid.*, p. 120.

Our model of the rule structure of language enables us to avoid this confusion. In the linguistic device [E], for example, the learner is not trying to decide about the applicability of the word 'bring' by comparing a present performance with a set of paradigm cases of bringing. Rather, he is carrying out, with respect to the present performance, certain tests and operations which together compose an algorithmic sequence which yields as its terminating step a determination of the applicability or inapplicability to that performance of the word 'bring'. In most normal circumstances this algorithm will yield either a definite "yes" or a definite "no." That is to say, when the learner is presented with sequences of actions taking place in a certain social context and asked to say whether or not they are cases of bringing, he will be able in most ordinary cases, by applying the rules of [E], to answer quite definitely "yes" or "no."

For the learner, then, 'bringing' is a word whose meaning is *precise*—the opposite of vague—for most ordinary situations. "Ordinary" situations here include Waismannian situations in which, for example, it later turns out that, perhaps because of a series of misunderstandings, what was going on in a given situation was not *bringing* at all. A word does not cease to be precise because some particular situation turns out, in the event, not to be one of the sort to which it applies: indeed, it is a mark of the word's precision that when the sceptic's forebodings are proved correct, it becomes as instantly apparent that the word does *not* apply, as it was previously, given the nature of the situation as it then appeared, evident that it *did* apply. A word is precise, in fact, just in case we know at once whether or not to apply it to any given state of affairs, including that which obtains (or seems to obtain) before some eye-opening revelation and that which obtains (or turns out to obtain) after it.

It is, I think, evident, once we cease to conflate epistemological considerations with those proper to the theory of meaning, that most general terms current in ordinary language are, in the above sense, precise with respect to most of the everyday states of affairs to which we have occasion either to apply or to refuse to apply them. And I think it is also evident that our model reflects this characteristic of ordinary language, whereas the model offered by the ETL does not. But it is equally true that, for most general terms, one can construct actual or imaginary states of affairs with respect to which the term is vague in that it is simply not clear whether or not it applies to that state of affairs. It remains to be seen what explanation of this fact our model offers.

We can construct a situation in which the rules of [E] would fail to yield an unambiguous "yes" or "no" as follows. Let us suppose that a sergeant asks a private soldier, who happens to be expert in the use of the boomerang, to bring him a boomerang. The soldier picks up the boomerang, takes a step or two towards the sergeant, but then throws the boomerang away from him. Before the sergeant can protest, however, the soldier marches smartly toward him. When he is three paces away from the sergeant, the boomerang returns, as he expected, to his hand: he catches it and hands it to the sergeant. The question now is, has the soldier, or has he not, failed to obey the order to bring the boomerang?

This is pretty clearly a case of vagueness$_{2L}$: we feel here equal and opposite temptations to say that the soldier has—in a way—brought the boomerang to the sergeant and that—in a way—he hasn't. The case is tailormade for the barrack-room lawyer.

It is fairly easy to see, from the point of view of the rule structure of [E], why the word 'bring' should be vague in its application to this case. The root of the trouble is that the rules of [E], when applied to this particular sequence of events, yield both affirmative and negative answers to the question "Is he bringing the boomerang?" depending on the point in the sequence at which we apply them. An innocent observer, knowing nothing of boomerangs but knowing how to operate the rules of [E], would produce the following replies to the question "Is he bringing the boomerang?": (1) at t_1, just after the soldier has picked the boomerang up and while he is taking his first few steps towards the sergeant, "yes"; (2) at t_2, just after the boomerang has been thrown, "no." And if (3) we introduce our observer only at some moment t_3, after the boomerang has been caught, his answer would again be "yes."

It would not be difficult to amend the rules of [E] in such a way that the device would generate consistent responses even in cases like that of the soldier and the boomerang. For example, we could add a further instruction, (vi), which makes the affirmative response contingent upon the object's remaining in the bringer's physical possession until he hands it to the receiver: we will call the version of [E] which contains this instruction [E_1]. The device [E_1], now, will be an altogether new linguistic device. We shall have arrived at it simply by deciding to alter [E], and we shall not (*pace* certain Austinians) be able to point to any justification for this decision in the "rules of ordinary language," for it is precisely the rules of ordinary language (the rules of [E]) which yield ambiguous results in the case of the soldier and the boomerang. However, [E_1] will be a much less useful device than [E], for its rules will yield a negative response in many cases (for example, the case in which someone, bringing me a parcel of books, puts it on the luggage rack of the compartment in which he is traveling) in which we would ordinarily want to speak of an act of bringing having been performed.

The degree of latitude open to us in reformulating the rules of [E] is considerably restricted, in fact, by the nature of the rules of [C]. We want the rules of [E] to be such that they yield an affirmative response in all and only those cases in which someone is correctly responding to a [C]-type command. [E] is perhaps an optimal device for this purpose, but certainly not a perfect one.

Philosophers often speak as though the possibility of altering the "rules of our language" were completely unrestricted and open at any point whatsoever in language and as if the question of how any given "rule of language" ought to be formulated could be settled piecemeal by an arbitrary decision, without reference to any other "rule of language." It has even absurdly been suggested that necessary truths may be true by virtue of this sort of arbitrary decision about the meanings of words. If we are correct, a language is an intricate and interlocking structure, and the process of reforming its rules a highly complex and unarbitrary one restricted by all manner of requirements having to do with the functions and the relationship to the world of particular linguistic devices and the relationships of particular linguistic devices to one another. The late J. L. Austin's sense of the relative unlikeliness of useful philosophical reform of "ordinary English" was, for this reason, I think, well-founded.

Finally, we must notice that although [E] is vague in the boomerang case, this vagueness does not, unlike the vagueness (vagueness$_{2E}$) of Waismann's main thesis, transfer back to any other case to which we might want to apply the rules of [E]. The rules of [E], in fact, continue to yield a definite, unambiguous response in the vast mass of everyday cases, despite the fact that they yield conflicting responses in the boomerang case.

We can now provisionally redefine 'vagueness' and 'open texture' for linguistic devices as follows. A linguistic device is *vague* with respect to some particular state of affairs if and only if its rules yield ambiguous or conflicting results when applied to that state of affairs. A linguistic device is *open-textured* if and only if it is logically possible that there exists some state of affairs with respect to which it is vague.

The particular mechanism underlying vagueness may differ from one linguistic device to another. In the case of labeling devices like [B], vagueness will reflect an inadequacy in the taxonomic schema or schemata which the device embodies. To see how this might work we must look more closely at the conditions of adequacy bearing upon taxonomic schemata.

If, *per impossibile*, I could define a word—again let us take as an example Price's 'crocodile'—by abstracting the common properties of a paradigm series, then, although the word so defined would be chronically vague$_{2E}$, it would be, by the same token, quite insusceptible to vagueness$_{2L}$. I would, that is, for all the familiar reasons having to do with epistemological scepticism, never be *quite* certain that any putative crocodile *really* resembles all the paradigm crocodiles in *all* the respects in which they resemble each other, and hence I would be chronically uncertain whether the putative crocodile really ought to be called a crocodile. But on the other hand, it would always be either true that the putative crocodile did have all the requisite properties or false that it had all of them; and if I could only find out with certainty which of these alternatives was the case, then I would either know definitely that the word 'crocodile' did apply to the putative crocodile or know equally definitely that it did not. The ETL theory of naming, in other words, makes it altogether inexplicable that there is sometimes *argument* about whether a word applies or not.

We are in a quite different position with a taxonomic schema. In choosing taxonomic characters for such a schema, we shall not be guided by a desire to isolate and specify in advance *every* characteristic possessed in common by all things worthy to be called crocodiles, or whatever. All we need to begin imposing a taxonomy on the field of animals is some pair of characteristics which are never in practice shared by the same animal. No animal we know of is both hairy and feathered. Thus, we can construct a very simple taxonomy for the animals we know of, as follows:

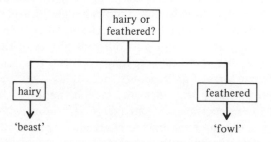

Of course we also know of many animals which are neither hairy nor feathered. Let us suppose that we are not very interested in these, since as it happens we neither hunt them nor eat them nor give them any significance in our religious activities. Then we shall get along very nicely with the following taxonomy:

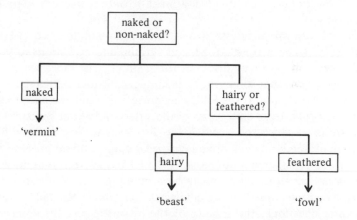

This taxonomy is perfectly satisfactory, given our assumptions about the natural world in which it functions, for the following reasons. First, the taxonomy is supposed to divide *individual animals* into groups, and second, no individual animal is in fact both hairy and feathered. Let us suppose that there does exist an animal which has two stages in its life cycle: a larval, feathered stage and an adult, furry stage. Provided that we are not concerned with constructing a taxonomy of *species* (that is, a taxonomy which ascribes the same animal name to all familially related individuals), this will not matter, for it will still be true that no *individual* animal is both furry and feathered: individuals belonging to different phases of the life cycle of (what a biologist would call) the same species will simply be identified as different sorts of animal.

In our postulated world, then, the facts of nature are such as to allow us to construct a quite satisfactory taxonomy of individual animals using the three taxonomic characters, 'naked', 'hairy' (or 'furry'), and 'feathered', although they are not such as to allow us to construct a satisfactory taxonomy of species using these taxonomic characters. The former taxonomy will be satisfactory just in that it assigns an animal name, 'vermin', 'beast', or 'fowl', to every animal we ever come across and only one such name to each such animal. So far, then, our usage as concerns animal names is in no sense vague but "perfectly in order as it is"; for it is not a *defect* of our taxonomy that it is an individual-animal taxonomy and not a species taxonomy.

Armed with this adequate taxonomy we can go on to discover both general facts about beasts, fowl, and vermin, and exceptions to such generalizations. We may discover, for example, that most beasts are quadrupeds but that some (the ones biologists would call kangaroos, for example) are not. If the ETL were correct, it would be hard to see how one could make discoveries of the latter kind about *beasts*, for if everything to which the word 'beast' has been applied hitherto had been quadrupedal, then a nonquadrupedal animal would presumably have to be considered a nonbeast. If the ETL is correct, indeed, then just as no semantic question can be a purely linguistic question, so there can be no question of empirical fact which can fail to raise semantic questions: the spheres of the linguistic and the empirical confusedly interpenetrate; every statement becomes in a sense "analytic," and at the same time the concept of analyticity comes to be incapable of clear definition.

We must now return briefly to vagueness. Suppose a very odd animal, perhaps extending its geographical range, enters the vicinity of the users of our crude taxonomy of beasts, fowl, and vermin. This animal has a feathered body and furry legs. With respect to *this* animal now, the taxonomy is vague, for it yields both the name 'beast' and the name 'fowl' for the animal. It is clear also that what is involved here is vagueness$_{2L}$, for the nub of the difficulty is precisely that, given the rules of the taxonomy, it is possible to argue equally plausibly that the animal is a fowl or that it is a beast. And, in practice, if we wanted our taxonomy to regain the property of assigning just one name to each and every animal with which we are acquainted, we should have to alter its rules in one or other of several obvious ways in order to remedy its vagueness in this particular instance.

8.4 In light of the theory of vagueness which we have just developed, it may be worth examining some contemporary controversies about the nature of philosophical analysis. Some philosophers, in particular Russell at one stage of his development, have held that it is the job of philosophical analysis to clarify the nature and extent of human knowledge, by systematically replacing the familiar sentences of ordinary language, which are held to be without exception vague (vague$_1$), by sentences in some language which is more "adequate" or "perfect," in that it more perspicuously represents the real epistemological and logical relationships which hold between the various parts of our knowledge and which are only vaguely and confusedly represented by the sentences of a natural language such as English. To paraphrase Russell, philosophical analysis replaces vague statements about a familiar subject matter with precise statements about an unfamiliar subject matter.

In *Philosophical Investigations*, Wittgenstein, arguing against the above view of analysis, appears to adopt a position which includes the following two contentions. (1) Ordinary language *is* inherently vague: it is "not everywhere bounded by rules."[12] Nevertheless, (2) we cannot "bring out the precise sense of" sentences in ordinary language by replacing them with sentences in a logically and epistemologically more adequate language, for ordinary language is not a feeble first attempt at the crystalline clarities of a logically perfect language; it is something which exists in its own right, and as such it is perfectly in order as it stands and neither requires nor can receive

[12] Wittgenstein, *Philosophical Investigations*, I.84f.

any *general* or *philosophical* clarification (although of course individual sentences in ordinary language can have their meaning clarified
by being supplemented by other sentences in ordinary language).
Both these contentions find expression in the following paragraph:

> On the one hand it is clear that every sentence in our language "is in
> order as it is." That is to say, we are not *striving after* an ideal, as if our
> ordinary vague sentences had not yet got a quite unexceptionable sense,
> and a perfect language awaited construction by us.—On the other hand
> it seems clear that where there is a sense there must be perfect order.—
> So there must be perfect order even in the vaguest sentence.[13]

On the face of it, (1) and (2) are just mutually selfcontradictory.
We might take (2) as a recommendation to pursue the sort of analysis
practiced by the late J. L. Austin. But Austin's program seems to
contain no *general* proof of the absurdity or inappropriateness of
Russellian or other forms of reductive analysis. Austinian analysis
works by demonstrating piecemeal, in particular cases, that once we
fully understand the logic of ordinary language, we see that there is
simply no point at which the need for reductive analysis arises and,
indeed, that any analysans which the reductive analyst could supply
would, in the present case, distort and obscure, rather than clarify,
the logical character of its analysandum. Austin claims, with good
reason, that " our ordinary words are much subtler in their uses, and
mark many more distinctions, than philosophers have realised...."[14]
But he gives no general ground for supposing that they mark all the
distinctions that anyone ever could, for whatever purpose, conceivably want to make. It has been exhaustively pointed out that neither
Austin nor Wittgenstein were against scientists' redrawings of our
conceptual map; only against philosophers'. Why this discrimina-
tion? Admittedly, philosophers have wanted to carry out *absolutely
general and comprehensive* redrawings; but why should this in itself
prejudice us against such metaphysical enterprises? Austin can point
here only to the scholasticism and the ignorance of the actual logical

[13] *Ibid.*, I.98.

[14] J. L. Austin, *Sense and Sensibilia* (New York: Oxford University Press,
1962), p. 3.

subtleties of ordinary language with which such philosophers sometimes approach their task. But might not someone who possessed a
completely sophisticated grasp of these subtleties still want to embark
on a program of reductive analysis?

In any case, the most casual reading of the relevant parts of the *Investigations* suggests that Wittgenstein believed himself to have a quite
general argument against at least Russell's sort of reductive analysis;
and his suggestions that ordinary language is not an unsuccessful
"*striving after* an ideal" which a logically perfect language might
realize, that a game with vague rules might still be a perfectly good
game, and that a vaguely delineated boundary might still, for certain
purposes, be a perfectly good boundary and not a feeble stab at the
production of some more exactly delineated form of boundary,[15] seem
to be parts of this argument. Certainly, I think, Wittgenstein did not
intend to put forward the sort of argument against the possibility of
reductive analysis which Waismann advances in "Verifiability" and
which depends upon Waismann's (I think mistaken) interpretation of
Wittgenstein's dictum that language is "not everywhere bounded by
rules" in terms of epistemological scepticism.

Our conception of a linguistic device is in some respects analogous
to Wittgenstein's conception of a language game. I want to propose,
with considerable caution, that it may suggest to us how a proper
interpretation of Wittgenstein's argument might run.

The linguistic device [E] and our crude taxonomy are, as we have
seen, both precise and vague. They are vague with respect to a few
rather out-of-the-way states of affairs, and precise with respect to a
great many commonplace states of affairs. In most ordinary situations, therefore, they fulfill their function perfectly: they are, with
respect to these situations, "perfectly in order as they stand." Russellian analysis, now, begins as an attempt to introduce precision into
our ordinary everyday uses of words. Russell's claim is, in effect, that
once we begin to pursue clarity in discourse, the pursuit of it will lead
us by insensible steps to the construction of a logically perfect language in which the elements of knowledge will be clearly displayed
in their true relationships: in which, for example, all proper names
(except "logically proper names") are displayed as hitherto disguised

[15] Wittgenstein, I.99, I.100.

definite descriptions, and all definite descriptions resolved into the familiar Russellian components. This claim, that the pursuit of clarity will necessarily lead us towards certain sorts of analysis, is an empirical one: it will only be true if the unclarity of ordinary language is of a specific type—the type which we earlier labeled vagueness$_1$. The vagueness of [E] is not vagueness$_1$; hence, if we try to make [E] more precise, we shall not be led by our enterprise in a Russellian direction. We shall not, that is, be led to replace expressions such as ' He is bringing *x* ', *wherever they occur in discourse*, with different expressions of some other logical type. What we shall be led to do is, as we have seen, simply to (attempt to) find some further instruction which we can add to the rules of [E](2) and which will be such that the rules thus supplemented will continue to yield exactly the same responses as previously in all ordinary cases, but will now yield unambiguous responses in the case(s) with respect to which the device was previously vague. This sort of "clarification" of language has no epistemological implications. For here we are manifestly not altering ordinary usage so as to display epistemological or logical relationships. Indeed, we are scarcely altering *ordinary* usage at all, for in the bulk of normal cases our revised linguistic device will function exactly as did its predecessor. Moreover, the drive to make ordinary language more precise in this sense will lead us to make, not general and wholesale reformulations or ordinary-language locutions (such as are involved in, for example, phenomenalist translations of material-object statements into the language of sense data), but limited and specific modifications introduced not for purposes of general *philosophical* clarification but in order to resolve limited concrete problems of communication, such as are likely to arise as science and other forms of inquiry extend our knowledge, and with it the range of phenomena which we wish to talk about. Actual occasions for this sort of reformulation are not all that common. Where vagueness does occur in ordinary language it is most often a trivial phenomenon, which allows great scope for verbal humor (syntactic puns, synecdoche, and so on) but offers no obstacle to communication in any field whatsoever. Often such vagueness is more troublesome to cure than to endure, as witness the " bringing " case, and it is seldom, relatively, that one finds an actual case analogous to our imagined ones of the sand tetrahedra, or the furry–feathered beast–fowl, in which it is helpful to alter the rules governing the application of a word. To this extent one can agree with Austin that ordinary language enshrines all but a minute proportion of the distinctions which we need to make in dealing with and understanding the world. In any case, if we are right, the business of making language a sharper and more precise instrument for expressing what we know about the world is always a matter of making minute extensions to the vast extant corpus of rules and devices and not, as has been the traditional practice of metaphysicians, of replacing the whole corpus with the rules of some quite different (and usually far simpler) language, such as that of phenomenalism, or Russellian atomism, or the logical languages of Carnap or Quine. And in the end these changes do not take us *toward* anything: they do not make language a closer and closer approximation to any ideal of perfect epistemological or logical perspicuity; they merely change it.

Some such argument, it seems to me, is, in part, what Wittgenstein is driving at in *Investigations*, I.80–I.100. Consider, for example, the following remarks:

> The sign-post is in order—if, under normal circumstances, it fulfils its purpose. [We would say: "The linguistic device is in order if under normal circumstances it yields consistent responses."]
>
> If I tell someone "Stand roughly here"—may not this explanation work perfectly? And cannot every other one fail too?
>
> But isn't it an inexact explanation?—Yes; why shouldn't we call it "inexact"? Only let us understand what "inexact" means. For it does not mean "unusable". And let us consider what we call an "exact" explanation in contrast with this one. Perhaps something like drawing a chalk line round an area? Here it strikes us at once that the line has breadth. So a colour-edge would be more exact. But has this exactness still got a function here: isn't the engine idling? And remember too that we have not yet defined what is to count as overstepping this exact boundary; how, with what instrument, it is to be established. And so on.[16]

The extra exactness of the chalk line and the color edge might have a function in certain special circumstances (compare the extra exactness of the new rule in the sand tetrahedron case)—and then of course

[16] *Ibid.*, I.87–I.88.

we would know what is to count as overstepping the boundary; how it is to be established, and so on, for the practical context would answer these questions for us (Wittgenstein's implied point here is that in the case of the conceptual revisions of metaphysics, where no practical context exists, the answers to such questions must often only be assumed to exist). This leads us to I.88: " No *single* ideal of exactness has been laid down...."

There are many ideals by reference to which we can make conceptual revisions, all of them suggested by the practical contexts in which the need for such revision arises. Hence:

> it may now come to look as if there were something like a final analysis of our forms of language, and so a *single* completely resolved form of every expression.... It can also be put like this: we eliminate misunderstandings by making our expressions more exact; but now it may look as if we were moving towards a particular state, a state of complete exactness; and as if this were the real goal of our investigation.[17]

Wittgenstein's most fundamental point in these passages is, I think, this: to make a language game more *useful relative to the purpose which it serves* is not to move toward a state in which that language game is *in some absolute sense* useful (as it might be, for example, if its structure exactly mirrored the structure of human knowledge, or of reality). For we have no criteria for establishing the absolute utility of a language game—only its utility relative to some set of practical purposes. We have been making a related set of points about linguistic devices. Thus, for example, I should be inclined to say that one function of the ETL has been to persuade the metaphysically inclined analyst that his search for some absolute and epistemologically significant species of clarity is not merely a metaphysical but also a practical pursuit, since—so the ETL makes it appear—there exists throughout ordinary language a species of vagueness which demands his species of clarity as its natural and proper remedy. Thus, analytical metaphysics is enabled to avoid the awkward questions which Wittgenstein raises at I.88, concerning the determination of the sense of 'exact' by representing itself (to use Kantian terms) as an activity at one and the same time transcendent and phenomenal.

[17] *Ibid.*, I.91.

9 Cognitive discourse

9.1 Someone might object that we have so far managed to make the conception of language as a system of linguistic devices plausible only by careful choice of examples. First of all, the analysis of linguistic capacity as the ability to generate utterances or pieces of behavior by carrying out sequences of instructions does not seem *prima facie* to offer a very convincing account of what it is to understand informative discourse. When I understand and assimilate the information conveyed by a simple descriptive sentence (for example, 'The flowers in the garden are red') it does not seem *prima facie* as if I *do* anything: I just understand. Secondly, there is a difficulty connected with our use of the terms 'function', 'use', and 'purpose'. We have chosen to characterize linguistic devices as systems (of rules), each of which determines, and is in turn determined by, a certain sort of social intercourse. The system of rules, and the type of social intercourse which it mediates, are on this view to be regarded as a single indissoluble unity: a "form of life," in Wittgenstein's phrase. We can only fully explain the function or use of such a device by explaining its rules in detail, in relation to all the various roles which its users can assume in relationship to it (as, for example, the roles of requester and bringer in [C] and [D] and in relationship to the form of social intercourse which it mediates. Obviously, however, when someone makes use of a linguistic device, his use of it may have a function, relative to his system of purposes, which is not identical with the "function of the device." Thus, for example, the function of the "bringing" device (the system of devices [A]-[D]) is to make it possible for bringing, and asking for things to be brought, to exist as a type of social intercourse. But my purpose in asking you to bring me the parcel on the hall table (the function of this request for me) may be to get rid of you, since I know that the parcel is really a bomb, containing plastic explosive and set to explode as soon as anyone touches it. We need to keep the functions of devices and the functions which particular utterances may have for particular users clearly apart in our minds, for if we fail to do this, we may trivialize our entire analysis. We shall do this, in fact, if we allow the domain of functions of linguistic devices to become coextensive with the domain of functions which particular utterances may have for particular speakers. Thus in our example above, we might postulate a linguistic device the function of which we might characterize as: "murdering people by asking them to bring plastic bombs disguised as parcels." The rules of this device would simply be an elaboration—in the direction of much greater specificity—of the rules of devices [A]-[D]. Clearly, if we adopt this line, linguistic devices will be as cheap—and exactly as numerous—as specifiable intentions. Moreover, we shall be implicitly committed to a thesis which seems *prima facie* false: that people have to be taught a separate set of rules for furthering each of their purposes, so far as its furtherance depends on the use of language. What seems in fact to be the case is that people, once they have acquired the capacity to use a language, are capable of adapting this capacity in original ways, so that whatever purpose they may acquire in particular and often unforeseen circumstances, they are able to produce utterances which assist in the realization of those purposes. This is simply another aspect of the quality of fertility which, as we have earlier observed, perhaps *ad nauseam*, is characteristic of fully developed linguistic competence.

The second of our two difficulties is, now, that it is hard to see any way of separating the functions of devices from the functions (for users) of particular utterances in the case of informative discourse.

What, after all, is the function of the device or devices involved in the giving of information? One is tempted to say "to inform": but a moment's reflection on the complexity of informative discourse will reveal the impossibility of constructing, on the lines of the model devices which we constructed in Chapter 7, any simple set of rules for a device whose function is so specified. Informative discourse must involve the interplay of numerous subordinate linguistic devices. But how are *their* functions to be specified? The only possible way forward at this point seems to lie in the specification of the purposes for which people actually utter informative sentences, but if we take this route it seems that we shall end up with functions like 'getting one's wife to sew one's buttons on', 'reminding someone to take his umbrella', 'getting someone to admit that his hypotheses are ill-founded', and so on. And now we have trivialized our thesis in the manner described above, by making our criterion for the postulation of a distinct linguistic device the existence of a distinct specifiable intention. We are faced in fact with Strawson's well-known question whether, for example, "the special use involved in sending an old man to sleep by reading aloud from a translation of a play"[1] is the sort of use of language which corresponds to a distinct language game.

9.2 As a necessary preliminary to the solution of these difficulties, we must develop a further series of model linguistic devices, ones in which something clearly recognizable as interchange of information is taking place.

[F]—a variation of [C]   Someone asks, 'Where is ____?' The blank in this schema may be filled by any of the labels given an application in **[B]**. The teacher only asks this when the object labeled is not close at hand and/or in sight. The learner generates his response by carrying out the following instructions:

---

[1] P. F. Strawson's review of *Philosophical Investigations* in *Mind* (1954). There is, of course, an even quicker way of trivializing the thesis, by saying that the utterance 'The flowers in the garden are red' corresponds to a linguistic device, the function of which is "telling people that the flowers in the garden are red" and the rules of which tell the learner when to use that particular sentence; but I think the futility of this is sufficiently evident.

(1) Walk in some randomly chosen direction, scrutinizing the objects
you see and carrying out the following operations for each object:
  (i) Generate its [B]-label.
  (ii) Detach 'Where is ___?' from the teacher's utterance and
  compare the remainder with the result of (i).
  (iii) If (ii) yields a match, take the object in question to the
  teacher; if not, proceed to the next object.
(2) If none of the objects seen in the course of carrying out (1)
qualify to be taken to the teacher, choose another direction to
walk in, repeating the operations of (1).[2]

The rules of [F] introduce the learner to the notion of *searching*
('searching', that is, like 'bringing', is not the name of a sequence of
bodily movements). Utterances of the form 'Where is ___?' are
given, by [F], a function as cues serving to initiate, and to determine
the objects of, searches. Once he has mastered [F], the learner possesses, as it were, a conceptual slot into which he can fit a device for
giving and receiving *directions for searching*. Such a device might
run as follows:

[G] The teacher introduces such utterances as '___ is upstairs' or '___ is in
the garden', the blanks being fillable by [B]-labels. The learner learns
the following rules:
(1) If, while you are conducting a search with the object of finding x,
someone says 'x is upstairs', then (assuming you think him trustworthy):[3]
  (i) Go to the foot of the stairs.
  (ii) Climb them.
  (iii) Carry out [F](1), (2), ..., (n) in the regions in which you then
  find yourself but without crossing the following boundaries:
  (a), (b), ..., where these boundaries will include injunctions
  against, for example, climbing through windows and searching
  on the roof.

---

[2] [F] should, of course, contain heuristic rules for switching from one direction
of search to another if the first proves fruitless. I have omitted these for the sake
of simplicity of exposition.

[3] Knowing what a man *means* when he asserts p is something quite different
from knowing whether his assertions are worthy of being taken on trust. Knowing
what his utterance *means* is knowing what I would do *if* I trusted the speaker and
if I wished to profit by the information contained in it.

(2)–(*n*) Instructions similar to (1), defining the use of 'in the garden', 'in the kitchen', 'in the bath', and so on.

The learner now knows a list of specifications of locations. It would be unwise to say that he now knows the *meaning* of this set of phrases, for to say this would imply that he knows how to employ and respond to them in all linguistic contexts, whereas he as yet knows how to respond to them only in one context, that provided by the device [F]. Again, it would be a mistake to say that the learner had learned a set of *names* in learning [G]. There are two reasons for this. First, talk of naming suggests ostensive definition and association. But it is clear enough that the learner could not be taught the device [G] by having volumes of space or areas of ground singled out for his attention[4] (by a sweep of the arm? a tour of inspection?) while the appropriate noise was uttered by the teacher. For, on the one hand, there is simply no way of ostensively singling out the "referent" of a word like 'upstairs' or 'garden'; and on the other hand, even if there were, what such an ostensive procedure would teach the learner would not be the rules of [G] but the rules of a recognition game of a type related to [B], and hence it would not teach him how to respond to an occurrence of '*x* is upstairs', or any other such phrase, in the course of operating [F]. Second, if we succumb to the temptation to regard [G] as a naming procedure, we shall no doubt succumb to the same temptation in the case of [B], and we shall thus probably fail to notice that we are grouping together expressions of radically different logical types for the sake of marking resemblances which are important enough for the purposes of conventional lexicography but relatively trivial when we are trying to understand the rule structure of a language. 'Doll' and 'upstairs' are of different logical types precisely because [B] and [G] are different sorts of linguistic devices, with different structures of rules. The rules of [B] are (roughly) rules which tell one which taxonomic characters license the utterance (in certain circumstances) of which words; the rules of [G],

---

[4] My view here is related to Kant's on space in the *Aesthetic*. Kant regards space as an *a priori* intuition in part on the ground that our concept of space is not "constructed" by noting the "similarities" between spatial volumes. Like Kant, I hold that acquiring the concept of space is not a matter of noticing similarities. My positive view would be (roughly) that space is the permanent possibility of giving specifications of relative location.

on the other hand, tell one how to get (in certain circumstances) into certain locations and stay there. There is, it seems to me, no reason why we should wish to interpret these very different functions and rule structures in terms of a single model, even if it were possible to do so. The word 'reference' in particular, cuts very little ice at this level of the discussion of language (which is not to say that it may not cut quite a lot at other levels, in the discussion of other problems).

To return to the argument. The learner, having mastered [G], knows how to make use of certain specifications of location in conducting searches. He may now learn to ask for such specifications:

[H] To generate a request for a specification of the location of some object which you have been asked to find, carry out the following operations in sequence:
   (1) Utter the words 'Where is ____?'
   (2) Generate the [B]-label of the object you have been asked to find.
   (3) Utter the [B]-label.

There is, now, a sense in which the learner who has mastered [F], [G], and [H] has acquired the capacity to understand informative utterances of a certain sort and to request others to provide him with the sort of information which such utterances convey. But those of us who are not predisposed in favor of use theories of meaning will, I suspect, feel severe qualms at any proposal to identify this sense of "understanding" with the sense in which we ordinarily speak of a linguistically competent adult as understanding informative utterances in his own language. These qualms have to do, I think, with the first of the two difficulties which we canvassed at the outset of this chapter.

The heart of this difficulty, it seems to me, is the temptation which we feel to interpret the business of understanding an informative utterance in terms of a certain picture. We want to say that an informative utterance creates in the mind of the understanding hearer a certain mental state: the state of knowing whatever information it is that the utterance conveys. Any action which the hearer may now go on to take on the basis of the information he has just acquired is now determined not by the rules which govern the meanings of the words used in the utterance in question but by the nature of this state of knowing. Moreover, the knowledge which the hearer has acquired from a given utterance may equally well determine his future actions as it may his present ones. The hearer, although he understands the utterance, may do nothing at all about it, beyond absorbing the information it conveys, for days, or years, and then engage in some action directly conditioned by the knowledge acquired through hearing it.

Our account of [F]–[H] may seem at first blush to be diametrically opposed to this familiar picture. We seem to be claiming that the actions which a person performs in the light of a given informative utterance are conditioned directly by the rules establishing the meaning of the words contained in the utterance. This, it would seem, must commit us to the view that no one can truly be said to understand an informative utterance unless he *immediately* takes some action in the light of it: hence on this view, it seems impossible to understand how the information conveyed by the utterance could simply be stored by the hearer and perhaps only issue in action at some considerably later date. And, finally, we seem in our account to have left no place for knowledge at all.

The short answer to these objections is that our theory in fact entails none of these views, since it is not a theory about knowledge, belief, intention, action, and their interrelationships, but a theory about the nature and content of linguistic convention. Our view is not in conflict with the traditional account of these matters, because it is not in competition with any account of them.

Any philosophical analysis, or at any rate, any which refrains from making the claims of complete and final explication characteristic of rationalism in its more grandiose forms, must aim at clarifying certain concepts against a background of other concepts which are left unanalyzed. In the present case, these include the concepts of knowing, believing, intending, and in general all those with which the philosophy of mind is concerned. I would wish to claim, and shall argue more fully later on in this chapter, that it is essential to separate the attempt to give an account of the conventional basis of language from the attempt to give philosophical analyses, behavioral or otherwise, of mental concepts. The philosophy of language cannot usefully be treated as a branch of the philosophy of mind: the fundamental misconception here is that to inquire what it is to possess linguistic competence is much the same thing as to inquire what it is to think.[5]

An example may make clearer the sort of division I have in mind here. Suppose that the learner, having mastered [F]–[H], asks (1) 'Where is my pet pig?' and receives the answer, (2) 'In the garden'. His *linguistic competence* consists in (among other things) his being familiar with a set of instructions for making use of (2). However, whether he exercises this competence at once or at some later date depends upon his situation and upon his needs, desires, intentions, and so forth. He may just have been asked to fetch the pig; or he may be inquiring its whereabouts in order to be able to fetch it at some later date; or any of an indefinite number of other sets of circumstances may obtain. It is worth noticing, however, that whether he chooses to exercise his competence at once or at some later date, his exercising it does not constitute a case of action guided by inference based upon past experience but a case of rule-following. The learner has not, that is to say, learned from repeated past experience that whenever anyone is heard to utter the string of noises (2) it invariably, or almost invariably, turns out that the pig is in the garden. For he has had, *ex hypothesi*, no training of the kind necessary to set up such an association. What he has been trained to do is to use the rules of [F] and [G] to generate, given the utterance (2), a search procedure which will end in (or at least increase his chances of) finding the pig.

At the same time, possessing this strictly linguistic competence, the learner *knows*, in a quite familiar, everyday sense of 'know' (which it is not our busines to clarify or analyze, although it might well be the business of a philosopher of mind or an empirical psychologist to do so) a great many things connected with his possession of such a competence. He knows (a) that, if he chooses to act on (2), the rules of [G] will lead him to go into the garden. He knows, perhaps, from his general acquaintance with the workings of nature and the habits of this particular pig, that (b) if the pig is not fetched out of the garden, it will uproot all the carrots; (c) that if it rains, the pig will get wet; (d) that in all probability the pig has

---

[5] I know of no convincing evidence that Wittgenstein made this assimilation, although, of course, many Wittgensteinians have done so.

already escaped into the road through the hole in the fence; and so on.

We need to bear in mind two points about (a)–(d). First, what the learner knows, in knowing (a)–(d), is in no sense licensed by, or derivable from, the rules of any linguistic device. There is, for example, no rule of **[G]** which instructs the learner, on hearing the utterance 'The pig is in the garden', to look for his pig in the road; still less is there a rule whose content is "On hearing utterance U, *believe that* your pig is in the garden (or, the road)." In fact, (a)–(d) represent essentially inductive knowledge, acquired by the learner from past experience, including experience acquired in the course of operating such linguistic devices as **[F]** and **[G]**.

Second, although the rules of **[G]** do not *license* the learner's belief that, for example, his pig is in the garden, it is nevertheless true that *his informant's utterance of the words* 'Your pig is in the garden'[6] may serve for the learner as the ground of his belief that his pig is in the garden, and that the learner may be right to take it as grounds for that belief. The connection between this event (the utterance of the words) and the beliefs which the learner grounds in it, is simply this. The learner knows what he would have to do (the rules of **[G]** being what they are) if he were to set about making use of (2): namely, go into the garden and conduct his search for the pig within its boundaries. Hence, if he thinks (2) worth making use of at all (that is, if he knows from experience that his informant's specifications of location are generally trustworthy; or more simply, and what is not at all the same thing, if he trusts his informant), he must think it likely that he will find the pig in the garden. But to believe this is to believe, given what he knows of the general order of nature, that the pig is (or has recently been) in the garden waiting to be found; and hence that if it should rain, it will get (would have got) wet; that it may have escaped through the hole in the fence; and so forth.

We can distinguish, then, between on the one hand, the *rule-licensed procedures* appropriate to a given utterance; and, on the

---

[6] It is important for the understanding of this bit of the argument to notice that I am *not* saying that the *sentence*, or the *statement*, 'Your pig is in the garden,' is, or gives, grounds for anything.

other hand, the *experience-licensed implications* that an utterance possesses, in the event that it is taken as trustworthy, in virtue of the fact that it generates certain rule-licensed procedures.

If we are correct, now, it follows that, when someone understands a given informative utterance U, the fact that he knows how to generate the rule–licensed procedures appropriate to U is always prior to, and is the ground of, his knowledge of the experience-licensed implications of U. Thus, to say of somebody that he understands U may mean simply that he possesses the strictly linguistic capacity to carry out the rule-licensed procedures appropriate to U. Or it may, or may also, mean that he has seen, or is capable of seeing, a greater or smaller number of experience-licensed implications of U. The existence of the distinction between rule-licensed procedures and experience-licensed implications accounts, I think, for the fact that it is possible to say of a man that he understands *what is being said* without necessarily understanding its *significance*. For example: " Of course I understood the meaning of Smith's words when he said that Arbuthnot was in danger of being dismissed, but it was not until later, when I came to realize the gravity of the political dissension in the university, that I understood the significance of what he had said."

We can now see more clearly why it is that the study of what is involved in linguistic competence—or to put it another way, the attempt to exhibit the form and content of the rules of a natural language, conceived as determining semantics as well as syntax— may not throw any light on the analysis of intentional concepts. Someone who has been told that his pig is in the garden, and who fears in consequence that the pig may be getting wet, will certainly be able, given that he knows English, to say what it is that he fears. But what is involved in the ability to say, in appropriate circumstances, such things as 'I fear my pig may be getting wet'? It does not seem at all clear that someone who knows how to comment on the plight of an actual pig which is presently getting wet before his eyes will necessarily *a fortiori* be able to comment on the possible plight of an envisaged future pig.

Teaching someone to talk about envisaged future contingencies must presumably involve teaching him simple uses of the future tense. I may, for example, repeatedly show someone colored lights after sounding a buzzer in his hearing. I now get him to answer the question, 'What will happen now?' asked after the buzzer has sounded, by giving the name of the color which he expects to appear. But in order to learn this very simple device the learner must *in some sense* already be able to envisage the future. We need not, of course, interpret "envisage the future" in a mentalistic way: we can, perhaps, if we are ingenious enough and can solve certain theoretical difficulties, adopt a behavioral, perhaps even a stimulus-response, account of what "envisaging" involves; or equally well we may, on the other hand, adopt an account which proceeds in terms of images —and this may be some sort of unregenerate, or Pricean, account in terms of mental images, or it may be the sort of account which has lately led some psychologists to call themselves "subjective behaviorists."[7] The point is simply that, whatever analysis we choose to give, the business of establishing that analysis must proceed quite independently of the business of establishing the nature of the rules which govern talk about envisaged contingencies.

Now, part of what the learner will do in extracting the experience-licensed implications of 'Your pig is in the garden' will be to envisage contingencies which must obtain if the way to recover the pig is really to perform the rule-licensed procedures appropriate to 'Your pig is in the garden'. If he knows how to comment verbally on envisaged contingencies, then he will know how to comment verbally on *these* contingencies. This, it seems to me, is as far as our theory will take us.

9.3 We can now deal with the two objections which we raised in Section 9.1. The answer to the first is that the linguistic devices which make up the system of informative discourse all hinge on the possibility of constructing sets of rules which enable the recipient of utterances of one sort or another to put such utterances to use in *doing* something or other: thus, their rules are of essentially the same sort as those of the devices we constructed in Chapters 3–7. Hence, the only part of the process of understanding an utterance which can count as an exercise of *linguistic* capacity is that part which consists in the learner's *doing* what is *to be done* (given the rules of the appropriate linguistic device) with utterances of that

---

[7] Miller, Galanter, and Pribam, *Plans and the Structure of Behavior*.

sort. There are, of course, a great many other things which the recipient may on occasion do, think, feel, and so on, *as a result of* exercising his linguistic capacity on a given utterance (an indefinite number of things, in fact, which explains why dispositional-behavioral analyses of belief are so unhelpful) and in ordinary usage we would no doubt class these as manifestations of his understanding of that utterance, but, nevertheless, none of these are in themselves exercises of linguistic capacity.

What is to be done in putting utterances to use will vary a great deal, of course, from one linguistic device to another. We have suggested that the recipient of a specification of location uses it to construct a search pattern, the degree of precision of which will vary with the degree of precision of the specification. What the recipient of a vast class of descriptive statements is supposed to do with them is to use them in various ways in *generating or constructing pictures*. But the the *mode of generation* of different elements of pictures will vary; compare, for example: (1) 'x is square', (2) 'x is red', (3) 'x is trembling', (4) 'x has branches', (5) 'x is seven-branched'. The rules that the recipient must follow in performing the rule-licensed procedures appropriate to (1)—in constructing his schematic square on paper or in the sand, or in his mind's eye—will require him to drop perpendiculars from points identified by reference to other spatial criteria, and so forth; the corresponding rules in the case of (2) will mention color charts or paradigm cases of redness; in the case of (4) they will again determine the construction of a spatial figure but in ways different from (1); in (5) some sort of counting procedure will be interpolated at some point; and so on. Again, when I am told 'x belongs to John', this utterance finds its place in a series of linguistic devices which involve (one could equally say, define) the notion of property. To be told that x belongs to John is (in part) to be told who to give it to if I wish to return it to its owner.

This is obviously only a very sparse and rudimentary sketch of how a complete explanation of informative discourse as a system of linguistic devices might look. However, it will serve to suggest the general strategy of a solution to the second of the two difficulties of section 9.1. The function of a linguistic device is determined by the character of whatever it is that the rules require me to do in performing the rule-licensed procedures appropriate to the utterances which are introduced into the language by that device; and, secondarily, by reference to whatever social function is served by the existence of a linguistic device having such rules. This definition enables us to avoid assigning to all informative utterances the function of "informing" *simpliciter*. But at the same time it enables us to distinguish between the functions of a linguistic device and the purposes which someone may have in employing that device. I may tell you that your pig is in the garden in the hope that you will go there at once, since unbeknown to you the garden is presently dissected by withering rifle fire from warring members of the Maoist and Soviet wings of the West Finchley Y.C.L.; but nevertheless the utterance 'Your pig is in the garden' remains functionally a specification of location and not, as it might be, an incantation to send you to your death. It has the latter function for me—or it may have, if I am lucky—because of a great many contingent facts about you and your intense anxiety about your pig; your congenital habit of going at things like a bull at a gate; the relative proximity and ease of access of the garden; the internecine strife of the West Finchley comrades; and so on. It has the former function, in the sense of linguistic, or semantic, function, because of the character of the rules of the linguistic devices which introduce it into the language.

Wittgenstein, in a familiar passage, remarks on the immense diversity of linguistic function:

> Think of the tools in a tool-box: there is a hammer, pliers, a saw, a screwdriver, a rule, a glue-pot, glue, nails and screws.—The functions of words are as diverse as the functions of these objects. (And in both cases there are similarities.)[8]

Philosophers have not, in general, found this claim easy to swallow. If one opens an elementary logic book, one finds a classification of the functions of language into the following few categories: "cognitive," "performative" (this is a newcomer), "evaluative," "imperative," "emotive," with a few additions or omissions to suit the author's taste; and it is not unknown for similar things to be said in seminars on the philosophy of language. It appears, however, if what we have

---

[8] Wittgenstein, *Philosophical Investigations*, I.11.

argued here is correct, that a little investigation might uncover a vastly more complex classification, one not too far removed in degree of complexity, in fact, from that adumbrated in the opening remarks of *Philosophical Investigations*.

9.4 It might look at first sight as if the distinction between rule-licensed procedures and experience-licensed implications might serve to clarify the distinction, which we drew in Chapter 2, between telling and revealing. What we are *told* by person A is, we might argue, equivalent to the class of rule-licensed procedures appropriate to A's utterance, whereas what A's utterance *reveals* is equivalent to the class of experience-licensed implications.

This would be quite inadequate. For one thing, the rule-licensed procedures appropriate to A's utterance are not (that is, are not, as a matter of logical type) the sort of things that could qualify for identification with *what A has told me*, and neither, for that matter, are classes of rule-licensed procedures. For in performing the rule-licensed procedures of an utterance, I *do* things (conduct a search; locate someone to be the recipient of something; measure off a length against a measuring rod; for example), whereas what A has told me must surely be identified not as an action, or set of actions, but as the *meaning*, or *content*, or *cognitive content*, of A's utterance. We can only exhibit the cognitive content of an utterance U, it seems to me, by producing other utterances which state the cognitive content of U. The distinction between what a man tells me and what his utterance, considered as an inductive sign, reveals to me, is only intelligible to us by virtue of the fact that we can state what it is that we have been told and thus can distinguish what we have been told from what we have assumed, inferred, invented, imagined, and so forth.

We must say then, it seems to me, that to say that someone understands the meaning of an informative utterance U is to say at least the following things: (1) that he is able to perform the rule-licensed procedures appropriate to U, and (2) that he can say what it was that the speaker who uttered U told him in uttering U.

We must, then, give some account of how a learner comes to be able to produce indicative sentences, *oratio obliqua* constructions, and so on, which express the cognitive content of other indicative sentences. We must moreover do this without postulating the existence of rules of language which explicitly stipulate that one utterance shall express the cognitive content of another. For if relationships of content between sentences depended upon such rules, then (1) there would have to be an indefinite number of such rules, whereas it appears that in fact a finite term of instruction in a natural language can equip a learner with the ability to answer all questions concerning relationships of content between different indicative sentences; and (2) anyone who uttered a new indicative sentence would have himself to decide *ab initio* what its cognitive equivalents, implicates, and so on, were—and then the meanings of sentences would depend upon the arbitrary will of speakers.

So far we have considered the device of specifying locations mainly from the point of view of the recipient of such specifications. But the parcel of linguistic devices which includes [F] and [G] will also contain devices whose rules result in the construction of specifications of location; and in general, someone who understands how to extract the rule-licensed implications of a given informative utterance will also understand how to construct utterances of that sort.

Let us postulate a device [I] for constructing specifications of location with a few simple location terms: 'upstairs', 'in the garden', and so on. Its rules will be roughly as follows:

[I] The learner is asked 'Where is ____?', the blank being fillable by [B]-labels. The learner learns the following rules for constructing replies:
  (1) Fill in the schema '____$_1$ is____$_2$' by inserting in place of '____$_1$' the [B]-label which replaces the blank in the schema 'Where is ____?' from which your questioner's utterance is derived.[9]
  (2) To determine what to insert in place of '____$_2$', carry out the following operations.
    (i) Ask yourself whether you would have to climb the stairs to get the object O whose [B]-label you have just inserted in place of '____$_1$'.
    If the answer is "no," proceed to . . .
    If the answer is "yes," proceed to (ii).

[9] This could, of course, be rewritten as a series of operations, without making any mention of the filling-in of a syntactic schema, although what was learned would still *amount to* the capacity to fill in certain schemata under certain circumstances.

(ii) Having climbed the stairs, would you have to cross any of the following boundaries to get O? (a), (b), ..., as specified in [G]. If the answer is "yes," proceed to .... If the answer is "no," fill in '____$_2$' with 'upstairs'.... And so on.

The reader can no doubt continue the system of rules of [I] and supply appropriate branches at the yes/no nodes for himself. And it will no doubt be evident that what we have in [I](2)(i)–(iii) is simply an application of the content of [G](1)(i)–(iii) to a new purpose. Instead of being expressed in a series of rules designed to govern actions, this content is here expressed in a series of rules designed to govern the construction of utterances.

Rule [I](2) requires the learner to carry out a series of operations— to ask himself certain questions. What utterance he produces in reply to the question "Where is O?" will depend upon the results of these operations: on whether the answers to the various questions have turned out in each case to be "yes" or "no."

I wish to speak in general of operations as *yielding* either the *result* "yes" or the result "no" and of an operation as having been *satisfied positively* or *negatively* when it has been determined whether it yields the result "yes" or the result "no."

It is evident, now, that to any utterance produced in obedience to the rules of [I] will correspond a determinate pattern of positive and negative satisfactions of the various operations prescribed by [I](2). Thus, we could represent the rules of [I] as a branching tree structure with yes/no decision points as its nodes, and, if we introduced symbolism for indicating the presence of either a "yes" result or a "no" result at each node, then any utterance capable of being generated by the rules of [I] could be mapped onto the tree by determining a specific array of its nodes in accordance with the rules of this symbolism.

We can therefore take any given utterance produced in obedience to the rules of [I] as representing a determinate array of positive and negative satisfactions of a specific set of operations. Now suppose the teacher says to the learner, 'Elsie the pig is in the garden'. The learner can take this utterance as *equivalent to* the satisfaction, positive or negative as the case may be, of a determinate array of operations and hence, if he wishes to state what it is that the teacher has told him, he can do so by producing any utterance whose generation would demand the positive or negative satisfaction of precisely the same operations and by applying to that utterance the grammatical transformations which govern the conversion of direct speech into reported speech, to get, perhaps: 'He told me, in effect, that Elsie was outside the house but inside the garden fence'. I am, of course, here taking 'What did he tell you?' to be equivalent to 'What was the force (the content) of his words?' and not to the stricter 'What did he say to you?' ('What were his precise words?').

In general, then, I wish to suggest that any informative utterance functions as what I shall call an *operation satisfier* with respect to some specific array of operations, each of which may be specified by the rules of one or more linguistic devices. Two informative utterances express the same content when they satisfy precisely the same array of operations: those which are satisfied positively by one being satisfied positively by the other, and those which are satisfied negatively by one being negatively satisfied by the other. Again, one informative utterance U *implies* another, U', in virtue of its meaning just in case the set of operations which U satisfies contains the set of operations that U' satisfies, provided that to each operation that U' satisfies positively there corresponds a positive satisfaction of the same operation by U, and similarly for negative satisfactions. Thus, for example, 'Elsie is in the garden' implies 'Elsie is outside the house'.

We can now give a very simple explication of the distinction between telling and revealing, in the senses which we gave to those words in Chapter 2. What a man tells me depends on what operations his utterance satisfies, which in turn depends upon the rules of the linguistic devices governing it. What his utterance, considered as a natural event, reveals to me, depends upon what sorts of circumstance I have in the past found to be generally associated with events of that sort.

10 Synonymy

10.1 The notion of informative utterances as satisfiers of operations may also throw some light on the concept of cognitive synonymy. Quine[1] has argued very plausibly that the criterion of interchangeability in all contexts *salva veritate* yields an acceptable account of cognitive synonymy only in a language which includes the adverb "necessarily" taken as yielding truth when and only when applied to an analytic statement. In such a language, to say that two terms 'T_1' and 'T_2' are freely interchangeable *salva veritate* entails that they can be interchanged *salva veritate* in the sentence,

(1) 'Necessarily all T_1s are T_1s'

to yield

(2) 'Necessarily all T_1s are T_2s'

[1] W. V. Quine, "Two Dogmas of Empiricism," in *From a Logical Point of View* (Cambridge, Mass.: Harvard University Press, 1961).

If (2) is true, then clearly 'T_1' and 'T_2' *are* synonymous, but to say that (2) is true is merely to say that

(3) 'All and only T_1s are T_2 s '

is analytic. Interchangeability *salva veritate* works, that is, only in a language in which we can, in effect, derive our concept of synonymy from a prior concept of analyticity (which of course stands itself in need of explanation). In an extensional language,

> interchangeability *salva veritate* is no assurance of cognitive synonymy of the desired type. That 'bachelor' and 'unmarried man' are interchangeable *salva veritate* in an extensional language assures us of no more than that (3) ['All and only bachelors are unmarried men'] is true. There is no assurance here that the extensional agreement of 'bachelor' and 'unmarried man' rests on meaning rather than merely on accidental matters of fact, as does the extensional agreement of 'creature with a heart' and 'creature with kidneys'.[2]

The idea that synonymy has *something* to do with interchangeability of synonyms dies hard despite these arguments of Quine's, I think; but plainly it will not take us very far unless we can answer the question, "interchangeability *salvo quo*?"—and clearly *veritate* will not do as an answer.

What I want to suggest is that what is saved when synonyms are interchanged is not truth, but the satisfaction of operations. The definition, or rather series of definitions, which I propose, runs as follows:

Definition 1: An *expression* in a language is any part of any phonemic string which can be used to fill any blank in any syntactic schema in accordance with the rules of any linguistic device having a place in that language.

Definition 2: An expression, E_1, functioning in the context of a linguistic device L_1, contains an expression E_0 as a *semantic component* when the array of positive and negative satisfactions of operations determined by E_1 depends in part on the rules of some other linguistic device L_2 in

---

[2] *Ibid.*, p. 31.

the context of which E_0 possesses a function, either in isolation, or as a component of some other expression E_2. Otherwise E_0 is a *formal component* of E_1.

Definition 3: Two expressions, E_1, and E_2, are synonymous if and only if there exists no expression E_3 having E_1 as a semantic component such that the total array of positive and negative satisfactions of operations determined by E_3 is altered by substitution of E_2 for E_1.

As we shall see in a moment, these definitions give us at least the beginnings of a solution of Quine's difficulties over analyticity. Meanwhile, it is worth noticing that they also enable us to avoid certain difficulties concerning the occurrence of words in quotation and as components of compound names, which also plague accounts in terms of substitutability *salva veritate*. Quine points out[3] that such truths as "'Bachelor' has less than ten letters" become false under substitution of 'unmarried man' for 'bachelor' and that similar difficulties are raised by 'bachelor of arts', 'bachelor's buttons', and so on. He suggests that although these difficulties might be overcome by treating "'bachelor'", "'bachelor's buttons'", and the rest as single indivisible words, this approach is likely to founder upon the difficulties of explicating the concept of a word.

Quine's apprehensions are, I am sure, well-founded. Any account of wordhood which made both "bachelor" and "'bachelor'" into a single indivisible word would be an odd one, for it would have to rest upon a demonstration that it is somehow simply mistaken to treat expressions like "'bachelor'" as instantations of the schema "'___'"—and this seems on the face of it to be a perfectly reasonable way of treating them. Of course, it might be thought tempting to say that any *name* must be a single indivisible word but—temptation apart—there seems to be very little indeed to recommend such a view.

What we have done in definition (1) is to introduce the concept of an expression as, in effect, any element of a language to which the rules of any linguistic device make any reference which is significant from the point of view of the function and workings of that device. Expressions will include syntactic schemata, sentences, morphemes, and

[3] *Ibid.*, p. 28.

various sorts of punctuation mark; the definition of these classes of entity in terms of linguistic devices might be feasible, would certainly be complex, and is no concern of ours. All that we need to do is to distinguish the case where an expression, as it were, "carries its meaning with it" into some expression of which it forms a part from the case in which it is merely "formally present" in the larger expression, and this we have done in definition (2). Confronted with Quine's difficulties over quotation and compound names, then, all we need say is that 'bachelor' is not a semantic component of ''bachelor'' or of ''bachelor's buttons'' but merely a formal component and that synonymy, as common sense suggests, and definition (3) expresses, is a relation holding only between semantic components of expressions.

Let us return to our original problem. Definitions (1)–(3) are in no way concerned with the truth of propositions, and hence *a fortiori*, no questions concerning analyticity or syntheticity arise in connection with them. Certainly they do not presuppose any account of analyticity. According to our definition, what is saved in all transpositions of synonymous expressions is not the truth of propositions but the *functional equivalence of expressions with respect to the rules of the language from which they are drawn*. This is what entitles us to claim that what we have defined is identity of meaning, since meaning is what is conferred upon expressions by the convention that they are to be used in accordance with these rules.

We can put this another way. To define synonymy in terms of substitutability *salva veritate* is to equate the assertion that two terms, say 'bachelor' and 'unmarried man', are synonymous, with the assertion that whatever is true of bachelors is true of unmarried men. Now, *if* it is true that whatever is true of bachelors is true of unmarried men, then it must be an empirical truth; for it is certainly an empirical truth that whatever is true of bachelors and unmarried men respectively is true. Unless we can deploy some convenient theory of necessary truth at this point, then we are committed to the view that if two terms are synonymous, then the fact that they are so is an empirical fact which rests upon the contingent truth of certain very general statements about what is and is not 'true of' the entities which they denote or stand for.

But, of course, synonymy is a *linguistic* relationship dependent upon the nature of the rules of language and not upon the truth of contingent propositions about the denotata of synonyms. Once again we have made a mistake characteristic of the ETL: we have attempted to represent the rule structure of language as if it were a mere reflection of the empirical nature of the referents of basic terms. The mistake is precisely parallel to the one Waismann makes in supposing that the vagueness of meaning of a word such as 'cat' is to be explicated in terms of the difficulty of deciding whether certain things are really true of any given cat that may be presented to us. In each case questions of meaning (likeness of meaning, vagueness of meaning) become inextricably confused with questions of truth. But, as Wittgenstein saw clearly in the *Tractatus*,[4] it must be possible to settle all questions concerning the *meaning* of statements in a language before we begin to investigate the question of what statements are true.

10.2 If we try to apply our account of synonymy to the problem of defining analyticity, we encounter a problem which arises with equal force no matter whether we say that what is saved in the mutual substitution of synonyms is truth or the satisfaction of operations. On either view, 'x is a man', 'x is a bachelor' will presumably be truth-functionally related as follows:

$$x \text{ is a man} \cdot \sim x \text{ is married} : \equiv x \text{ is a bachelor}$$

But from this it follows that

$$\sim x \text{ is a bachelor}$$

is equivalent to

$$\sim x \text{ is a man} \vee \sim \sim x \text{ is married}$$

But no model which assigns this meaning to the English expression 'x is not a bachelor' can possibly be correct. 'x is not a bachelor'

---

[4] Ludwig Wittgenstein, *Tractatus Logico-Philosophicus*, trans. D.F. Pears and B.F. McGuinness (London: Routledge and Kegan Paul, 1961), 2.0211, 4.024 4.064.

does not mean 'Either x is married or a woman' but 'x is a married man'. Even this formulation is not quite correct. If someone were to say, 'Frances is certainly not a bachelor' and it later emerged that Frances (spelled with an "e") was a young unmarried woman, we should not say that the speaker had used the word 'bachelor' correctly (as we should have to if the truth-functional analysis above were correct), but we should not, either, say (or say simply) that he had uttered a falsehood but, at worst, that he had made a misleading verbal joke. I think one would have to say, just on the basis of linguistic intuition, that the basis of this joke is that the maleness of the subject of reference is in some sense *presupposed* by assertions of bachelorhood and nonbachelorhood but is not part of what such assertions assert. Our reluctance to claim that the joker was actually *lying* stems, on this view, from the fact that 'Frances is certainly not a bachelor' *could* be taken as expressing the claim that Frances does not satisfy an essential presupposition for ascriptions of bachelorhood and is thus in *that* sense 'not a bachelor', although, of course, she is not a married man either.

But what does *presuppose* mean? Linguistic intuitions of this kind are cheap enough, in other words: the problems arise when we try to show how—and whether—they are grounded in the rule structure of language.

I think we can overcome these difficulties as follows. Let us suppose that we have a linguistic device [L_3] whose rules amount, in effect, to directions for filling in the syntactic schema:

'——$_P$ is married'

where '——$_P$' is fillable by proper names, personal pronouns, noun phrases composed of a demonstrative 'person' or definite descriptions identifying persons, for example, 'The man who broke the bank at Monte Carlo'. There is, of course, no rule of language which *specifies* that these expressions are to be considered appropriate fillers of this particular blank. We shall see in more detail in Chapter 12 why we cannot postulate rules of this type: the reasons have to do with the need to avoid *ad hoc* rules which limit the fertility and simplicity of the system of linguistic devices and the need to give an intelligible account of semantic anomaly and semantic category.

Instead, what determines that the blank in the schema governed by [L₃] can be filled by the output of certain other devices, [L₄] ... [Lₙ], let us say, and not by the output of other devices again (devices whose output, inserted into the schema governed by [L₃] might yield, for example, 'The pot in the corner is married'), is simply the actual character of the rules of [L₃]: that is, the fact that, having set them up, they are in fact workable in conjunction with certain devices and not workable in conjunction with certain others. We shall examine this solution in greater detail in Chapter 12. All we need note here is that, if successful, it enables us to construct a complete description of the semantics of a language simply by stating the rules of the linguistic devices without the need for extra rules relating the devices to one another: that is, rules specifying for every possible syntactic schema what expressions can fill what gaps.

The rules of [L₃] will refer to the ceremonies, provisos, and so forth, which define the institution of marriage and by reference to which we determine whether a person is married or not. Similarly, the rules of other linguistic devices will determine whether the person identified by the expression which fills the blank in

'—— is married'

is male or female.

We now introduce what I shall call a *verbal substitution convention* (VSC). This will run as follows:

VSC1: In expressions of the form '*x* is unmarried', for 'unmarried' substitute 'a bachelor' just in case the person identified by the expression '*x*' is male and 'a spinster' just in case the person identified by the expression '*x*' is female.

We shall, of course, encounter problems concerning the point in the rule structure at which we are to introduce such a convention in order for it to govern all possible occurrences of 'bachelor' in contexts where it bears the sense which we wish to define, but I assume that these can be solved in some non-*ad hoc* way.

We must notice, now, that VSC1 is not a linguistic device and does not confer meaning upon the expressions 'bachelor' and 'spinster' in the way in which a linguistic device confers meaning upon the phonemic strings assigned by its place-filling conventions to occupy the places defined by its place-defining rules. A linguistic device confers meaning upon a phonemic string by associating it with a set of rules which in various ways mention and are connected with the world. A verbal substitution convention is, like a linguistic device, a machine for generating utterances, but its rules do not refer directly to the world, but only indirectly, *via* reference to the rules of linguistic devices. Thus, 'bachelor' enters into longer English expressions not by being used to fill a blank in a syntactic schema but by being substituted into a blank already filled by another expression; and the instructions of VSC 1 which specify the conditions licensing this substitution refer to the results of carrying out other sets of instructions drawn from linguistic devices fully specified elsewhere in the structure of semantic rules of the language.

Verbal substitution conventions are, then, second-order linguistic devices. 'Bachelor' and 'spinster', like other words introduced into the language by verbal substitution conventions, have no independent empirical content of their own: that is, none beyond that which they acquire simply by being placed in a conventional relationship to other words in the language. In this they differ from 'married', 'unmarried' 'man', and so on, which are meaningful "in their own right" and independently of any other words in the language. 'Bachelor' and 'spinster' are mere definitional shorthand, in fact, and could be deleted from the language without any ill-effects save a certain slight increase in the long-windedness of discourse about marriage.

VSC 1 specifies an *operation*, which we may call O_{subst}. The effect of this operation is to transform one expression into another, the first expression being the *base* of the operation and the second the *result*. Now, since 'bachelor' has no function in language other than that specified for it by the rules which govern O_{subst}, it has no meaning of its own, and hence its substitution into the base expression cannot in any way change the meaning of that expression. It follows, therefore, that

'x is a bachelor'

is equivalent in meaning to

'x is unmarried'

But can this really be so? For surely, to say that 'x is a bachelor' and 'x is unmarried' are equivalent in meaning is to say that

$$x \text{ is a bachelor} \equiv x \text{ is unmarried}$$

But that no such truth-functional relationship holds is evident from the fact that

$$x \text{ is unmarried} \cdot \sim x \text{ is a bachelor}$$

expresses the form of many true propositions.

To this objection we can only reply that truth-functional equivalence, although it is often a consequence of equivalence of meaning between sentences, is neither entailed by nor "the same thing as" equivalence of meaning. To state the meaning, or the sense, of a statement is to give another sentence, or sentences, whose sense is the same as that of the first. We can only derive an equivalent sentence from, for example,

'John is a bachelor'

by carrying out O_{subst} upon it, and this yields

'John is unmarried'

But what, now, is the relationship between these sentences and the sentence

'John is a man'

which has been commonly believed to "enter into the meaning" of 'John is a bachelor'? The connection is, I believe, this. The rules of VSC 1 do more than state the content of a certain substitution operation; they specify a precondition which must be met before this operation can be performed upon a sentence of the form 'x is umnarried': namely, that the individual specified by the expression which takes the place of 'x' in the sentence must be male, that is, must be such that the expression 'male' applies to it, given the nature of the rules governing the application of that expression. The precondition of an operation must not be confused with the base on which the operation is performed or with the result of performing it. Thus, the base of O_{subst} is not

'x is an unmarried man'

but

'x is unmarried'

But the precondition for applying O_{subst} is that

'x is a man'

be true.

It follows that we cannot say that 'x is a bachelor' *means* 'x is unmarried and x is a man'. It *means* 'x is unmarried' but it can never be *properly asserted of x* (that is, its assertion of x will not be licensed by the rules of English) unless x is a man.

It follows that ' $\sim x$ is a bachelor' is not equivalent in meaning to ' $\sim x$ is a man $\vee$ x is married'. We can interpret our intuitive sense of the inadequacy of this account as a more or less obscure awareness of the difference between the relationship holding between the base and the result of an operation, and that holding between an operation and its preconditions. The reason why the information that x is not a bachelor strengthens rather than weakens the presumption that x is a man is that if this information were false it would presumably be possible to say truly of x that he is a bachelor. But we can only generate the expression 'x is a bachelor', given the rules of English, by applying the operation O_{subst} to the expression 'x is unmarried', and the application of this operation is licensed by the rules of English only if 'x' in fact specifies an individual who happens to be male.

But by the same token someone who says of a woman that she is not a bachelor is not asserting a falsehood, as he would be if 'bachelor' meant 'unmarried-and-a-man': he is simply breaking a rule of English, by refusing to observe the restriction on the application of O_{subst} to sentential bases and hence asserting by his utterance, not a falsehood, but nothing at all. Or nothing, at least, about the marital status of the woman to whom he refers, for we can if we wish take what he says as a whimsical way of asserting something about the logic of 'bachelor': namely, that it is such that the word is inapplicable to women, including this one.

10.3 We can now deal with Quine's difficulties about synonymy and analyticity as they arise in connection with 'All bachelors are unmarried men'.

If we are correct, then the expression 'bachelor' and the expression 'unmarried man' are synonymous in the sense which we defined in section 10.1: that is, they determine exactly the same positive and negative satisfactions of operations. Moreover, their synonymy is grounded purely in convention: the reason why 'bachelor' necessarily satisfies the same operations as 'unmarried man' is that the meaning (use) of 'bachelor' is defined solely by an arbitrary rule (VSC1) which specifies that it may be substituted for 'unmarried' when and only when the subject term of the sentence of which 'is unmarried' is the predicate designates some man or other. Hence, it is trivially true, or "true by (linguistic) convention," that anything which can be said to be a bachelor will be both unmarried and a man.

It must be emphasized that I am not claiming to have shown that 'All bachelors are unmarried men' is true *by definition*. I share the qualms expressed by Quine, Kneale, Pap,[5] and others about the notion that necessary truths can somehow be founded upon or "made true by" definitions or by any other species of direct linguistic fiat. As Quine rightly points out, a definition must either assert the synonymy of two words on the basis of a prior judgment of synonymy, or else it must simply stipulate that a new *notation* is to bear the same sense as one already used to represent some expression in a language. But in the former case, the notion of definition fails to explicate, and must, indeed, itself be explicated by reference to, our prior notion of synonymy, and hence fails to explicate the notion of analyticity; while in the latter case the definition merely expresses a notational convention.

[5] See, for example, Quine, "Two Dogmas," pp. 24–27; William Kneale, "Are Necessary Truths True By Convention?" *Aristotelian Society Supplement*, Vol. 21; Arthur Pap, *Semantics and Necessary Truth: An Inquiry into the Foundations of Analytic Philosophy* (New Haven: Yale University Press, 1958), chap. 7.

We *can*, if we wish, state notational conventions using the language of necessary truth, by means of some such formula as "It is necessarily true that *a*'s are *b*'s," but we shall only be able to avoid misleading by such statements if we add some such addendum as "in Quine's terminology" or "in legal discourse," which gives the game away. Real necessary truths of the kind which philosophers have wanted to label "analytic" require no such deprecatory qualification. 'All bachelors are unmarried men' is not "analytic in English" or "analytic in Kant's terminology," but simply analytically true by virtue of the meanings of its terms. That is, in any language which contained terms having just those meanings, together with appropriate grammatical machinery, it would be possible to formulate a corresponding sentence which would express the same—necessary—truth.

If what we have said so far about the rules of linguistic devices is correct, then a system *S* of linguistic devices augmented by a verbal substitution convention such as VSC 1 will contain nothing which might be called a definition, if by *definition* we understand a rule prescribing that a given phonemic string is to have a given "meaning" assigned to it or that two phonemic strings are to have the same "meaning" assigned to them. For, if we are correct, the rules of *S* (place-defining rules) which determine meanings will not mention any phonemic string; while the rules which mention phonemic strings (place-filling conventions) do nothing to determine meanings, but simply assign phonemic strings to places in *S*, in the sense of "place" established earlier. It would be, indeed, rather difficult even to make sense, in terms of *S*, of the notion of "assigning a meaning to" a phonemic string, for even if we were to identify the class of "meanings" with the class of places and say that, in effect, the place-filling conventions assign meanings to the phonemic strings in assigning them to fill places, we should still have explained the meaningfulness of a very small class of expressions: none of the sentences in this book, for example, would be assigned to places in the system of linguistic devices of English by the place-filling conventions of that system.

In fact, we must drop the notion of definition from the discussion of meaning and synonymy altogether. The meaning of an utterance is its function as defined by a complete representation of the rules of the linguistic devices which introduce it into the language. We can define this function for cognitive discourse by reference to the notion of the satisfaction of operations. In a system of linguistic devices without verbal substitution conventions, there will be no semantic redundancy and hence no synonymy, since any possible expression will define a unique set of positive and negative satisfactions of operations. A verbal substitution convention, however, gives us a rule by which, for any member of an indefinitely large class of utterances which can be generated by following the rules of a given set of linguistic devices, we can generate another utterance which satisfies exactly the same set of operations.

If the verbal substitution convention simply authorizes indiscriminate substitution of one word for another in any context, as in the case of slang or dialect ('spud' for 'potato'; 'pot' for 'marihuana') we get the sort of *mere* synonymy which we envisaged a few moments ago as issuing from stipulative definitions. Thus, we feel no temptation to regard 'All potatoes are spuds' as a necessary (analytic) truth, and by the same token we feel no hesitation in adding "in the mouths of stage Cockneys."

But if, on the other hand, the verbal substitution convention authorizes substitution only on certain preconditions, we get the sort of synonymy that yields apparently necessary truths and so leads to philosophical talk about analyticity, truth-in-virtue-of-the-meanings-of-terms, and so forth.

The reason for this is that the restrictions on the substitutability of a word like 'bachelor' are felt, and rightly felt, as part of its meaning. The rules of VSC 1 do after all specify operations which have to be satisfied in deciding whether or not to insert 'bachelor' at a given point in discourse: it is just that these operations are concerned not with things in the extralinguistic world but with other parts of the total system of linguistic rules. Thus we feel, and rightly, that 'bachelor' is a concept "in its own right," even though we may at the same time be vaguely aware that this concept would have no place in a language which contained no semantic redundancy. And hence, we feel that any language which contained this concept along with those of 'man', 'woman', and 'marriage', would be such that we could construct in it a sentence which would have the same meaning as 'All bachelors are unmarried men' and which would also be analytic. And so, finally, we conclude that in some strange and obscure way 'All bachelors are unmarried men' is *both* a *necessary* truth (that is, one which is not just "true in" a particular language) and yet a truth which is somehow solely dependent upon linguistic convention.

And no doubt we are right (though muddled) about all this: only it seems, if what we have said about linguistic devices holds water, that we are not really making large and obscurely based judgments about concepts, or meanings, or possible languages (or worlds) but merely observing, on the wall of the Platonic Cave of everyday English, the vast and flickering shadows thrown by the minutiae of the underlying rule structure of the very language in which we discuss these questions. In particular we need to see that any language which had just the same linguistic devices and verbal substitution conventions as English and so yielded the same analytic truths, would be only phonetically different from English: that is, would differ, apart from differences in phonology, only in its place-filling conventions.

10.4 As is well known, Quine concludes in "Two Dogmas of Empiricism" that there is no distinction between analytic and synthetic statements or, what comes to the same thing, that we are free to stipulate, within our conceptual scheme, any arbitrary boundary we choose between analytic and synthetic.

> . . . it is misleading to speak of the empirical content of an individual statement—especially if it is a statement at all remote from the experiential periphery of the field [of total science]. Furthermore it becomes folly to seek a boundary between synthetic statements, which hold contingently on experience, and analytic statements, which hold come what may. Any statement can be held true come what may, if we make drastic enough adjustments elsewhere in the system.[6]

If we are right, the possibilities for redrawing the boundary between synthetic and analytic statements are not as unlimited as Quine suggests. We cannot revise the logical status of each individual statement as we choose, even provided we are prepared to accept revision of the status of other statements. Our conceptual system, if we are correct, takes the form of a finite system of linguistic rules: we can abandon parts of that system and replace them with others but

[6] Quine, "Two Dogmas," p. 43.

we cannot by so doing alter the fact that when either set of parts is connected to the rest of the system, certain relationships, including relationships of analyticity, arise in (logical) consequence. For any system of linguistic devices we choose to adopt, that is, analyticity will enter at quite definite points in the system: those points, that is, at which there occurs semantic redundancy of the sort which we can represent in terms of verbal substitution conventions involving preconditions.

The difference between our view and Quine's on this issue is a particular consequence of a more general difference: namely, that on our view it is possible to state the meaning of any sentence in a language without saying anything about the truth of any statement in that language, simply by reference to a finite system of linguistic rules. On Quine's view this is not possible. To give the meaning of a proposition is, for him, in the end, to use it, or some other logically connected proposition, to *assert* some truth: the system of meanings and the system of true empirical propositions in their full array of logical and theoretical connections ("the field of total science") are in the end, for Quine, coextensive.

The discussion of these differences would, I think, raise many fundamental philosophical questions, but it will not be possible to pursue them further within the limits of this book.

11 Use, usage, and category

(1) John frightens sincerity

(2) Bring Thursday

(3) Socrates is prime

(4) He saw carefully that the door was open

(5) The seat of the bed is hard

(6) My door is red and green all over

(7) The sound of a trombone is blue

(8) The tail has a dog

(9) My fear of falling is three inches to the left of my belief that I shall be pushed

11.1 There is *something* wrong with all the above sentences. This much our linguistic intuition assures us with some certainty: any adult native English speaker could pick them out as ill-formed from a list in which they were randomly associated with such well-formed correlates as

(10) Sincerity frightens John

(11) Bring James

(12) Socrates is wise

(13) He saw clearly that the door was open

It is much harder to find any general term with which to characterize such sentences. To begin with none of them is *simply* ungrammatical. In most of them, the oddity seems to turn in some way on the *meaning* of the terms which they contain. Even in cases like (1) or (8), which we may feel tempted to class simply as exhibiting bad grammar, a strong suspicion remains that the ungrammaticalness has a semantic root. And in cases like (2) or (4), where we feel much more certain that a semantic error is being committed, it is not certain that syntax may not nonetheless be involved. Syntax and semantics are not easily separated in such cases.[1]

To describe (1)–(9) simply as "deviant" ("semantically deviant") or as "anomalous" ("semantically anomalous") suggests, what is open to question, that what is wrong with them is that they depart in some way from some more or less clearly understood norm or pattern. "Senseless" or "absurd" disguises the fact that not all such sentences fail to make any sort of sense, or lack even the possibility of being interpreted in such a way as to make sense. (8) might express a quip, or a piece of irony. (9) might turn out in certain circumstances— if, for example, the truth of some radical version of the brain–mind identity thesis had been established—to be a perfectly good way of expressing certain facts about the state of someone's brain. In what follows we shall adopt the relatively colorless expression "ill-formed," on the ground that it begs the fewest questions. Ill-formedness must be distinguished from ungrammaticalness. An ill-formed sentence, such as (4), may be perfectly grammatical, while an ungrammatical sentence may not be ill-formed. On the other hand, we may feel intuitively (and obscurely) that some cases of ill-formedness, such as (1) and (8), involve *something akin to* ungrammaticalness; and, of course,

---

[1] See, for example, Noam Chomsky, *Aspects of the Theory of Syntax* (Cambridge, Mass.: The M.I.T. Press, 1965), p. 160f.

it remains possible for a sentence to be both ill-formed and—for quite other reasons—ungrammatical: for example,

(14) He saw carefully that the door were blue

The class of ill-formed sentences can be taken as including all sentences which embody what philosophers sometimes call category mistakes.

The examples of ill-formedness offered by (1)–(9) do not all seem to be of the same type. But when we try to give a clear account of the differences we run into further difficulties, which stem from the fact that intuition yields no consistent classification or, rather, tempts us to classify in several different and conflicting ways. There is, as we have just seen, a temptation to regard some cases of ill-formedness as syntactic or quasi syntactic in origin. But what are the rules of syntax involved? And which sentences, exactly, break them? Intuition gives us no help here. Again, many people would want to say that whereas (1)–(3) are neither true nor false, but senseless, (6) and (9) are not only false but necessarily false, although the type of necessity involved is unclear. Asked whether (4) is of the same type as (6) and (9), even adult native speakers might vacillate, some claiming that it also is necessarily false, others that it is unintelligible. (8) might produce still more vacillation between the alternatives of necessary falsehood, un-intelligibility, and simple ungrammaticalness. Russell, in *An Inquiry into Meaning and Truth*, claims that (7) " is not nonsense but false "[2] (that is, presumably, expresses a contingent falsehood), and I have no doubt that many philosophers would be prepared to extend the same treatment to (1)–(4) and (8), although no doubt with some hesitation and wavering.

Our interest in these curiosities of language derives, as we have seen, from our interest in the fertility of linguistic systems. One aspect of this fertility is that the learning of language need not (indeed, could not) involve the explicit characterization, for the learner's benefit, of every ill-formed expression as ill-formed. Once someone knows a language (that is, after a finite period of language learning), he is able

[2] Bertrand Russell, *An Inquiry Into Meaning and Truth* (New York: Humanities Press, 1963), p. 197.

to recognize as ill-formed any ill-formed expression constructed from the basic components of that language. There are two questions which we must raise concerning this capacity:

Question 1: What is it, the learning of which confers upon the learner the capacity to recognize ill-formedness?

Question 2: When a linguistically competent adult judges an expression to be ill-formed, what exactly is he judging concerning it? Is his judgment, that is, a judgment of absurdity, of self-contradictoriness, of nonconformity to a rule, of contingent falsehood, or what?

Evidently these questions are not independently answerable, for our answer to question (1) will depend very largely on what answer we give to question (2). But we shall find when we try to answer question (2) that it will serve, in Johnson's phrase, to concentrate our minds, if we consider what sorts of learned systems of rules we might have to postulate in order to render intelligible the genesis of the normal adult capacity to recognize ill-formedness, given one or another account of what is involved in that capacity.

It is not likely that we shall find answers to either of these questions simply by attending to the deliverances of linguistic intuition. We can rely on linguistic intuition to tell us *that* an utterance is ill-formed; and, indeed, we must rely on it to provide us with data for any linguistic or philosophical theory of well-formedness in natural languages or of the relations between syntax and semantics. This much is granted by the practice of linguists in constructing generative grammars. Thus, Chomsky at one point remarks that "It is obvious to anyone who knows English" that expressions like

(15) The boy may frighten sincerity

(16) Sincerity may admire the boy

and others "have an entirely different status from" expressions like

(17) Sincerity may frighten the boy

(18) The boy may admire sincerity

And he continues:

> The distinction between [them] is not at issue, and clearly must be ec-
> counted for somehow by an adequate theory of sentence interpretation
> (a descriptively adequate grammar). [Such expressions as (15) and (16)]
> deviate in some manner—(not necessarily all in the same manner) from the
> rules of English.[3]

As we have seen, however, it is much harder to get intuition to
yield a clear and unambiguous division of the class of ill-formed expressions into subclasses, each of which represents a different type of
ill-formedness (or " manner of deviation from the rules of English").
Ryle, in a celebrated paper on categories, discusses what he calls the
" absurdity" of certain types of ill-formed expression and concludes
with the despairing cry: " But what are the tests of absurdity?"[4] And
indeed, it has seemed to many philosophers that all attempts to
distinguish types of ill-formedness on intuitive grounds must be inherently hopeless, because the exercise of intuition in such cases amounts
to no more than the savoring of different "flavors of absurdity."
But things are not really quite as bad as this. Even if the intuition of
different speakers appears to differ or that of a single speaker to leave
him undecided between two alternatives, it is usually possible to agree
on what the alternatives are between which intuition leaves us sus-
pended, where the intermediate cases lie, and what the various temptations are to which we feel intuitively subject with respect to the classification of particular sentences. For example, native speakers of English will commonly be prepared to admit that on the one hand they
feel tempted to claim that (1) is neither true nor false but senseless,
but that on the other hand they feel tempted to say that (1) is necessarily false on the ground that

(19) Nothing can frighten sincerity

is necessarily true. Native speakers who wish to claim that (1) is contingently false will grant that they *feel* both the above temptations

[3] *Ibid.*, p. 76.

[4] Gilbert Ryle, "Categories," in A. G. N. Flew, ed., *Essays on Logic and
Language*, 2nd series.

but consider that there are serious philosophical difficulties[5] which confront us if we succumb to either temptation and that therefore we should give in to neither. They will grant, moreover, that (1) seems intuitively to be a statement of a quite different sort from any ordinary contingent falsehood, such as

(20) Chamberlain frightened Hitler

but will contend that the promptings of intuition ought to be disregarded in such cases on the grounds that they are too vague and subjective to be made the basis for philosophical discussion.

What any theory which pretends to account for the adult native speaker's capacity to recognize ill-formedness must do, then, is to show why, in each particular case, just those conflicts and ambiguities must appear in the native speaker's intuition which do in fact appear. If, for example, native speakers feel equally tempted to regard an expression as senseless and to regard it as necessarily false, while at the same time finding themselves unable to give any clear account of the type of necessity involved, then a good theory of language should explain why this is so. Hence, since one criterion of an acceptable answer to questions (1) and (2) is that it should explain, in some nontrivial way, the actual deliverances of linguistic intuition, it is plain that such an answer cannot itself be extracted from the deliverances of intuition.

11.2 Let us return to question (1). A moment's reflection suggests two obvious possible answers:

Answer i: What one can and cannot do with a word in the way of combining it with others depends on, and is evident to the learner from, the nature of the things that it refers to. If sincerity cannot be frightened by John, that is because, and is evident given the fact that, John and sincerity are the sorts of things that they are.

Answer ii: The learner is at some time or other taught a set of rules of the form, 'S_1 must not occupy syntactic position ___ with respect to S_2'.

---

[5] These are thought to involve on the one hand, the admission of a very odd kind of necessary truth and, on the other, the possibility of basing " ontological " conclusions upon what appears to be merely " linguistic " premises.

Neither of these suggestions is in the end tenable. The first is open
to the following objections. Presumably, if answer (i) is correct, we
know that (1) is ill-formed in virtue of knowing the truth of some such
statement as (19). It is of interest that Chomsky, in discussing these
matters, gives the following variants of (19):

(21) It is nonsense to speak of (there is no such activity as) frightening
     sincerity

(22) Sincerity is not the kind of thing that can be frightened

(23) One cannot frighten sincerity

remarking that "a descriptively adequate grammar must indicate
that" (1) is deviant and that (21)–(23) are not.[6] If answer (i) is correct, now, (21)–(23) must be construed as stating facts about sincerity.
We cannot, however, construe these as *contingent* facts about sincerity, for the following reasons.

Let us suppose, for the sake of argument, that gorillas happen as a
matter of fact to be absolutely fearless creatures. We would express
this contingent fact in sentences like the following:

(24) As it happens it is nonsense to speak of frightening gorillas

(25) A gorilla is not the kind of thing that can be frightened

(26) One cannot frighten a gorilla

I think it is intuitively obvious that whereas the 'cannot' of (26) is the
'cannot' of contingent matter-of-fact, the 'cannot' of (23) is much
more like the 'cannot' of logical impossibility ('One cannot put a
quart into a pint pot'; 'One cannot construct a triangle whose angles
total more than 180°'). Moreover, intuition appears to be supported
here by the fact that it is possible to think of a state of affairs in
which (25) would become false; gorillas, or some gorilla, might turn
timid. But could sincerity turn timid? 'Sincerity has turned timid'
suffers from the same disquieting oddity as (1). I should imagine that
it was the difficulty of imagining sincerity turning timid which made

[6] Chomsky, *Aspects*, p. 157.

Chomsky insert the clause "(there is no such activity as)" in (21). For although, given the truth of (24)–(26), it would be quite sensible, if clumsy, to say

(27) There is no such thing as a frightenable gorilla

it would nevertheless be very odd to say

(28) There is no such activity as frightening gorillas

Sentence (28) suggests, not that gorillas are absolutely fearless but that 'I intend to frighten that gorilla' somehow fails as a specification of a possible (conceivable) intention. But this is not what we want to say. All that we are justified in saying, given the truth of (24)–(26), is that, while 'I intend to frighten that gorilla' certainly specifies a possible intention, it specifies one which for all practical purposes is impossible to execute. And this is what (27) does say.

We can make (28) roughly equivalent to (27) by adding (as we have done in (24)) a disclaimer clause, thus:

(29) In practice, there is no such activity as frightening gorillas

This makes it clear that we are not making a conceptual point, to the effect that the expression 'frighten a gorilla' is conceptually odd, but a point about the practical difficulties of frightening gorillas. Nonetheless, (29) possesses a wry ironic flavor precisely because the suggestion of conceptual oddity is not entirely canceled out: it implies, without saying explicitly, that frightening gorillas is *next door to* logically impossible or conceptually absurd. Note that no such disclaimer is appropriate, or for that matter possible, in the case of (21)–(23). For

(30) In practice, one cannot frighten sincerity

is again ill-formed. Here the "in practice" seems to have no function at all: what sort of practical experience could it be that would lead to the conclusion that, after all, it might be the most sensible course to cease attempting to frighten sincerity?

The protagonist of answer (i) may object that the whole of the above argument ought to be dismissed on the ground that it appeals to intuition and is therefore viciously "subjective." But this objection is not to his purpose. Answer (i) is supposed to provide an answer to the question "How does the learner acquire the adult English speaker's capacity to recognize ill-formedness?" If, while accepting answer (i), we maintain that (21)–(23) and (24)–(26) all express contingent truths, then the explanatory force of answer (i) evaporates. We are left, that is, with no means of explaining how it comes about that whereas knowing (24)–(26) to be (contingently) true leads the adult English speaker to judge that

(31) John frightens gorillas

is false, knowing (21)–(23) to be contingently true leads him to judge in some moods that (1) is necessarily false ar.d in other moods that it is neither false nor true but absurd. Nor do we have any explanation for the fact that adult speakers of English certainly feel tempted to represent (21)–(23) as (in some sense) necessarily true. Answer (i) yields a partial explanation of these disparities only when taken in conjunction either with the view (a) that (21)–(23) are necessarily true, or with the view (b) that for some reason the learner comes to take (21)–(23) as necessarily true. If we can accept either (a) or (b), that is, we can argue that it is because the learner sees, or takes, (21)–(23) to be necessarily true that he judges (1) to be necessarily false. But on either view, this explanation shrouds in deeper darkness more aspects of the adult speaker's competence than it explains. Why is it, for example, that some adult speakers, or the same speaker on another occasion, may judge (1) not to be necessarily false but rather ill-formed: neither true nor false? Moreover, if we accept view (b), we must accept it as an unexplained *ad hoc* addendum to answer (i), for that answer offers us no explanation of why the learner should come to take (21)–(23) as necessarily true or of what it is about (21)–(23) which makes it possible for the adult English speaker to so regard them, given that their alleged necessity is not of any easily explicable type. If we adopt view (a), on the other hand, we are even worse off. For now, apparently, the truths about John, sincerity, and so forth, in virtue of which we recognize as ill-formed ill-formed combinations of the words 'John', 'sincerity', and so on, really are necessary truths. If we ask how it is that we can possibly come to know necessary truths about contingent existents, no answer presents itself, unless it be one involving the postulation of some sort of rational intuition of the essences of John, sincerity, and the rest.[7] And once again the ground and nature of the necessity which such truths allegedly possess is left wholly obscure.

We may conclude that answer (i) sheds more darkness than light and proceed to the examination of answer (ii). To begin with, answer (ii) seems not to account for the adult speaker's capacity to recognize *any* ill-formed sentence as ill-formed. We cannot suppose that there exists a rule of language expressly characterizing as ill-formed every ill-formed expression capable of being constructed by juxtaposing basic components of the language. Hence, there must be an upper bound upon the length of the strings represented by S_1 and S_2. But if there is such an upper bound, what enables the learner to infer from the ill-formedness of the simple expressions expressly characterized as ill-formed by rules of the form, 'S_1 must not occupy syntactic position _____ with respect to S_2', to the ill-formedness of longer and more complex expressions?

Answer (ii) is open to a still more serious objection. If it is correct, then the rules which determine that words may not be combined in certain ways are quite independent of the rules establishing the meanings of words. On such a view, one would have to distinguish between, on the one hand, the learning of the meanings of words and, on the other hand, the learning of what one might call "combinatorial conventions." Now it is beyond doubt, I think, that we detect ill-formedness in an expression by reflecting upon the meanings of the words involved. But we have already seen that "reflecting upon the meanings of the words involved" cannot be taken as equivalent to "reflecting upon the empirical nature of the referents of the words involved." We seem to need an account of the rules which introduce meaning into a language from which it will be apparent that, and how, someone who knows those rules will be able to recognize ill-formedness. This is precisely what answer (ii) fails to provide. How could a rule of the

---

[7] Or, of course, a Kantian one; but the resuscitation and multiplication of the pure categories of the understanding seems a stiff price to pay for the retention of answer (i).

form, 'S_1 must occupy syntactic position ____ with respect to S_2', be derived from the meaning rules of a language? One would suppose that such a rule would simply have to be inculcated *ad hoc*, independently of any other rules. But then the status of such rules becomes that of mere arbitrary conventions. But if (4), for example, is ill-formed, it is so not in virtue of an arbitrary convention established among English speakers (the sort of convention, for example, which at the turn of the century in England forbade well-bred people to pronounce the terminal "g" in *hunting* and *fishing*) but in virtue of the meanings of the words contained in it.

The class of theories of meaning which attempt to exhibit the ability to recognize ill-formedness as the outcome of the assimilation of a system of rules governing meaning is no longer an empty one. Much recent work on semantic description by Fodor, Katz, Postal,[8] and others seems to be in part an attempt to provide such a theory and must therefore now be examined.

Fodor, Katz, and Postal's semantic theory is intended to constitute the semantic component of an integrated system for the description of natural languages, the other parts of which are a syntactic component and a phonological component. The syntactic component these authors have in mind is some form of transformational grammar. The general aim of the system is that of transformational grammar: to describe in its full complexity what is involved in the linguistic competence of someone who has complete mastery of a language. "The problem for the linguist, as well as for the child learning the language, is to determine from the data of performance the underlying system of rules that has been mastered by the speaker-hearer and that he puts to use in actual performance."[9]

Katz, Fodor, and Postal propose that we account for the adult speaker's capacity to understand the meaning of indefinitely many well-formed sentences in his language by representing his semantic competence as involving the following features:

---

[8] See Jerrold J. Katz and Jerry A. Fodor, "The Structure of a Semantic Theory," *Language*, vol. 39 (April–June 1963), 170–210; Jerrold J. Katz and Paul M. Postal, *An Integrated Theory of Linguistic Descriptions*, Research Monograph No. 26 (Cambridge, Mass.: The M.I.T. Press, 1964).

[9] Chomsky, *Aspects*, p. 4.

(1) An assignment of one or more meanings to each of the morphemes of the language.

(2) A set of rules by means of which, given a knowledge of (1) and of the syntax (transformational grammar) of the language, he is able to generate a meaning for any syntactically well-formed string of morphemes.[10]

A semantic theory, then, will consist of two parts: "first, a *dictionary*, that provides a meaning for each of the lexical items of the language, and second, a finite set of *projection rules* ... [which] assign a *semantic interpretation* to each string of formatives generated by the syntactic component."[11] Our interest for the moment is in the dictionary:

> The normal form for a dictionary entry is as follows: an entry consists of a finite set of sequences of symbols, each sequence consisting of an initial subsequence of *syntactic markers*, followed by a subsequence of *semantic markers*, then, optionally, a *distinguisher*, and finally a *selection restriction*.[12]

What Katz and Postal have in mind can be seen more readily by considering the following schematic representation of a sample dictionary entry:[13]

[10] "Since the set of sentences is infinite and each sentence is a different concatenation of morphemes, the fact that a speaker can understand any sentence must mean that the way he understands sentences he has never previously encountered is compositional: on the basis of his knowledge of the grammatical properties and the meanings of the morphemes of the language, the rules the speaker knows enable him to determine the meaning of a novel sentence in terms of the manner in which the parts of the sentences are composed to form the whole." ("The Structure of a Semantic Theory," in Fodor and Katz, *The Structure of Language* (Englewood Cliffs, N.J.: Prentice-Hall, Inc., 1964), p. 482.)

[11] Katz and Postal, *An Integrated Theory* p. 12.

[12] *Ibid.*, p. 13.

[13] Copyright © 1964 by the Massachusetts Institute of Technology, from Jerrold J. Katz and Paul M. Postal, *An Integrated Theory of Linguistic Descriptions*, Research Monograph No. 26 (Cambridge, Mass.: The M.I.T. Press, 1964), p. 14, diagram 2.7.

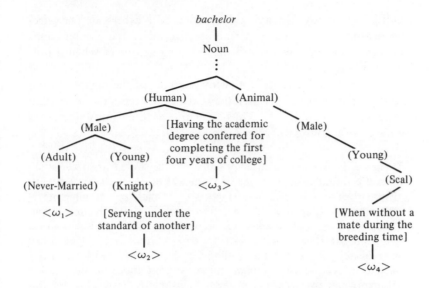

Here, elements not italicized or in brackets are syntactic markers; those within parentheses are semantic markers; those within square brackets are distinguishers, and those within pointed brackets are selection restrictions. Each path in the tree represents a *reading* for the lexical item in question; thus, this diagram defines four readings for *bachelor*.

Every formative in a sentence will have an entry of this sort associated with it. The task of the projection rules is to amalgamate the entries for any given sentence, discarding parts of them and perhaps transforming them in other ways, so as to yield one or more readings ("reading" here seems to mean roughly "paraphrase") for the sentence as a whole. Katz and Postal claim, among other things, that the resulting paraphrase or paraphrases will provide, for any given sentence, "a full analysis of its cognitive meaning."[14]

The success of this enterprise turns to a quite considerable extent on the formulation of selection restrictions. Katz and Postal define a selection restriction as "a formally expressed necessary and sufficient

[14] *Ibid.*, p. 12.

condition for [a given] reading to combine with others. . . . The selection restriction attached to a reading determines the combinations with other readings into which that reading can enter when a projection rule is applied."[15]

Katz and Postal give the following example of the operation of a selection restriction; and from it they extract an account, or definition of " semantic anomaly," by which they appear to mean roughly what we have been calling ill-formedness.

> If the readings in the dictionary entry for the lexical item *honest* are correctly formulated, then one of them will be: *honest* ⟶ Adjective (Evaluative) ⟶ (Moral ⟶ [Innocent of illicit sexual intercourse] ⟨(Human) and (Female)⟩. The selection restriction in this reading is construed as saying that an adjectival occurrence of the lexical item *honest* bears the sense (Evaluative) ⟶ (Moral) ⟶ [Innocent of illicit sexual intercourse] just in case the reading for the nominal head which this adjectival occurrence modifies contains both the semantic marker (Human) and the semantic marker (Female). If the reading for this nominal head lacks one or both of these markers, no combination occurs, and there is no *derived reading* which represents the meaning of the modifier-head constituent in terms of the meanings of its components. Thus, an expression such as *honest woman*, in one of its senses, means ' a woman who is not guilty of illicit sexual intercourse' because the lexical item *woman* has a reading containing both (Human) and (Female). But an expression such as *honest geranium* has no meaning because the reading of the lexical item *geranium* fails to satisfy the selection restriction for *honest*. In cases where syntactically compound expressions are assigned no derived reading, we shall say that the semantic component marks them as *semantically anomalous*.[16]

This sort of semantic theory meets our first objection to answer (ii) and might appear to meet the second as well. What the learner learns, in learning the meaning of any word, according to Fodor, Katz, and Postal, is a set of possible readings expressed as a string of semantic markers and distinguishers, with, attached to each reading, a rule

[15] *Ibid.*, p. 15.

[16] *Ibid.*, p. 16.

or rules to the effect that the word in question can only bear the reading in question when it stands in a given syntactic relation to a further word, if that further word contains, in one of its readings, certain other semantic markers. The speaker's ability to recognize ill-formedness thus appears, satisfactorily enough, as a function of his knowledge of the meanings (the trees of readings) of the words (or, formatives) wrongly combined in ill-formed expression; and his judgment of ill-formedness stands revealed as a judgment to the effect that the rules of the language fail to assign a sense to the ill-formed expression, because that expression fails at some point to meet the criteria for assignment of sense (derived reading) expressed in the selection restrictions attaching to its component formatives.

So far so good: Fodor, Katz, and Postal are going in the right direction. But, it seems to me, their view leaves a crucial question unanswered. On what grounds do we determine which selection restrictions to attach to which readings? Why does "*honest* $\longrightarrow$ Adjective (Evaluate) $\longrightarrow$ (Moral) $\longrightarrow$ [Innocent of illicit sexual intercourse]" have "⟨(Human) and (Female)⟩" attaching to it, rather than "⟨(Vegetable)⟩"? If we claim that the choice of selection restrictions is merely a matter of linguistic convention, we meet the difficulty that they can be attached in no other way, or, rather, that attaching them in any other way leads to the generation of ill-formed expressions. Incoherency of sentence construction is, in other words, exactly mirrored by incoherency of selection-restriction attachment; and the one needs explication just as much, and for exactly the same reasons, as the other. Or suppose we claim that the choice of selection restrictions is governed by the meanings of the words to which we attach them. For Fodor, Katz, and Postal a meaning (reading) of a word is simply a string of syntactic markers, semantic markers, and distinguishers. But I cannot discover that the selection restriction to be attached to the reading "*honest* $\longrightarrow$ Adjective $\longrightarrow$ (Evaluative) $\longrightarrow$ (Moral) $\longrightarrow$ [Innocent of illicit sexual intercourse]" ought to exclude "⟨Vegetable⟩" from the selection restriction unless I know that, as a matter of fact, it is absurd to ascribe to a geranium innocence of illicit sexual intercourse with the force of a moral evaluation. And knowing this, of course, just amounts to knowing that 'honest geranium' is ill-formed—at least, so long as we insist on 'honest' bearing a certain sense.[17] In practice, Fodor, Katz, and Postal presumably obtain their assignments of selection restrictions by juggling alternative restrictions until they discover a reasonably compendious one which appears to generate, at least within the limits of an example, results conformable to their linguistic intuition. And no doubt this is the only possible way of arriving at an assignment of selection restrictions to readings. But then, to say this is simply to say that the notion of selection restriction throws no light on what is involved in the capacity to recognize ill-formedness, for we can equally well ask either "How does it come about that the adult speaker can recognize ill-formedness?" or "How does it come about that the adult speaker can assign selection restrictions to readings?"

If we want an answer to the latter question, there seem again to be two possible alternative moves which we can make. We can say that the adult speaker, or the linguistic community, assigns semantic markers by reference to the empirical nature of the things which words refer to, which gives us a version of the thesis which we have labeled answer (i) and already rejected. Or we can say that the attachment of semantic markers is a function of some class of semantic rules whose form and content are determined without reference to any intuitive judgment of ill-formedness. But then, these rules must be quite different from any of the types of rule provided for by Fodor, Katz, and Postal's theory. Chomsky comes close to formulating this difficulty. In *Aspects of the Theory of Syntax*, he remarks:

> I have described the semantic component as a system of rules that assign readings to constituents of Phrase-markers—a system that has no intrinsic structure beyond this. But such a description is hardly sufficient. In particular, there is little doubt that the system of "dictionary definitions" is not as atomistic as is implied by this account. ... it seems obvious that in any given linguistic system lexical entries enter into intrinsic semantic relations of a much more systematic sort than is suggested by what has been said so far. . . . Thus, for example, consider Adjectives that are mutually exclusive in some referential domain, for example, color words.

---

[17] 'Honest geranium' is not, of course, ill-formed in any absolute sense. A gardener who asserted that the new green and black varieties were all very well as a curiosity but that for his part he preferred a plain honest geranium, would be talking perfectly good English.

Such "antonymy sets" . . . provide a simple example of a field property which cannot be described naturally in terms of separate lexical items, though it obviously plays a role in semantic interpretation.[18]

Chomsky himself has proposed a way of taking account of ill-formedness within the framework of transformational grammar.[19] He points out for example, that sentence (1) is not as extreme in its violation of grammatical rules as is the following:

(32) John sincerity frightens

although, equally, it is not as perfectly grammatical as (10). He suggests that a grammar might be reasonably expected to assign to an expression such as (1) or (32) a structural description which would indicate "its degree of grammaticalness, the degree of its deviation from grammatical regularity, and the manner of its deviation."[20] Chomsky's suggestion is as follows: A grammar may characterize the units (*formatives*) in terms of which it generates structural descriptions of utterances according to a hierarchy of categories of formatives. Thus, on the first level, we may have a single category C_1^1 embracing all formatives; on the second a set of categories $C_1^2, \ldots, C_{n2}^2$; on the third a set $C_1^3, \ldots, C_{n3}^3$, where $n3 > n2$, and so on. Thus, for example, C_1^1 might be the class of all words, C_1^2 nouns, C_2^2 verbs, $C_i^3, \ldots, C_j^3$ subcategories of verbs (transitives, verbs with inanimate objects) and so on. Now, any sequence of words will find a representation at some level in this hierarchy, even if it is only at the first level (at which any sequence appears as $C_1^1 C_1^1 C_1^1, \ldots$). A grammatically deviant sentence will lack a representation at some level or levels of the hierarchy: a *completely* ungrammatical sentence, such as 'abundant loves company' will find a representation only at the first level. The distance of the level(s) at which an utterance receives a representation from the highest (m^{th}) level of the categorial hierarchy thus, obviously enough, offers us a measure of the degree

[18] Chomsky, *Aspects*, p. 160.

[19] Noam Chomsky, "Degrees of Grammaticalness," in Fodor and Katz, *The Structure of Language*.

[20] *Ibid.*, p. 386.

of remoteness of the utterance from the set of perfectly well-formed sentences: a " degree of grammaticalness." [21]

It is not my purpose to criticize this suggestion of Chomsky's, considered simply as a proposal for establishing a measure of deviation from a standard of grammatical regularity as established by some generative grammar. But difficulties do arise if we attempt to take such a system as explaining our ability to recognize such deviations by describing the rules which a learner must " internalize " if he is to be able to exercise such a recognitional capacity.[22] First, for the system to be genuinely explanatory in this respect, it would be necessary for the choice of categories and selectional rules (just as much as for the choices concerning the attachment of selection restrictions to readings in Fodor, Katz, and Postal's theory) to be exhibited as determined by some set of rules whose introduction into a system of linguistic description can be explained and justified without involving the need to account for our actual intuitive judgments of ill-formedness or semi-grammatical status. In other words, a description of the rules which enable the learner to construct well-formed utterances in a language ought, if it is adequately formulated, to yield, as a by-product, an explanation of our intuitive judgments of ill-formedness, thereby obviating the need for the introduction of a further class of rules for avoiding ill-formedness. For, such a further class of rules can at best only systematize our intuitive judgments of ill-formedness, without explaining the basis of such judgments.

Second, Chomsky, in a note to the above passage, raises the question, " What is the natural point where continued refinement of the category hierarchy should come to an end?" and remarks that there is no obvious answer to this question but that

> As the grammatical rules become more detailed, we may find that grammar is converging with what has been called logical grammar. That is, we seem to be studying small overlapping categories of formatives, where each category can be characterized by what we can now (given the grammar) recognize as a semantic feature of some sort.[23]

[21] I have paraphrased Chomsky's suggestion from his "Degrees of Grammaticalness," pp. 386–387.

[22] I do not suppose that Chomsky himself would make such a claim.

[23] Chomsky, "Degrees of Grammaticalness," p. 387, n. 8.

The question of whether, and what, "categories" are revealed by the study of "logical grammar," or conceptual analysis, is a disputed topic in philosophy. Typical of the claims that have been made by conceptual analysts is, for example, Ryle's claim that "achievement words" ('sees', 'wins') constitute a category (or "family of concepts")distinct from the category of "performance words" ('looks', 'runs').[24] A good many familiar theses of contemporary philosophy could quite easily be expressed in this Rylian vocabulary of categories, provided we treat it as no more than a *façon de parler*. Thus it might be claimed that a predicate like 'is yellow' belongs to a different category from predicates like 'has a wavelength of 240A' ("the concepts employed in the description of colored things form a family distinct from the family of concepts employed in the description of electromagnetic radiation"). But such talk of categories has ill-defined limits and rather notoriously lacks a clear theoretical basis.[25]

Ryle's usage suggests that language ought to divide neatly into mutually exclusive classes of expressions, each constituting a separate category (although his phrase "family of concepts" obscures this neat and simple picture by suggesting that there can be "family resemblances" between concepts—but perhaps these hold only between concepts belonging to the same category). The same neat exclusiveness is suggested by Chomsky's talk of "small overlapping categories of formatives, where each category can be characterized by ... a semantic feature of some sort."

But can we really fit the complexities of "logical grammar" into any system of neatly separable categories, even categories with overlaps (that is, presumably, ones with some expressions (words, formatives) in common)? Consider, for example, what Austin has to say about what he calls "dimension words":[26] for example 'proper', 'genuine', 'live', 'real', 'authentic', 'natural', 'fake', 'artificial', 'bogus', 'makeshift', 'toy'. Austin points out, among other things, that for any given substantive "we frequently have a well-founded antecedent idea in what respects the thing mentioned could (and

---

[24] Gilbert Ryle, *The Concept of Mind* (London: Hutchinson, 1949), p. 125.

[25] See my article, "Category Mistakes and Rules of Language," *Mind*, n.s.74, no. 295 (July, 1965).

[26] Austin, *Sense and Sensibilia*, pp. 71–72.

could not) be 'not real'." Thus, silk can be 'real' or 'artificial' but
not 'toy', and presumably there can be no such thing as an authentic
goat, a makeshift potato, fake afterimages, bogus silence, or natural
machinery, at least not *literally* (whereby hangs another, and longer,
tale). It is not at all easy to see how one could represent even this
relatively simple bit of Austinian conceptual analysis in terms of
categories. Do all of Austin's dimension words form one category?
Or a category subdivided into smaller categories? It the latter, where
do the dividing lines between subcategories come: does 'makeshift'
belong in the same category with 'proper', or do all of Austin's
"negative" dimension words form a category on their own? And
what about the substantives: do all the things that can be bogus
(Vermeers, credentials, accents, Marquesses, and so on) form one
category? Any such attempt to impose a compartmental structure on
the fluid and multifarious network of relationships which Austin is
concerned to expose seems to result merely in distortion and over-
simplification. And yet Austin's conceptual judgments are not, or
not often, merely idiosyncratic: they are part of the web of intuitive
linguistic knowledge which a fully competent speaker possesses and
which a decent descriptive theory of language ought to explain, belonging not on the *parole* but on the *langue* side of Saussure's distinction.

The lack of adequate theoretical backing for talk of categories is
still easier to demonstrate. Ryle gives the following criterion for
deciding when two expressions have significata belonging to different
categories:

> Two proposition factors are of different categories or types if there are
> sentence-frames such that when the expressions [sentence-factors] for
> these factors are imported as alternative complements to replacements
> for the same gap-signs (blanks), the resultant sentences are significant in
> one case and absurd in the other.[27]

J. J. C. Smart[28] has pointed out, however, that for almost any pair of

[27] Gilbert Ryle, "Categories," in A. G. N. Flew, ed., *Essays in Logic and
Language*, 2nd series, pp. 77–78.

[28] J. J. C. Smart, "A Note on Categories," *British Journal for the Philosophy
of Science*, nos. v, iv (1953–1954), p. 227.

sentence factors one can discover some sentence frame which will enable one, using Ryle's criterion, to assign these factors to different categories. Thus, we can differentiate between 'chair' and 'bed' using the sentence frame 'The seat of the ____ is hard'. But, asks Smart, if furniture words do not constitute a single category, what class of words does?

It is very hard to see what criterion different in principle from Ryle's we could have for assigning expressions, or formatives, to different categories. Smart's argument seems to show, then, that whatever list of words (expressions, formatives), we adopt as the headings of a dictionary of a natural language, our list of categories will contain exactly as many items as our dictionary, each "category," in fact, containing a single dictionary heading. Such an interpretation of the notion of category would certainly render it useless for Ryle's purposes, but it also presents severe difficulties for Chomsky. For as we have seen, Chomsky is aware that if the semantic component of a language is "atomistic" (if it consists simply of an unstructured list of items with associated meanings, or readings), it will be impossible to give any account of cases of ill-formedness which appear to turn on intrinsic semantic relationships holding between different items on the list. And such cases are unfortunately rather numerous; they include not merely such hoary philosophical warhorses as (6), but examples like (1)–(4), (8)–(10), and a host of others as easily constructed as these. Chomsky's suggestion in "Degrees of Grammaticalness" *might* offer a way of remedying the lack of structure displayed by a list of dictionary entries by supplementing the list with a hierarchy of categories, *if* it were true that the gradual refinement of the system of categories led in an orderly and clearly definable fashion from the purely syntactic categories of the upper levels to lower levels of categories clearly relevant to the concerns of logical grammar (conceptual analysis). But in fact, if we have argued correctly, any attempt to develop a hierarchy of grammatical categories in such a way would encounter severe theoretical difficulties. For if Smart is right, and I can see no way in which either Chomsky or Ryle could evade his argument, the lowest level of all would simply consist of the unstructured list of dictionary entries. And it would be very difficult (not just because of Smart's argument, but simply because of the difficulty—given the complexity of language—of fitting the results of conceptional analysis into *any* orderly schema of categories), to construct a plausible hierarchy of levels of categories connecting this lowest level with the upper levels of straightforwardly grammatical categories. We would be left, then, with a number of levels of grammatical categories at the top of our hierarchy; below them, a single level containing a category for each dictionary entry; and nothing at all in between. Once again, syntax and semantics seem to have fallen apart in our hands.

11.3 The notion of a semantic category seems so obscure and so beset with difficulties that perhaps we should abandon it. But it is not an entirely gratuitous notion. Philosophers have been led to talk in terms of semantic categories in an effort to explain what one might call the fundamental phenomena of category, including all those facts about native speakers' intuitions of ill-formedness which we discussed earlier on; and these facts remain to be explained.

One of the most curious of these facts is that to many expressions, such as (1), which Ryle would regard as embodying category mistakes, there correspond ranges of sentences like (21)–(23), which appear to express *a priori* truths but for which no obvious answer to the *Transzendentale Hauptfrage* can be discovered. It is worth noticing that odd sentences of the sort on which Smart's argument depends do not yield such correlative *a priori* truths. Thus, corresponding to (5), we shall presumably get, by analogy with (21)–(23), something like the following:

(33) It is nonsense to speak of the seat of a bed being hard   (There is no such thing as a hard seat of a bed)

(34) The seat of a bed is not the kind of thing that can be hard

(35) The seat of a bed cannot be hard

There are certain important differences between (21)–(23) and (33)–(35). (21)–(23) can all be taken as offering explanations of the ill-formedness of (1). No doubt the explanation which they offer (that one cannot say 'John frightens sincerity' because it is logically impossible to frighten sincerity) is not a very helpful one, but the reason why it is unhelpful is not that (21)–(23) are ill-formed in just the way that (1) is ill-formed. Quite the contrary—(21)–(23) are not only well-formed but necessarily true; they are unhelpful only because we feel that an adequate explanation of the ill-formedness of (1) would have to involve not merely some statement to the effect that (21)–(23) are necessarily true, but also some explanation of the ground of the necessity of (21)–(23).

Sentences (33)–(35), on the other hand, do not seem to be necessarily true, and they offer no explanation of the ill-formedness of (5), for if (5) is ill-formed, then (33)–(35) are ill-formed in exactly the same way. It is as much nonsense to say 'The seat of a bed cannot be hard' as 'The seat of the bed is hard': we feel inclined to retort, testily, that if beds had seats, no doubt some would be soft and some hard but that, of course, beds are not made with seats. And this, I think, brings us to the nub of the matter: to explain the ill-formedness of (5) we require, not the enunciation of a necessary truth together with some explication of the ground of its necessity, but a simple statement of contingent fact, namely:

(36) Beds do not have (are not made with) seats

It is clear, now, that whereas we can imagine no state of affairs in which (1) might be true, and hence well-formed (how could sincerity become timorous?), we can quite easily imagine a situation in which (5) would be true. Beds, or some beds, might come to be made with built-in seats (for sitting on to remove your boots before going to bed, perhaps) as well as sleeping surfaces. Of such a bed it might well be said, 'The seat of this bed is hard, although the mattress is soft'.

It seems to me that if a sentence is grammatical and if it is quite possible to imagine circumstances in which it would be literally true, then it is not ill-formed in any sense which requires linguistic or philosophical elucidation. Someone who says 'Monsignor Hagerty's wife is over forty' or 'The blade of John's spoon was blunt', is not displaying an imperfect grasp of the English language but rather a simple ignorance of certain commonplace (and by no means necessary) truths about the celibacy of the Catholic clergy and the anatomy of spoons.

We might simply reply to Smart, then, that the sentences he dis- ·
cusses are not ill-formed but merely odd in a philosophically uninteresting way, and hence that his argument is irrelevant to the problem
of category. But this would be to miss one important implication
of his argument. We cannot answer the question "Why is it wrong to
say 'He saw the ball carefully' or 'John frightens sincerity'?" by
pointing to any contingent fact about balls, seeing, John, sincerity or
fright. But yet, presumably, these sentences are ill-formed because
they break the rules of the English language, and it is surely a contingent truth that speakers of English conform to the linguistic rules to
which they do conform: descriptive linguistics is an empirical science
and not an *a priori* one. It appears, then, that just as (5) is odd because
certain facts about beds happen to be the case, so (1) is ill-formed
because certain facts about the usage of English speakers happen to
be the case. But we cannot rest happy with this conclusion. For although we can see how (5) might come to express a true statement
merely by postulating changes in the manufacture of beds, we cannot
by postulating changes in the usage of English speakers, see how (1)
might come to express a true statement. Even if we imagine all speakers of English assembling, like Russell's parliament of hitherto speech-
less elders, to decree that in future (1) is to be regarded as a well-
formed sentence, there remains the difficulty that this procedure
would be in an important sense *idle*, for it would still be impossible
for any English speaker to imagine any situation which, given the
meanings of 'John', 'frightens', and 'sincerity', could properly be
described by (1)—except, of course, by invoking some grammatical
dodge, such as that of regarding 'Sincerity' as a girl's name or as a
way of referring to the Sincerity Short-Term Loan Corporation,
which would alter the syntactic structure of (1). We could, of course,
try to explain this difficulty by talking about the empirical nature of
the referents of 'John', 'frightens', and 'sincerity', but we have already seen in some detail why this approach is fruitless: for one thing
it will not explain why (5) is not ill-formed in the same way as (1).
We are left, then, confronting a dilemma. Either we say that sentences
such as (1) and (4) are ill-formed and that they are ill-formed because
they break the rules of language, or else we must say that such sentences assert what is logically impossible, or inconceivable, and that
the inconceivability of what they assert stems from the nature of the

referents of the terms involved in them—in which case we ought perhaps to class them as necessarily false rather than ill-formed. The trouble is, now, that both of these paths seem to be closed to us: the latter because it leads into ever deeper metaphysical complexities and confusions; the former because we seem unable to produce an account of the logical character of rules of language which will enable us to explain precisely why (1) and (4) are ill-formed while (10) and (13) are not or even to discriminate between sentences like (1) and (4) and sentences like (5).

I want to suggest, now, that the theory of linguistic devices as we have developed it offers us a way of escaping from this dilemma and sheds a good deal of light on the other difficulties which we have encountered *en route* to it.

11.4   Let us for the sake of simplicity begin by considering the second of our initial list of examples: 'Bring Thursday'. Absurdly trivial as it appears, 'Bring Thursday' raises exactly the same questions as 'John frightens sincerity' or 'He saw carefully that the door was blue'. There is a corresponding range of apparently necessary truths ('One cannot bring Thursday', and so on); it is impossible to make 'Bring Thursday' well-formed by postulating changes of usage, except by employing syntactic dodges, and so on.

According to our model, 'Bring', or rather the syntactic schema, 'Bring _____ ', derives its meaning from the series of devices beginning with (A)–(D).

In order to introduce 'Thursday' into our model language, we shall require another device, which we shall label [J]. This is a device for keeping track of events by reference to a week of seven days.

[J] Stage 1: Learning to answer the question, "What day is it?" correctly.

(1) The learner first learns to recite the names of the seven days in a set and unalterable sequence. This is rather like learning a nursery jingle: as yet the learner does not know how to *use* the words involved.

(2) The learner is taught now an arbitrary base assignment of a day name to the day on which the learning is taking place. He is taught, for example, to answer 'Monday' to the question, 'What day is it today?'

(3) The learner is taught that, from the moment of the base day-name assignment on, the proper answer to the question, 'What day is it today?' is to give the day name arbitrarily assigned and to go on giving this answer up until the middle (determined by a clock or some other conventional means) of the period of darkness following the period of light during which the base day-name assignment was made; but that after this point the correct answer is to give the name which follows the day name assigned as base, in the set sequence of day names learned in (1).

(4) This procedure is now generalized in the following set of instructions, which enable the learner to generate a correct response to the question 'What day is it today?' on any occasion.

   (i) In order to answer the question, 'What day is it today?' on subsequent occasions, count off the number of days (that is, periods of light: a temporal periodicity of light and darkness in the environment is assumed) which have elapsed since the day of the base assignment; simultaneously subvocally uttering the day-name series so that one day name is uttered for each elapsed day, beginning with the day name next in the series to the one uttered on the base assignment day. When you reach the present day, utter (out loud) the last day name which you have reached in the series.

   (ii) If the number of elapsed days is greater than the number of names in the day-name series, repeat the series cyclically.

   (iii) To all repetitions of the question, 'What day is it?' within the same period of light, the same answer must be given.

Further stages would contain rules extending the device beyond the present, to allow, for example, for a correct response to questions like 'What day was it yesterday?' and so on.

The devices [A]–[D] and [J] are very different sorts of device. We can bring out some of the differences between them if we ask what sorts of environmental conditions will have to be present if we are to be able to teach someone how to operate [A]–[D] and [J]: let us call these the physical preconditions of [A]–[D] and [J]. The physical preconditions of [J] turn out to be quite different from the physical preconditions of [A]–[D]. We shall be able to teach someone the rules of [J] provided only that his environment exhibits some temporal periodicity: this may take the form of an alternation of periods of darkness with periods of light; or of periods of silence with periods when a steady, faint buzzing is heard; or anything else of the sort.

Provided his environment contains such a temporal periodicity, the learner will be able to carry out instruction (4)(i)—that is, to put the members of the day-name series in one-to-one correlation with units of the temporal periodicity—and it is evident that this is all that is required for him—and his teacher and anyone else who happens to be familiar with the rules of the device—to be able to use the device to keep track of events.

Different physical presuppositions are required for the operation of [A]–[D]. A world in which speakers can operate with [A]–[D] must contain objects to which [B]-labels can be assigned, and these objects must be relocatable. Moreover, they must be the sort of objects on which the operation specified in [A] can be performed: thus, a large class of objects which would satisfy our first condition—mountains, lakes, clouds, puddles of water or mercury, pillars of fire, and so on, would fail to satisfy the second. But, provided the world contains moderate-sized physical objects, with reasonably enduring characteristics, which can be fetched and carried, it will be possible for speakers to have [A]–[D] included among the component linguistic devices of their language.

Suppose, now, that a learner has learned [A]–[D], together with a limited range of [B]-labels; and [J]. It is certainly, in a sense, *possible* for the learner to produce the utterance 'Bring Thursday'. He knows these words, and he has not been taught any rule prohibiting him from combining them in that order. But it is obvious that, although he can *produce* this utterance, he cannot *generate* it using the rules of any linguistic device with which he is familiar. The device which generates utterances of the form 'Bring ____ ' is [D]. Instruction (2) of this device reads: "Look at the object[29] you wish your hearer to bring, and by using the rules of [B(2)] generate the phonetic string which you would utter if you were being shown the desired object in the context of [B]." Now there is simply no object with the [B]-label 'Thursday' to which this procedure might be applied. 'Thursday' is one of an arbitrary sequence of phonemic strings whose sole function in [J] is to be set in one-to-one correlation with units of a temporal periodicity in order that users of [J] may keep track of events relative to a base day-name assignment.

---

[29] "Object" here means only "entity which satisfies the physical preconditions of [A]–[D]."

'Bring Thursday' is clearly ill-formed with respect to our model language—or sublanguage—consisting of [A]–[D] and [J]. What I wish to suggest, now, is that to say that it is ill-formed with respect to this language is simply to say that it could not be generated by following the rules of any of the linguistic devices which make up this language.

We are now in a position to explain the puzzling aura of logical necessity which emanates from such statements as 'It is (logically) impossible to bring Thursday' or 'Days of the week are not the sort of thing that can be brought'. These statements are, it seems to me, simply oblique ways of saying that 'Bring Thursday' cannot be generated by any linguistic device in our language. But if this explanation is to satisfy, we must give some account of the logical force of the "cannot" in "cannot be generated."

It seems clear that we could not operate the string of devices [A]–[D], or teach anyone how to operate them, in a world which contained no objects satisfying the physical preconditions of [A]–[D]. And, similarly, we could neither operate nor teach anyone to operate [J] in a world which contained nothing satisfying the physical preconditions of [J]: which contained nothing, that is, in the nature of a temporal periodicity. Moreover, to say this is to say something which is necessarily true in a philosophically unpuzzling sense of the words "necessarily true." If while watching a game of chess I see two pawns of the same color standing in the same column then it is true, *a priori*, *given the rules of chess* and given also that the rules are being observed (that is, that what I am watching really is a *game of chess*), that one of them must have taken an opposing piece in a previous move.[30] Similarly, although we may choose to set up any linguistic device in any way we please, nevertheless once we have set up precisely *these* devices [A]–[D] and [J], it will be true *a priori* that they possess the physical preconditions which they do possess.

What makes it possible for a system of linguistic devices to generate infinitely many well-formed and meaningful sentences is the fact that it is possible to insert one linguistic device into another so that the inserted device functions as a subroutine of the device into which it is

---

[30] I am indebted for this example to Zeno Vendler, *Linguistics in Philosophy*, p. 17.

inserted. In this way, for example, [B] functions as a subroutine of [C] and [D].

Let us suppose, now, that the physical preconditions of two linguistic devices, [L] and [L'], are such that [L] could neither be operated nor taught in a universe containing *just* phenomena satisfying the physical preconditions of [L'], while [L'] could neither be taught nor operated in a universe containing *just* phenomena satisfying the physical preconditions of [L]. We shall say of such a pair of linguistic devices that their physical preconditions are *incompatible*.

Now, if 'Bring Thursday' were to be capable of being generated by the rules of the linguistic devices of our restricted model language, then [J] would have to be capable of being inserted into (functioning as a subroutine of) [D]. But neither of a pair of linguistic devices whose physical preconditions are incompatible can function as a subroutine of the other. This is because, no matter how long we continue operating either device, we shall never reach any point at which it will be possible to interpolate the other device, since we shall never reach any point in the operation of the first device at which the physical preconditions of the second device will be satisfied. Those features of the world, that is, with respect to which the operations specified by the rules of the first device are to be carried out form, as it were, the universe within which the second device is to be operated, and if the physical preconditions of the two devices are incompatible, then this universe will simply not have a rich enough content for the second device to be operable within it.

It seems to me that to say that two devices have incompatible physical preconditions or to say that two devices with incompatible preconditions are mutually incapable of being interpolated one into the other, is to say something which is necessarily true in exactly the same philosophically unpuzzling sense as the assertion that a given linguistic device has the physical preconditions which it has. We cannot *both* set up a linguistic device in a certain way *and* set it up in a quite different way. Hence, in setting up just the devices [A]–[D] and [J], we automatically ensure that our language will contain devices with certain physical preconditions, and hence we determine also that it will contain at least one pair of devices whose physical preconditions are incompatible. And if, as it happens, we also require, as a feature of the system of linguistic devices, that complex utterances are in general to be generated through the interpolation of one linguistic device into another, then it will follow that in ensuring that our language contains pairs of devices with incompatible physical preconditions, we shall also have ensured that certain "theoretically possible" utterances will not in fact be capable of being generated by following the rules of our language.

If we are right, then the fact that 'Bring Thursday' is ill-formed—that it is not generated by any linguistic device in our language—is purely and simply a linguistic fact: a fact about the way in which we have chosen to set up the rules of our language. And this makes it reasonable to claim that statements like 'You cannot bring Thursday' or 'Days of the week are not the sort of thing that can be brought', and so on, are merely portentous ways of stating this fact about our linguistic conventions. But now we must explain why it is that although we are presumably familiar, as native speakers of English, with the conventions of our language, such statements do not appear to us *intuitively* to be merely statements about linguistic convention. For as we saw in section 11.1, native speakers feel a strong temptation to regard such statements as expressing necessary truths about their ostensible—that is, extralinguistic—subject matter. When we are in this mood, for example, 'Nothing can be red and green all over', appears as a necessary truth about colors; 'One cannot *see* carefully' as a necessary truth about perception (or, more cautiously, perhaps, a point about our conceptual scheme as it relates to perception); and so on.

No doubt part of the answer is that we are not *familiar* with our linguistic conventions in the sense of being consciously aware of them, any more than the knot-tyer is aware of the movements which his fingers execute as he ties a half-hitch. But we must go further than this. We can state the putatively necessary truths which correspond to ill-formed sentences in two different ways. We can say, for example,

(37) It is impossible to bring Thursday

which suggests that we are capable of exercising some very strange species of rational intuition of the essence of Thursday. Or we can put the same statement in a form which suggests that, when we try to conceive of certain states of affairs, we find ourselves subject to certain inescapable (transcendental?) psychological limitations, thus:

(38) It is impossible to conceive of anything which would count as bringing Thursday

We are led into saying things like (37) by reflecting upon the fact that it seems impossible to make ' Bring Thursday ' well-formed merely by altering our linguistic usage. '*Nobody*', we say, could *decide* that henceforth ' Bring Thursday ' is to make sense, for this is not something that depends upon linguistic convention. If ' bring ' and 'Thursday ' are taken to mean what they ordinarily mean, then it is simply a fact that it is impossible to ' Bring Thursday '.

Now, of course, we are quite right to say this. We cannot retain the ordinary meanings of ' bring ' and 'Thursday ', *and*, merely by decree, bring it about that ' Bring Thursday ' makes sense. For what we can alter merely by arbitrary decree is the rule structure of our linguistic devices. But if we " alter our linguistic usage " in *this* sense, all that we shall achieve is the deletion of certain linguistic devices from our language and the substitution of new and different ones. These new linguistic devices may indeed generate ' Bring Thursday ' as a well-formed utterance, but it will remain true, and necessarily true, that ' Bring Thursday ' is not generated by the devices which we have just deleted from our language; but " retaining the ordinary meanings " of ' bring' and 'Thursday ' just means retaining the ordinary linguistic devices in which they function in everyday English. The fact which (37) expresses is, at bottom, the fact that we cannot (obviously) have the same linguistic devices and yet have their physical preconditions differently related. But this feature of our language presents itself to us in the guise of an intuitive sense of the impossibility of making ' Bring Thurday ' well-formed by direct fiat given the meanings of its component words: whence we in turn naively conclude that what cannot be altered by direct fiat must therefore be, not a feature of our linguistic conventions, but a feature of the world.

Something very similar happens with (38). It seems intuitively clear to us that we could not make ' Bring Thursday ' a sensible utterance by changing any contingent fact about the world. We can contrast

'Bring Thursday' with a request like 'Bring a cloud', which is in practice, but not logically, unfulfillable. Here we can conceive of contexts in which this utterance makes sense: perhaps it is said by Jupiter Pluvius to one of his divine asistants; or perhaps, in some science fiction future, a device—we may even be able to speculate quite plausibly about its nature—has been developed for moving large masses of water vapor about *en bloc*. No such mythological or science fiction goings-on seem possible in the case of bringing Thursday. "We simply cannot conceive of anything that would count . . . etc."

Again, of course, our initial intuition about the contrast between 'Bring Thursday' and 'Bring a cloud' is correct. No matter how radically technology or the physical properties of things might change, no such change would make the slightest difference to the fact that the physical preconditions of [A]–[D] and those of [J] are incompatible. For this incompatibility is not a consequence of any contingent matter of fact; rather, it is a consequence of the rules of [A]–[D] and [J]. Hence, in any world in which [A]–[D] and [J] were operable at all, their physical preconditions would be incompatible. (38), then, like (37), is in effect a comment upon a feature of our system of linguistic conventions, but the feature in question appears to us, because we do not fully comprehend the intricacies of our own linguistic convention, in the light of a peculiar transcendental limitation upon what states of affairs it is possible for us to conceive or imagine.

We can now see how to avoid the dilemma which confronted us at the conclusion of section 11.3. Ill-formed sentences do not assert what is logically impossible, or inconceivable, given the nature of the referents of their terms; nor do they *break* any of the rules of the language in which they are framed. Rather, it is simply that they are not generated by the rules of (the linguistic devices which make up) that language.

We can also distinguish clearly between sentences like (1)–(4) and Smart's 'The seat of the bed is hard'. The difference is not merely a subjective one having to do with differing "flavors of absurdity." It is simply that the absurdity of Smart's statement does not arise from an attempt to incorporate into a given linguistic device a different one with incompatible physical preconditions. If we were to attempt to construct the linguistic devices involved in the generation of (5), we should presumably need first a device [L(1)] for generating ascriptions of properties to physical objects: these would have the form 'The ____ is ____'. Then we should need a device [L(2)] for generating specifications of parts of objects: these would have the form 'The____ of the ____'. The physical preconditions of [L(1)] and [L(2)] will obviously be roughly the same: therefore, we shall be able to construct a third device [L(3)] which will generate property ascriptions similar to those generated by [L(1)] but with the expression 'The____' replaced by the [L(2)] specification 'The ____ of the ____' to give an ascription of the form 'The ____ of the ____ is ____'. Now of course beds do not have seats, and so we shall never, as things stand, find ourselves instantiating the first two blanks in the latter schema with the [B]-labels 'seat' and 'bed'. But equally obviously it is quite possible that beds might come to be made with seats, and then, in that case, we might.

11.5 We can now suggest answers to the two questions which we raised at the beginning of this chapter concerning the way in which a speaker learns to recognize ill-formedness and the character of an adult speaker's judgment of ill-formedness. Our answer to the first is that the speaker automatically learns to recognise ill-formed utterances in his language as a consequence of learning the rules which enable him to construct well-formed utterances: that is, the rules of the linguistic devices which make up his language. The learner does not, that is, have to learn a special set of rules which instruct him to avoid certain combinations of words. For, given any particular set of linguistic devices, the ways in which the members of the set can and cannot be interpolated into each other will be necessarily determined the moment we decide to set up the rules of the devices concerned in one way rather than in another. In setting up the devices in a certain way we determine that certain utterances will not be capable of being generated by these devices; and this fact is, as it were, *there to be discovered* by anyone who learns to use this particular set of devices—much as the fact that a King can be checked with a Knight and a Bishop alone but not with a Bishop alone, is *there to be discovered* by anyone who learns to play chess, although it is not itself one of the *rules* of chess but something which is necessarily true, given the rules of chess. The learner, having learned the set of devices which constitute his language, can thus discover for himself—by attempting to interpolate one device into another, and finding that the attempt sometimes succeeds and sometimes fails— that certain utterances, including some which have a superficial appearance of grammaticalness, are not capable of being generated by any device or combination of devices in his language; the learner can then say, with complete certainty, that those sentences are ill-formed, or absurd, or "don't make sense," or, most revealingly of all, that they are "just not intelligible English." What he is judging, in each case, is that there is no possible actual situation in which such an utterance would be generated by following the rules of English, and the reason he can make this claim with absolute certainty is that its truth follows simply from the rules of English being what they are. He need not hedge his claim with any of the qualifications appropriate to talk about matters of empirical fact, for he is not talking about a matter of empirical fact.

Our solution offers a way of dealing with what philosophers are accustomed to call category. We need not suppose, that is, that the study of category mistakes gives us any insight into " modes of being ": that, for example, the absurdity of ' Bring Thursday' reveals a sort of cleavage in the fabric of reality, on one side of which lie physical objects, "existing" in the ordinary sense; while on the other side lie days of the week, "existing" in a sense appropriate to their rarefied ontological status. The study of the limits or preconditions of significant utterance can reveal to us only the structure of our own systems of linguistic convention. All that we can know about the world in which these systems of conventions function must be discovered by the ordinary methods of science and common sense, and there is simply no such science as ontology. There is thus no point in attempting to divide the contents of the world into classes corresponding to different logical types or categories of entities, still less in attempting to discover a finite list of such categories; and any view which construes philosophical analysis as the attempt to construct such a classification, misconstrues it. To any language, conceived as a finite system of linguistic devices, there corresponds a practically infinite array of grammatical or semigrammatical utterances made up of words drawn from the language but not in fact capable of being generated by the linguistic devices of the language. If we interpret these ill-formed sentences as the results of attempting to "cross categories" and then attempt to list all those categories whose crossing yields nonsense and which may therefore be regarded as corresponding to ultimate cleavages in reality, we shall find that the immense variety of forms of nonsense will force us in the end to assign each word of the language to a separate category and to specify each such category by a set of rules expressly forbidding certain combinations of each word with certain other words. Such a theory will obviously be entirely *ad hoc* and uninformative. But if, on the other hand, we interpret ill-formed utterances as utterances which are not capable of being generated by the rules of our language, we shall be led to a theory which offers a finite description of language and is neither uninformative nor *ad hoc* but which will not be a theory of categories but a theory of linguistic devices.

A further objection to the notion of categories is that it commits us to thinking in terms of classes of entities which are mutually exclusive in the sense that nothing which can truly be predicated of any entity belonging to one such class can be truly predicated of any entity belonging to another; the trouble with this is, of course, that many sentences which are literally nonsense are perfectly sensible and indeed illuminating when interpreted metaphorically or analogically. Moreover, it is often the case that important discoveries, or changes in our way of conceiving natural or human phenomena, spring in the first instance from the discovery that certain metaphors are possible. The vocabulary of categories has the disadvantage both of suggesting that every " crossing of categories " must merely produce nonsense and of offering us no way in which we can conceive of the invention of new metaphors as a process of discovery, with definite criteria of success attached to it, rather than as a matter of arbitrary caprice. Some metaphors are fruitful and enlightening: others are strained, far-fetched, or amount to a mere play on words. A good metaphor or a good analogical extension of a word succeeds because of, and not in spite of, the prior meaning of the word chosen for extension or metaphorical employment. These distinctions, and others, must all be explained by any adequate theory of language.

The task of developing a theory of metaphor must await another occasion and we shall here offer only a programmatic suggestion. This is that the instructions of a linguistic device may prove capable of being obeyed in the context of some set of physical preconditions other than those for which the device was originally constructed, provided we make certain modifications to the instructions. Thus, I can speak of someone "bringing good news," provided I weaken the requirement that some object must be conveyed into the possession of the recipient of what is brought to allow the conveyance (another metaphor) of information to count as the conveyance of an object. Once I do this I shall, in effect, have constructed a new linguistic device, having different physical preconditions and hence different interpolation relationships with other devices (it will be absurd to say, for example, 'Where has he put the news you brought him?' unless a document is being referred to). But it will be a device intrinsically related *via* the structure of its rules to [A]–[D]. By contrast, if we make 'Bring Thursday' well-formed by treating 'Thursday' as a man's name we have not by so doing constructed a new linguistic device intrinsically related *via* the structure of its rules to [J]. All we have done is to take the phonemic string 'Thursday' and to make use of it as a counter in a different linguistic device which we already possess but which is quite unrelated to [J]: the device of assigning proper names to persons. These two cases may serve as paradigm respectively for the discovery of a way of extending the use (meaning) of a word and the arbitrary reassignment of meaning to a word so that its new meaning is unrelated to its prior meaning.[31]

Given what we have said so far, we can perhaps see how to offer Chomsky something close to what he has in mind when he demands a theory of meaning according to which the "system of dictionary definitions" is not wholly atomistic but involves a systematic order of intrinsic semantic relationships.[32] Linguistic devices, if we are correct, are internally related to one another both from the point of view of the interpolation relationships which flow from their physical preconditions and from the point of view of the manner in which a given linguistic device may develop extensions of one sort and

[31] In the light of our earlier distinction between place-defining rules and place-filling conventions, what is involved in the one case is the development of a set of new place-defining rules (of new places) intrinsically related to a pre-existing set and in the other case the conventional assignment of a phonemic string to a different but already existing place.

[32] Chomsky, *Aspects*, p. 4.

another—and no doubt in still other ways as well. The whole question of the possible relationships between linguistic devices is one which demands detailed and extensive study, of a kind which would take into account the results both of linguistics and of conceptual analysis.

A system of linguistic devices is, of course, something quite different from a system of dictionary definitions. But no semantic theory which bases itself on a system of dictionary definitions, conceived as a list of conventional associations between words or phrases in a language and either verbal definitions (or readings) or elements of the world, can account for ill-formedness; for if the semantic rules of a language are merely conventional associations of this sort, it is hard to see how the impossibility of combining certain of the lexical items of the language in certain syntactic structures can possibly be a consequence of the semantic rules of the language. Such a semantic theory leads us, then, straight into the system of blind alleys which we explored in sections 11.1–11.3 and ultimately into the dilemma of either introducing *ad hoc* selection restrictions, which may enable the theory to avoid, but do not explain, ill-formedness, or else treating ill-formedness as a consequence of the nature of the referents of the lexical items of the language. We ourselves have avoided this dilemma only by regarding the meanings of the lexical items of a language as arising not in virtue of any relationship in which they stand to elements of the world or to verbal definitions or sets of semantic markers, but rather in virtue of the places which they occupy in linguistic devices.

On the other hand, a theory of linguistic devices may present certain advantages for the linguist, besides offering him a semantic theory which accounts for intrinsic semantic relationships between lexical items. First it suggests an important parallel between syntax and semantics. With the rise of interest in generative grammars over the past decade, it has come to be widely accepted that a grammar of a given language is a system of rules which generate all and only the grammatical strings of that language. An ungrammatical combination of lexical items, then, is simply a combination of lexical items which does not happen to be generated by these rules: beyond this no *further* explanation of ungrammaticalness is required. Ill-formedness seems to disturb this neat and satisfying picture, since it seems that although we can introduce rules into our grammar which make it impossible to generate ill-formed sentences, these rules in practice tend to be cumbersome and rather *ad hoc* and in any case do not fully explain illformedness; for even when we have pointed out that the rules of our revised grammar exclude certain strings as ill-formed, we can still be asked what makes such strings ill-formed, for obviously it is their illformedness which has made us modify our grammar to exclude them and not the fact that English speakers conform to certain grammatical conventions which makes them ill-formed.

On our theory, however, ill-formedness is precisely analogous to ungrammaticalness: that is, an ill-formed sentence is simply one which is not in fact generated by the linguistic devices which make up a certain language. And, as in the case of ungrammaticalness, once we have shown that, and how, this is the case, no further explanation is required. Ungrammaticalness and ill-formedness can thus both be construed as failure to be generated by systems of linguistic conventions, although the systems in question are of somewhat different types.

Second, a theory of language, both on our view and on Chomsky's, states what must be taught to a learner if he is to acquire normal adult linguistic capacity. It is presumably desirable that such a theory should exhibit adult linguistic capacity as derivable from the smallest and simplest structure of learned rules possible. A semantic theory such as Fodor, Katz, and Postal's must introduce selection restrictions to exclude ill-formed expressions, and it must introduce them on an *ad hoc* basis, unless it contains machinery for distinguishing between the " semantic anomaly " of a sentence like (1) and that of a sentence like (5). For if beds come to be made with seats, (5) will cease to be anomalous and alterations will have to be made to the selection restrictions of ' bed ' and/or ' seats ', and/or ' hard '. On our theory, on the other hand, no rules beyond those which govern the generation of well-formed expressions are required to account for ill-formedness; and in particular no *ad hoc* introduction of rules is required, since on our view it is obvious that if a given sentence is ill-formed with respect to given linguistic devices, it will be ill-formed in any possible worlds or worlds in which those devices remain operable.

Thus, our theory satisfies (as, so far as I can see, a theory such as Fodor, Katz, and Postal's does not), a requirement which I take to be indispensable to the autonomy of linguistics as a science: namely, that it must be possible to state the rules of a language without referring in justification of any rule to any empirical matter of fact concerning the world in which the language is used. This principle has as a corollary that the rules of a language cannot be such that they change automatically accordingly as sentences in the language happen to express true or false propositions (that is, such that questions of the grammaticalness or ungrammaticalness, well-formedness or illformedness, of expressions simply *turn on* the truth or falsehood of contingent propositions). If the rules of a language did not satisfy these requirements, then sentences might become or cease to be grammatical or well-formed just in virtue of the fact that the statements expressed by the same or other sentences became or ceased to be true,[33] and thus the description of the grammar or semantics of such a language would, for obvious reasons, not be a finite task capable of being completed independently of the progress of other sciences.

This principle has long been familiar to structural linguistics as the principle of the independence of grammar from semantics. This formulation of the principle has helped to obscure what I have tried to show throughout this book: that the principle holds with equal force as a requirement for any theory which attempts to describe the semantic rules of a language.[34]

Third, a theory of linguistic devices may offer a clearer and less problematic method than has hitherto been available of distinguishing the syntax of a language from its semantics. It should be possible in terms of such a theory to sharply distinguish questions of illformedness from grammatical questions and to solve many outstanding questions concerning the interactions of the semantic rule system of a language with its grammar. All these topics, however, demand a great deal of further study, and we shall do no more than touch on them in Chapter 12.

11.6 It is open to critics to object that 'Bring Thursday' is a *very* easy example to deal with. It may therefore be worthwhile to conclude by showing that even such a notorious

[33] See Wittgenstein's remark at *Tractatus*, 2.021.

[34] Although Wittgenstein makes this point clearly in the *Tractatus* and I think could easily be shown to assume it throughout his later writings.

philosophical chestnut as 'Nothing can be red and green all over' can be dealt with in much the same way.

'Nothing can be red and green all over' has enjoyed a considerable reputation as a plausible candidate for the status of a synthetic *a priori* truth. It has seemed to philosophers to be necessarily true that no homogeneously colored surface which we were prepared to call red could at the same time be homogeneously colored green. A few of the more tough-minded have suggested that this may merely reflect a contingent defect of our powers of imagination. Perhaps somewhere in the universe or given in the visual experience of creatures with differently constituted sense organs, there exist colors unknown to us, which we are presently unable to imagine but which once we had been made acquainted with them, we should have to concede to be genuine red-greens. Various attempts have been made to produce empirical counterexamples to 'Nothing can be red and green all over'. Irridescent surfaces and leaves with red pigmentation superimposed on green abound in the literature, which abounds also in sage demonstrations that such examples are beside the point since they invariably involve reference to things which are not *in the ordinary meaning of the words* 'red all over' or 'homogeneously red'. Almost all writers agree, however, that 'Nothing can be red and green all over' is not an analytic truth, and that, indeed, its truth does not flow in any obvious way from the conventions of our language. For, it is argued, we simply find the colors red and green in our experience. All that linguistic convention does is to place the phonemic strings 'red' and 'green' in arbitrary association with certain natural resemblances which things exhibit. Once we have done this we simply discover that nothing which resembles those objects which we have designated 'red' in respect of color can possibly resemble in respect of color those objects which we have designated 'green'; and we are here obviously not discovering something about language but something about the world.

Now, all of this bears a strong resemblance to our earlier reflections about sincerity and John, and it should further raise our suspicions that corresponding to 'Nothing can be red and green all over' we can formulate a class of statements like (6), which have as good a claim to be regarded as unintelligible as they have to be regarded as necessarily false.

What, then, is the flaw in the above discussion? It is, I think, this.

Philosophers have assumed that we are, as it were, presented in our experience with colors, or color properties (whether these are regarded as universals or as classes of resemblances makes no difference), and that we define color words ostensively simply by setting them in one-to-one correspondence with colors. The truth seems to me to be rather that we are presented in our experience with a more or less continuous spectrum of hues which can be arranged in a circle on which reds merge into oranges, oranges into yellows, and on through greenish yellows, greens, greenish blues, blues, and purples back to reds. Any hue on this circle stands in relationships of resemblance to the shades on either side of it: for any given hue these relationships extend for a considerable distance round the circle, though they become weaker the further one gets from the shade in question.

If we wish to set up a vocabulary of color words having a reasonably precise and definite meaning we shall have to impose arbitrary divisions on this continuous circle of related hues. It is obvious that we cannot do this if our rule for the application of a given color word simply singles out an object of a particular shade and instructs the learner to apply the word to any object resembling this paradigm in color and, equally obvious for reasons explained in Chapter 3, that we shall only make matters worse if we introduce further paradigm objects exhibiting different shades. What we must do is to make use of two types of instruction. The first type will single out a paradigm object exhibiting a certain shade and instruct the learner to apply a certain color word to everything that resembles that shade. The second type of instruction will arbitrarily specify two points on the color wheel beyond which resemblances between the shade of the paradigm object and other shades shall no longer be regarded as licensing the application of the color word in question.

Now it is clear that by setting up a linguistic device which generates utterances of color words in this way, we can divide the color wheel up as finely as we like. We can have two color words in our language, or two dozen. But in either case, the boundaries between colors will be arbitrarily determined by the operation of rules of our second type. And equally obviously, the colors which we define in this way will be incompatible: that is, for example, if something displays a homogeneous expanse of a given shade which our rules compel us to call 'turquoise' our rules will forbid us to call it 'green'; for although it certainly resembles greens (as it resembles blues, or bluish turquoises), the resemblances in question extend beyond the points on the color wheel which we have designated as the arbitrary cutoff points beyond which resemblances to the green paradigm shall no longer license the application of the word 'green'.

A linguistic device containing our two types of rules, operating as we have suggested, will have as its physical precondition the existence of a spectrum of properties displaying continuous resemblances such as those of the color wheel. The device which generates expressions of the form, '____ is ____ and ____ all over', will presumably only be operable in a world which contains at least some properties which are *not* related each to each in a continuous gradation like that displayed by the color wheel. Thus, the expression 'My door is red and green all over' and its ilk are simply incapable of being generated by these devices.

Let us now try to separate what is necessarily true of this whole situation from what is contingently true. It is true that the physical preconditions of the system of linguistic devices which govern our talk about colors is satisfied. That is, it is true that there exists a spectrum of continuously related shades. But this is surely a contingent truth, for it is quite possible that no such spectrum of properties should exist. And, in any case, it is not a truth about incompatibilities of colors.

It is necessarily true, on the other hand, that certain sentences will not be generated by the linguistic devices which we have just described, since their physical preconditions are incompatible. But this is a truth about the internal consequences of adopting certain linguistic conventions.

It might be objected[35] that my account of color incompatibilities has the defect of demonstrating, what is patently false, that a musical sound cannot be both A^b and E^b. Clearly, when these two notes are played simultaneously on, say, a piano, the resulting sound has this property. We can, if this is correct, restate the problem about incompatibilities of colors: if different pitches can occur simultaneously in time, why cannot colors occur coextensively in space?

The answer to this objection, it seems to me, is that what occurs simultaneously in time in such cases is not two pitches but two sounds

---

[35] I owe this objection to Dr. Aaron Sloman.

of differing pitch. The "necessary" truth about sound which corresponds to the familiar philosophical chestnut about colors is "one sound cannot have two pitches"; and the apparent necessity of this proposition derives from the fact that pitches form a continuous spectrum of the same type as the color spectrum. The sounds played by a musical instrument are separable in a variety of ways which do not involve recourse to the arbitrary divisions which our language imposes upon the spectra of color and pitch alike. If this were not possible—if music were a continuous skein of sound separable only by arbitrary division into "notes" or "sounds"—then talk about notes or sounds would have to be governed by a linguistic device having the same logic as those which govern our talk about colors and pitches; and then, of course, it would be logically impossible for two notes to sound simultaneously.

It seems, then, that the tough-minded philosopher's readiness to entertain the possibility that there may exist a surface displaying a color which we are contingently unable to imagine but which in the event of our being made acquainted with it we should be compelled to describe as 'red and green all over', is as ill-judged as the tender-minded philosopher's willingness to accept 'Nothing can be red and green all over' as a synthetic *a priori* truth. What the tough-minded are demanding, in effect, is that the self-same linguistic devices should possess different physical presuppositions. And this demand is straightforwardly self-contradictory.

12 Linguistic devices: summary and recapitulation

In section 1.7, we summarized the main tenets of the ETL. We are now in a position to look back at this list of tenets, and to say, with reference to each of them, in what respects our theory of linguistic devices differs from the ETL. The numbering of the remarks below corresponds to the numbering of the points in our earlier summary of the ETL.

Tenet 1: In a system of linguistic devices there can be no distinction between basic utterances, through which meaning is introduced into a language, and nonbasic utterances, whose meaning is not derived from any direct relationship to the world but only from their standing in some relationship or other to the basic utterances. Any given linguistic device is directly "related to the world" by the concrete procedures (rule-licensed procedures) which its instructions specify and by the way in which it fits into the structure of human social life so far as this has to do with communication by means of language. Utterances are "connected to the world" by the relationships in which they stand to the linguistic devices by whose rules they are generated: no utterance is "given meaning" by standing in any relationship, definitional or otherwise, to any other *utterance* whatsoever, except in the case of the semantically redundant utterances introduced by verbal substitution conventions.

Linguistic devices, as we have seen, form series of related devices, in which the later members in a sense 'presuppose' the earlier: thus [H] in this sense presupposes [F] and [G]. 'Presupposes' here, however, means only "can be rendered intelligible only by reference to":[1] in this sense an account of endgame strategies presupposes the rules of chess. There is no question of the later devices in such a series being "connected with the world" only through their relationship with the earlier ones: [H] is "connected with the world" in ways obvious to inspection, quite irrespective of its relationship with [F] and [G].

Tenet 2: It follows, then, that there is no special class of utterances through which meaning "enters" language, which would otherwise be a mere formal calculus. Any utterance whose use is governed by a linguistic device is, as much as any other, a point at which we can make the "exit from the maze of words."

Tenet 3: Meaning is not introduced into a language through associations between its utterances and things in the world. On our view, indeed, there is something wrong with the very phrase "a connection between language and the world," for this suggests that meaning must consist in some sort of relationship between the units of some level of linguistic description—words, morphemes, sentences—and something extralinguistic, and that the main task of semantic theory must be to elucidate that relationship. For us, no such relationship exists. What is "connected with the world"—insofar as this phrase makes sense at all—is not anything which can be given a phonemic representation, but is the linguistic device. We can regard the linguistic device as an abstract system of instructions and procedures which defines a set of roles which vocal noises—or other sorts of things—can be made to assume. Thus, people who want to operate the device [B] will have to decide (arbitrarily) on a set of noises (or gestures, or marks on paper) to play the part of [B]-labels. Similarly, would-be users of [F] must decide (arbitrarily) to make some noise (gesture, mark) play the role played in our example by the expression 'Where is ____?' Vocal noises, then, are connected (arbitrarily) not with

---

[1] It should also be emphasized that to say that devices presuppose each other in this sense is not to say anything about the order in which they may or may not be learned by actual children. We are not concerned with genetic questions of this kind but with questions of how simple systems of rules of a given sort can be combined in intelligible ways to form larger systems of the same sort.

"elements of the world" but with linguistic devices. Linguistic devices, in turn, can be (loosely and rather misleadingly) said to be "connected with the world" in virtue of the fact that their instructions mention, in a great variety of ways and for a great many purposes, all sorts of things in the learner's environment. Thus many, even most, of the instructions of a linguistic device can be said to connect the device with the world, but the mode of connection is never associative linking. For example, consider instructions (2)(i)–(v) of [E]. These read in part:

(2) Determine which answer ["yes" or "no"] to give by reference to the following instructions:
  (i) Determine whether the person P to whom the request 'Bring a' was addressed has moved his position.
  If he has not, answer "no."
  If he has, proceed to (ii).
  (ii) Determine whether P has any object visibly in his possession, or attached to him.
  If he has not, answer "no."
  If he has, proceed to (iii).

Clearly, these instructions "connect [E] with the world," if that phrase has any sense at all. For example, instruction (i) instructs the learner to determine whether something has moved its position and to act in various ways depending on the result of the determination. The person P and P's movements are certainly things in the world; and the device [E] is "connected to the world" as a whole because its instructions mention them and other things similarly "in the world." But it would be quite false to say that the instructions of [E] *associatively link* any element of language with P, or with P's movements, or any other "element of the world." For what could the requisite element of language be? The noise "yes"? "no"? One—or each—of the large family of utterances of the form 'Bring a'? All these suggestions seem patently absurd, for none of these utterances functions in the device as a terminus of an associative linkage.

In short, then, although there are associative conventions operating upon phonemic strings (place-filling conventions), they associate the strings in question not with elements of the world but with places defined by the rules of linguistic devices. And although language is in a sense "connected with the world," the connections are not associative and do not operate on phonemic strings.

Tenet 4: Again, in a system of linguistic devices all questions of concatenation are settled once and for all when we specify the rules of the devices comprised by the system. All questions of concatenation in a given language can be settled, that is, merely by stating the rules of the language, without its being necessary to refer to the truth or falsity of any proposition which may subsequently be asserted *in* that language. At the same time, the consequences of specifying certain rules for a system of linguistic devices are not immediately evident from the rules themselves since, although *within* each linguistic device certain concatenations of words (certain fillings-in of syntactic schemata, that is) are *in effect* licensed by the rules of the device (although, of course, the device contains no rules explicitly referring to syntactic schemata or to their filling-in with expressions of the language and, hence, no rules explicitly decreeing that certain concatenations of words shall be held to be well-formed), there are no rules which govern the relations between linguistic devices. What can and cannot (sensibly: that is, successfully—in such a way that the main device can still work) be inserted in the blanks of a syntactic schema is in the end something which the user of a language has to discover for himself. Hence, there can be discoveries about "conceptual geography" or "our conceptual scheme" which are not discoveries about a particular language but about any language (provided we add the saving clause "having the same linguistic devices"), yet which nevertheless do not rest upon, or embody the results of, inductive generalization but are available to the native speaker as a consequence of his having acquired a grasp of a certain system of learned conventional rules.[2]

Tenet 5: It follows that, if we are right, no questions of concatenation depend in any way upon the empirical nature of referents of words and that the contents of the rules of a language cannot change *just in virtue of* the discovery of any matter of empirical fact, but depend solely upon convention.

Tenet 6: In a system of linguistic devices there is no distinction between syntactic and semantic rules of the sort proposed by the ETL. That is, there is no distinction between rules which *just* make the (associative) connection between language and the world and rules which are *just* concerned with relationships between expressions and

---

[2] *Cf.* R. M. Hare, "Philosophical Discoveries," *Mind* (1960).

other expressions. The rules of a device prescribe a sequence of operations which results in the generation of a class of well-formed utterances; they are thus simultaneously "semantic" (in that they make the connection between language and the world) and "syntactic" (in that they determine how expressions are to be combined), but there is no way in which we can separate these two functions and assign them to separate classes of rules within the device.

At the same time our theory does not imply that the distinction between syntax and semantics customarily made by linguists is in any sense mistaken or unfounded. Indeed, if we are correct, this distinction can be drawn more sharply than hitherto. The set of linguistic devices composing a language will generate an indefinitely large set of well-formed sentences in that language. There is nothing to prevent us from considering this corpus of sentences from the viewpoint of the linguist and proceeding to construct a description of its grammar or phonology in the ordinary way. The description of a language as a system of linguistic devices, that is, is simply not in competition with any of the other customary modes or "levels" (syntactic, phonological) of linguistic description. It may, of course, be in principle incompatible with other modes of semantic description but since no clear and accepted theory of semantic description at present exists, this possibility need not detain us.

The description of a language as a set of linguistic devices may, however, I want to suggest, supplement the description of language at other levels of linguistic description and may, in fact, fill the gap which is customarily left for "semantic description" in projected "integrated theories of linguistic description." If we are correct, we may expect to find connections at a fairly abstract level between the syntactic structures of natural languages and the formal characteristics of systems of linguistic devices, and I shall try in Part III to suggest what some of these might be. At the very least, such a theory of semantic description should clarify the limits of syntactic description by enabling us to distinguish far more clearly than hitherto between semantic and syntactic questions and to distinguish both sorts of linguistic question from empirical questions of other types. The ETL has traditionally provided a sharp distinction between syntax and semantics, and one which could be represented as holding at an ultimate level of linguistic description, but only at the cost of shrouding the relationship between syntax and semantics in impenetrable mystery so far as practical linguistic inquiry was concerned. With our theory the position is reversed: there are levels of linguistic description at which the syntax–semantics distinction evaporates; but, at the same time, the distinction can (hopefully) be drawn more clearly at the levels of description at which the practical linguist operates.

Tenet 7: If we are right, then, the conventional rules introducing meaning into a language do not make up an unstructured list, each item of which introduces a "meaning" in logical isolation from the introduction of any other meaning. The stipulations which make up the rule structure of a linguistic device are related to one another in a systematic way, so that what gives meaning to an utterance is not any single semantic rule but the place which it occupies in the device as a whole. Moreover, individual devices are not isolated from each other but are connected in a network of relationships of various sorts, so that one could regard the whole of a language as a single immensely complex linguistic device containing a very large number of subordinate systems and subroutines. We can see this clearly in the case of a device like [B]. The function of [B] is not to establish the meanings of words, if establishing the meaning of a word is taken to involve determining how it is to be used in discourse. The device [B] simply establishes a ritual of uttering a stereotyped noise when a given object is indicated in a certain way. The purpose of this ritual only begins to emerge when we introduce into the learner's repertoire other linguistic devices whose instructions mention the instruction of [B], that is, contain the instructions of [B] as a subroutine. We could, if we wished, represent the instructions of [B] simply as a subset of instructions common to the instructions of many other devices, according to the following diagram:

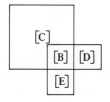

[B]-labeling in isolation from these other devices is a mere idle ritual, which throws no especial light on the concept of meaning. When we consider [B]-labeling in the context of [C] or [D], it seems much more natural to regard [B]-labels as words, having a meaning: but then, what confers this status upon them is the total set of rules of [C] or [D], of which the rules of [B] are merely a subset, or sub-routine. Our objection to the ETL theorist's claim for the primacy of naming as the sole means of introducing meaning into language is, then, that it entails the claim that the rules of a device like [B] can do duty for the rules of every other linguistic device, a claim which distracts us from the actual complexity of language by focusing our attention on a specious theoretical simplicity.

We can reasonably ask what other sorts of relationship subsist between linguistic devices. This is a difficult question to answer at all fully, as it requires a comprehensive study of particular devices. I am inclined to suggest that at least the following three sorts of relationship hold between the members of the system of devices which we constructed in Chapters 7–9, but this must be regarded as a very tentative and preliminary classification which may not in every case have a clear or consistent application beyond the particular examples from which it is derived.

(1) *Subroutine inclusion*: The instructions of one device may be included as a subroutine in the instructions of another. Such relationships can be represented as a tree structure and seem to hold among our examples as follows:

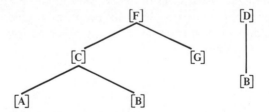

(2) *Complementarity*: The purpose of a device can only be stated by reference to some other device; thus, for example, there is no point in knowing how to request specifications of location unless one knows what

to do with such specifications when one has them. If one represents complementarity by a curved arrow indicating the device from which a given device derives its point, the following relations hold:

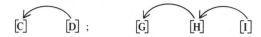

(3) *Rule-structure determination*: The rules of one device directly reflect the rules of another; they are what they are because the rules of the other devices are what *they* are. Representing this relationship by a broad arrow, we get:

Tenet 8: Finally, if we are correct, the rules of a language are not *intrinsically* inductive in character. This is not to say that it would be impossible to give an *account of the learning of* such rules in terms of induction or association, although for other reasons it is very difficult to see how this could in fact be done: the plausibility of associative accounts does seem to depend, that is, on the associationist being able to hold that the rules of a language can be put into the form of a set of inductive generalizations. It is precisely this that we are denying. The " principle of inductive abstraction " cannot, if we are right, itself function as a rule of language: the semantic rules of a language are not inductive generalizations about the way in which a linguistic community associates utterances with elements of the world, and the syntactic rules of a language are not inductive generalizations about the way in which the linguistic community chooses to combine, or to refrain from combining, words into sentences. For the rules of a language are not inductive generalizations at all but sequences of operational instructions.

part three
Linguistics and psycholinguistics

13 Linguistic devices and grammars

13.1 The past decade has witnessed a revolution in structural linguistics, brought about by the development, largely through the work of Noam Chomsky[1] and others, of the theory of generative-transformational analysis. The reverberations have been felt strongly in psychology, so that there now exists an embryonic science, psycholinguistics, which utilizes the new linguistic techniques and which has already achieved some highly interesting and unexpected results at the expense of a quite modest outlay of research effort;[2] and somewhat less strongly in philosophy.[3]

No book on the philosophy of language can afford to ignore these developments, least of all this one, for I shall try to show that the ideas

---

[1] Noam Chomsky, *Syntactic Structures* (The Hague: Mouton, 1957), *Current Issues in Linguistic Theory* (The Hague: Mouton, 1964), and *Aspects* (1965).

[2] Most of these results are summarized or presented, with copious bibliography, in Frank Smith and George A. Miller, eds., *The Genesis of Language* (Cambridge, Mass.: The M.I.T. Press, 1966).

[3] The best, because the least programmatic, attempt to apply linguistic techniques in philosophy known to me is Zeno Vendler, *Linguistics in Philosophy*.

and theories developed in the foregoing pages flow naturally into confluence with those deriving from the study of generative-transformational grammars.

13.2 Chomsky's contribution[4] to linguistics rests on the demonstration that any adequate generative grammar must contain transformational rules, or rules of a scope and power equivalent to transformational rules. If we regard a language L as a (finite or infinite) set of sentences, each of which can be represented by a finite sequence of phomenes, then the aim of a generative grammar of that language is to state rules which generate a class of structural descriptions whose members uniquely specify all and only the members of the class of sequences which are grammatical, and hence sentences of L, thus separating them from the members of the class of sequences which are ungrammatical, and hence not sentences of L. Linguistics is concerned not merely with devising grammars for particular languages but also with the theory of grammar. The theory of grammar does not refer to any particular language but contains means of representing abstractly the formal structures utilized by the grammars of particular languages and, ideally, should state theorems which concern these formal structures and which are thus independent of the particular languages whose grammars may utilize such structures. Chomsky's discovery is intended as a contribution to the theory of grammar.

We might construct a "grammar" for a language consisting of a finite set of sentences (or one with an upper bound—say one million—on the number of phonemes to be drawn from a finite set which together can constitute a grammatical sequence) simply by introducing into the grammar, in coordination with each possible grammatical sequence, a rule which asserts that that particular sequence *is* a grammatical sequence. Such a "grammar" would be completely trivial and would offer no explanation of the fact that a particular sequence of phonemes was ungrammatical, beyond reiterating that it was not grammatical (that is, not on the list of grammatical

---

[4] The brief summary of Chomsky's ideas contained in this section is intended solely for readers not yet familiar with his work. It is not supposed to be a full-dress exegesis or to provide a sufficient basis for the evaluation of the arguments which follow.

sequences). Moreover, such a "grammar" would offer no explanation of the fundamental fact that someone who has completed the
presumably finite task of mastering the grammar of a language can
thereafter tell whether any sentence in that language is grammatical
or not, no matter whether or not he has been presented with that
particular sentence as a grammatical example during the process of
learning the grammar. And, of course, such a grammar would be
adequate *only* if we were to accept some arbitrary limitation on the
number of grammatical sequences of phonemes possible in the
language to which the grammar refers.

It follows that any adequate grammar of a natural language must
contain recursive devices, since only by means of such devices can we
expect to generate an infinite set of sentences by means of a finite
system of rules. The simplest grammar capable of meeting this
requirement would be one based upon a *finite state machine*.[5] A
finite state machine is one which can switch from one to another of
a finite number of internal states. We can suppose that there is a
machine of this type which produces an English word each time it
switches from one state to another. The performance of such a
machine might be represented by the following diagram,[6] in which the
nodes represent states and the connecting lines transitions between
states.

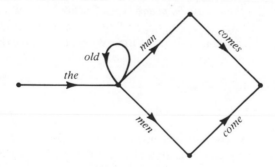

[5] See C. E. Shannon and W. Weaver, *The Mathematical Theory of Communication* (Urbana: University of Illinois Press, 1949); C. F. Hockett, *A Manual
of Phonology*, Memoir LL, Indiana University Publications in Anthropology
and Linguistics (Baltimore, 1955).

[6] © Copyright by Mouton & Co., Publishers, from Noam Chomsky, *Syntactic
Structures* (The Hague, The Netherlands: Mouton, 1966), p. 19, diagram (8).

The machine in effect generates sentences by tracing a path from the initial point on the left of the diagram to the final point on the right. The closed loop ' old ' supplies a minimal recursive device which ensures that the machine will generate infinitely many sentences, thus:

The man comes

The old man comes

The old old man comes

The old old old man comes

⋮

Such a machine can thus be regarded as representing a *finite state grammar*, whose rules generate sentences from left to right and in which the decision as to what word or words can occupy a given sentence depends solely on the choices which have already been made to leftward of the point of decision. At each stage in the generation of a sentence, that is, we move one step to the right, and in so moving we limit the choice of words which can be added to the developing structure of the sentence by further rightward steps.

A language for which an adequate finite state grammar can be constructed is a *finite state language*. It can easily be shown that English is not a finite state language. This is because, among other things, English contains the sort of logical dependencies exhibited by the following sentences:

(1) Either S_1, or it will rain

(2) If S_2, then blue sky will appear

Such sentences contain dependencies (between ' either ' and ' or ' and ' if ' and ' then ' in our example) which extend across the comma. If we replace S_1 and S_2 with ' X ' and ' Y ' and use lower case letters to represent mutually dependent expressions, then we can symbolize (1) and (2) as

(3) aXa

(4) bYb

But now we can replace S_1 or S_2 with any English sentence, say, (1) or (2). This gives us

(5) Either if S_2, then blue sky will appear, or it will rain

(6) If either S_1, or it will rain, then blue sky will appear

Obviously, with appropriately chosen sentences, there is no theoretical limit to nesting, or embedding, of this type.

Now (5) and (6) will appear in our notation as

(7) *ab Yba*

(8) *baXab*

That is, (5) and (6) involve "mirroring": the occurrence of a string of symbols followed by the identical string in reverse. No language in which embedding procedures, such as those above, can be reapplied n times to the same sentence where n is an indefinitely large number, can have its grammar represented by a finite state machine, since such a machine could only work by listing all the possible cooccurring halves of mirroring strings capable of being generated by the embedding procedures, and obviously if n were not a finite number, no finite list would be possible. If we were arbitrarily to identify n for English with some finite number, then a trivial and uninformative finite state grammar of English would of course be possible.[7]

If, now, we consider the type of grammar (phrase structure grammar) which is presupposed by conventional methods of constituent analysis (parsing), we find that it is essentially more powerful than a finite state grammar. A phrase structure grammar contains a finite set Σ of *initial strings*, together with a finite set F of *instruction formulas*, or *rewriting rules*, of the form $X \longrightarrow Y$ (interpreted as "rewrite X as Y"), each of which permits us to form a string Y by rewriting a single symbol of a string X, which may, but need not, itself consist of a single symbol.

---

[7] A more detailed summary of this argument can be found in Chomsky, *Syntactic Structures*, pp. 18–25; and a formal proof of the inadequacy of finite state and Markov process models to the description of certain types of language in Noam Chomsky, "Three Models for the Description of Language," I.R.E. *Transactions on Information Theory*, vol. IT-2 (1956).

Thus, for the following grammar (9), Σ contains the single symbol *Sentence*, and F contains the instruction formulas (i)–(vi):[8]

(9) (i) *Sentence* $\longrightarrow$ *NP* + *VP*

    (ii) *NP* $\longrightarrow$ *T* + *N*

    (iii) *VP* $\longrightarrow$ *Verb* + *NP*

    (iv) *T* $\longrightarrow$ *the*

    (v) *N* $\longrightarrow$ *man, ball*, etc.

    (vi) *Verb* $\longrightarrow$ *hit, took*, etc.

The following is a *derivation* of the sentence, "The man hit the ball," making use of (9).

(10) *Sentence*

NP + *VP*	(i)
T + *N* + *VP*	(ii)
T + *N* + *Verb* + *NP*	(iii)
the + *N* + *Verb* + *NP*	(iv)
the + *man* + *Verb* + *NP*	(v)
the + *man* + *hit* + *NP*	(vi)
the + *man* + *hit* + *T* + *N*	(ii)
the + *man* + *hit* + *the* + *N*	(iv)
the + *man* + *hit* + *the* + *ball*	(v)

The derivation of (10) can be represented as a diagrammatic phrase marker which exhibits the parsing of 'The man hit the ball' into its syntactic constituents, although it does not represent the order of application of the instruction formulas of (9).

---

[8] This example, and the following three—(10), (11), and (12)—are taken from Noam Chomsky, *Syntactic Structures* (The Hague, The Netherlands: Mouton, 1966), pp. 26–30, examples (13), (14), (15), (18).

(11)

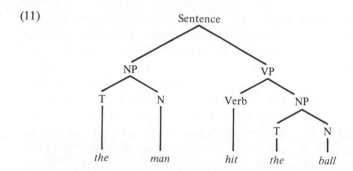

A phrase structure grammar affords us, in principle, at least, a clear criterion of grammaticalness. A grammatical sentence will be one for which a derivation can be found, and an ungrammatical sentence one for which no derivation is possible. A descriptively adequate phrase structure grammar for a given language, then, will be one which yields a derivation for every sentence in that language, and no derivation for any ungrammatical sentence.

That a phrase structure grammar is more powerful than one which exemplifies the finite state model ("more powerful," that is, in that many grammatical constructions which cannot be described at all in terms of a finite state model can be described in terms of a phrase structure model) can easily be demonstrated as follows.

Consider a language whose alphabet contains just the letters a, b, and whose sentences comprise ab, $aabb$, $aaabbb$, ..., and in general all and only those strings comprising n occurrences of a followed by n occurrences of b. Such a language, for the sort of reason discussed earlier, is not a finite state language, but all its sentences can be generated by the following phrase structure grammar:

(12) $\Sigma : Z$
$\quad F: Z \longrightarrow ab$
$\qquad Z \longrightarrow aZb$

The salient feature of a phrase structure grammar is that its rules, unlike those of a finite state grammar, operate on symbols (NP, S, Z, for example) which do not occur in the sentences of the language. Phrase structure grammar thus introduces a new "level of linguistic representation." At the level of constituent analysis a sentence may have more than one representation (parsing), whereas at the level of phonemic analysis, or for that matter finite state analysis, it can have only one.

It is possible that English may be completely describable by a phrase structure grammar. If this is the case, the phrase structure grammar is in the strict sense adequate to the description of English; but in a weaker sense it may still be inadequate. That is, it may be the case that a formally adequate phrase structure grammar of English would be extremely complex and *ad hoc* and would not possess much explanatory power. And in fact it can be shown that this is the case.[9] To show this requires the discussion of many examples, but a fair idea of the drift of all these discussions and of the conclusions to which they lead can be gained from any one of them.

If we have two sentences of the form $Z + X + W$ and $Z + Y + W$, it is often the case that we can form a new sentence of the form $Z - X + and + Y - W$.[10] Thus, given the sentences

(13) The house—where I was born—has been demolished

and

(14) The house—where I grew up—has been demolished

we can form

(15) The house—where I was born and where I grew up—has been demolished

The possibility of carrying out this sort of conjunction provides an important criterion for deciding initially what counts as a sentence constituent in English. It happens that the resulting grammar is very considerably simplified if we choose to set up constituents in such a way that the following rule holds, or holds approximately.

[9] *Cf.* Chomsky, *Syntactic Structures*, pp. 34–48.

[10] Here " + " functions as a concatenation operator on the level of phrase structures.

(16) If S_1 and S_2 are grammatical sentences, and S_1 differs from S_2 only in that X appears in S_1 where Y appears in S_2 (that is, $S_1 = \ldots X \ldots$ and $S_2 = \ldots Y \ldots$), and X and Y are constituents of the same type in S_1 and S_2, respectively, then S_3 is a sentence, where S_3 is the result of replacing X by $X + and + Y$ in S_1 (that is, $S_3 = \ldots X + and + Y \ldots$).

But a grammar which contains a rule like (16) is no longer a pure phrase structure grammar. For as we have seen, each of the F rules of a phrase structure grammar operates on single constituents of strings without reference to any other constituent of the string in question and can be applied at any point in a derivation without reference to any preceding step in the derivation. This is not the case with (16). In order to apply (16), we must know that two sentences have related phrase structures, or constituent analyses. Knowing this essentially involves reference to earlier steps in the derivations of S_1 and S_2. This will appear clearly if we reflect that X and Y will be constituents, but not constituents of the same kind, of S_1 and S_2 respectively, just in case each has a single point of origin in the derivations of S_1 and S_2, but these points of origin are differently labeled.

Reference to more than one sentence, to more than one constituent, and to more than one stage in a phrase structural derivation are essential characteristics of what Chomsky calls *transformational rules*. In general, a grammatical transformation operates on a given string with a given constituent structure (phrase marker) and converts it into a new string with a new, derived constituent structure. It is important, I think, in grasping the distinction between the rewriting rules of phrase structure grammars and transformational rules, to see that whereas the former operate on *constituents*, the latter operate on *constituent structures*, their function being essentially to map one or more phrase markers onto a single derived phrase marker.[11]

The grammar of a natural language thus appears to fall naturally into two components. The first of these, the *base component*, is essentially a phrase structure grammar which yields as its output *base strings* (that is, the terminal strings of the derivations which its rules

---

[11] For a more extended, semi-formalized explication of the notion of a transformational rule, see Noam Chomsky, "On the Notion 'Rule of Grammar'," reprinted in Fodor and Katz, *The Structure of Language*, pp. 119–136.

permit). The base strings are then further operated on by the rules of the *transformational component*.

We may distinguish between *optional transformations* and *obligatory transformations*, which must be applied to given base strings if the grammar is to generate sentences in English, as distinct from the strings of morphemes interspersed with grammatical symbols which occur as the output of the base component. It has become conventional to apply the term *kernel sentence* to sentences formed from the base strings by the fewest applications of obligatory transformations necessary to produce English. Kernel sentences should not be confused with base strings.

We can also distinguish between *generalized* and *singulary* transformations. Generalized transformations produce a derived phrase marker from a pair of base phrase markers, by embedding in one such phrase marker a transform of the whole or a part of the other. Thus, the phrase markers corresponding to

(17) The man was fired

(18) The man persuaded John of Δ

(19) John was examined by a specialist

can be successively embedded one in another by a series of generalized transformations to yield a phrase marker corresponding to

(20) The man who persuaded John to be examined by a specialist was fired

The "transformational history" which connects (20) to (17)–(19) can be represented by a diagram such as the following (a transformational marker), in which the sequence of transformations is indicated by the symbol T_i ;

(21)

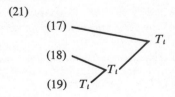

A singulary transformation converts a single phrase marker into a derived marker, as in the following example,[12] in which a single transformation converts (a) to (b):

(22)(a)

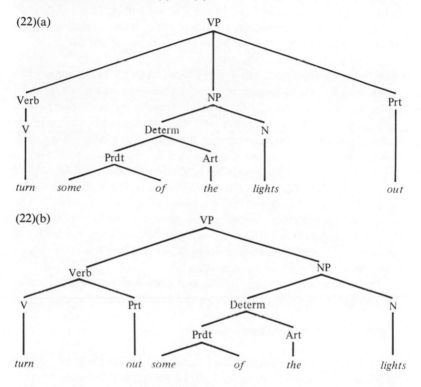

(22)(b)

In *Aspects*, Chomsky proposes a simplification of the general structure of transformational grammar. Generalized embedding transformations, and hence transformational markers, are to be dispensed with, their functions being fulfilled by allowing the symbol #S# ("Sentence") to replace constituents of base strings, and the

---

[12] From Noam Chomsky, "On the Notion 'Rule of Grammar'," in Fodor and Katz, *The Structure of Language*, p. 135, figure 3.

rules of the base to reapply cyclically to any such embedded occurrence of $\#S\#$.[13] The grammar further contains a transformational component consisting of a set of singular transformations which must be applied in an ordered linear sequence either to a constituent structure before it is embedded in a matrix, or to the matrix and constituent structure after the embedding has been carried out.

It is important to see that although these changes simplify generative grammar they make no essential difference to its character. The essential feature of a transformational grammar, which is expressed in earlier versions entirely through the transformational component and in the version of *Aspects* partly through the introduction of recursive embedding procedures into the rules of the base component, lies in the fact that for any sentence in a language which has such a grammar, it is invariably possible to distinguish between the *surface structure* of the sentence and its *deep structure*. The surface structure is given by the phrase structure analysis of the sentence itself. The deep structure is given by the phrase structure analysis of the base string or strings from which it has been derived, together with the sequence of transformations or reapplications of the base rules which have been employed in its derivation.[14]

The distinction between surface and deep structure affords a way of accounting for syntactic ambiguity. Thus the sentence,

(23) They are flying planes

although it is plainly syntactically ambiguous, can only be given a single structural description by a phrase structure grammar. A transformational grammar, however, allows us to regard this description

---

[13] Chomsky, *Aspects*, p. 132f.

[14] *Cf.* Chomsky, "On the Notion 'Rule of Grammar'," p. 129: "The motivation for adding transformational rules to a grammar is quite clear. There are certain sentences (in fact, simple declarative active sentences with no complex noun or verb phrases—or, to be more precise, the terminal strings underlying these) that can be generated by a constituent structure grammar in quite a natural way. There are others (e.g., passives, questions, sentences with discontinuous phrases and complex phrases that embed sentence transforms) that cannot be generated in an economic and natural way by a constituent structure grammar, *but that are systematically related to sentences of simpler structure*" (my italics).

as merely expressing the surface structure of (23), which we can further represent as possessing two alternative deep structures: that is to say, as being related by two distinct, possible transformational histories to two structurally quite different base strings.

The grammar, consisting of base and transformational components, can be regarded as a device for generating abstract sequences of symbols which stand in need of both phonological and semantic interpretation. Linguists are agreed that semantic interpretation applies only to the output of the base component: that is, to deep structure.[15] Transformations neither add nor delete meaning-bearing elements of the language but merely interrelate phrase markers whose semantic interpretation is already determined. On the other hand, phonological interpretation is applied only to the surface structure. We can give, then, the following diagrammatic representation of the relationships which appear to exist between the syntax, semantics, and phonology of a natural language.

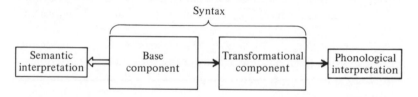

13.3 We have argued that the rules of linguistic devices are both (that is, indifferently) "semantic" and "syntactic" in function, although in neither case quite in the sense which traditional empiricism might lead us to attach to these terms. A learner who has mastered a set of linguistic devices will be able to generate, in appropriate circumstances, a set of well-formed English sentences. The possibility of interpolating one device within another ensures that the possessor of even a moderately numerous array of linguistic devices will be able to generate, and to understand, infinitely many such sentences; or rather, that his capacity to generate and understand well-formed English sentences will be bounded only

[15] *Cf.* Chomsky, *Aspects*, p. 132.

by whatever arbitrary limit we may choose to impose upon the length of the strings which we are prepared to consider well-formed English sentences. Some interpolations will be reflexive and indefinitely recursive. Thus, in constructing a device which yields specification of locations of the form,

(24)(a) the a_1 to the left of the a_2

it will evidently be possible to formulate the rules of the device in such a way that they can be reapplied cyclically to generate

(24)(b) the a_1 to the left of the a_3 to the left of the a_2...

It will of course be possible to treat a (finite or infinite) set of sentences generated (or generable) by a system of linguistic devices as a corpus of text in a language and to try to construct a grammar of this language. And hence we can reasonably ask what sort of grammar would be adequate to the description of a corpus of sentences so generated.

On our account, a natural language consists of a finite set of linguistic devices. Each of these contains rules for generating utterances, and each utterance generated by these rules will either be a single word (for example, the utterances of [B]-labels) or else will be generated by a process which will amount to the filling in of one or more blanks in a syntactic schema.

Let us for the moment regard recursively generated expressions such as (24)(b) as involving more than one occurrence of a syntactic schema. Now, if we take, singly and separately, each of the syntactic schemata mentioned by the (finite set of) linguistic devices, and generate all of the English sentences which result from filling in the blank or blanks in each schema by following the rules of the linguistic device which introduces that schema into the language, then we shall end with a very large, but finite, set of simple English sentences. We may, not unreasonably, call these *basic sentences* of English.

It might seem as if the grammar of these basic sentences would be fairly simply and elegantly describable in terms of the phrase structure model, once the notions of a morpheme and of a set of form classes have been defined in the usual way with respect to the corpus of basic sentences. For such a grammar, it would appear, will be adequate just if it allows us to construct a phrase structure description (phrase marker) corresponding to all and only the members of a finite set of syntactic schemata, and if it provides for this in such a way that where a given blank in a given syntactic schema is fillable by any member of one or more form classes, the constituent which takes the place of the blank in the structural description corresponding to the schema in question is such that the rewriting rules of the grammar allows its replacement by constituent symbols corresponding to those particular form classes. Just because the corpus of basic sentences is founded upon a finite set of syntactic patterns, there would seem to be nothing in the way of increased simplicity or elegance to be gained from introducing transformational or context-sensitive rules into the grammar, since the patterns in question are, as it were, the ultimate sources of syntactic structure in the language. They do not "refer back" to simpler patterns or sentence types and hence, presumably, are not intrinsically related to one another in any way. Some problems may arise over the exclusion of semantic anomaly, in cases where this comes about through the substitution into a given blank of some members of a given form class rather than others, but given the finite nature of the language, these could no doubt be solved by an appropriate choice of form classes (if, indeed, we treat semantic anomaly as a problem to be solved by the syntactic component of an integrated description of language—which, as we shall see in a moment, we need not do).

Now in fact, it seems to me, the assumption that there would be nothing to be gained by introducing context-sensitive or transformational rules into the grammar of the set of basic sentences is false. The error here consists in supposing that the syntactic patterns (syntactic schemata) on which the basic sentences are based are *arbitrarily* introduced into the language: that is to say, that there are no deeper linguistic considerations which determine the structure of these patterns, and hence that the structures which the patterns exhibit will not be intrinsically related.

This supposition is false, for the following reason. If a natural language is a system of linguistic devices, then understanding an utterance in a natural language is essentially a matter of selecting one or more devices whose rules are to be applied to the utterance in question in order to generate a certain result: a search pattern; the identification of an object; of a person to whom an object is to be taken; the construction of a geometrical figure; the generation of a reply ("yes," "Thursday"); and so on. If it were merely a matter of selecting one device per utterance, there would be no need for the utterances of a language to possess any syntactic structure at all. A language which conformed to this condition would, as we have seen, be infertile: it would simply consist of a repertoire of sterile and circumscribed rituals conditioned to a set of cues which need only be phonetically distinct from one another.

A natural, human language, on the other hand, is fertile; and, if we are correct, its fertility arises from the fact that every (or almost every) device within it is related to other devices in the way in which, in our model, [C] and [D] are related to [B]: that is, through the relation which in Chapter 12 we called subroutine inclusion. Hence, in order to understand a phonemic string S (that is, in order to carry out the rule-licensed procedures appropriate to it), the learner must be able to answer the following questions:

(1) Which devices are to supply which sequences of instructions to be used in interpreting S?
(2) Which sequence of instructions is to function as the main sequence, and which sequences are to function as subroutines, sub-subroutines, and so on?
(3) At which points are the subroutines to be inserted into the main sequence and how is the output of each subroutine to be utilized in continuing the main sequence?

It must, moreover, be possible for someone who knows the language to answer these questions immediately, simply by inspecting S (that is, without knowing whether S is true or not). This condition can be met if and only if phonemic strings associated with the devices which yield the subroutines which must be executed in interpreting S enter in a systematic way into the actual phonemic composition of S. It must be possible, that is, to apply to S a *decoding process* which will refer the learner to various linguistic devices in a certain order, and this will only be possible if S is actually composed of phonemic strings drawn from the linguistic devices in question and combined in a way determined by the rules of those devices.

If S exhibits a structure of this type, then the rules of the device to which S belongs can be made to determine a main sequence of operations requiring, at certain points, a transition to subroutines drawn from other devices identified by the *types* of phonemic string occupying given positions in the internal structure of S, while the conduct and outcome of these subroutines will depend on *what* particular phonemic string of a given type occupies that position. But if S exhibits no such structure, then it will be impossible for the learner to derive answers to (1)–(3) simply from an inspection of S.

We can see why this is so if we consider the relationship between [C] and [B]. The rules of [C] are such that they require the learner, when presented with such phonemic strings as

(25) (a) Bring dog

    (b) Bring book

    (c) Bring doll

to generate a set of [B]-labels until a match is obtained between some [B]-label and a part of the presented phonemic string and then to perform certain further operations; this amounts to saying that the rules of [C] determine a main sequence of operations, identify the subroutine, and determine how it is to be inserted into the main sequence. Suppose now that we were to replace the phonemic strings of (25) with the following set of " structureless " strings, each consisting of a single phoneme:

(26) (a) ā

    (b) ē

    (c) ō

There is no way in which the rules of [C] could be applied to (26) (a)–(c). For, *ex hypothesi*, it is impossible to derive from any of them an element which " refers back to " [B] in the way in which, for example, 'dog' in (25)(a) refers back to [B]. And hence, even if we were to make it a rule that the learner, upon hearing one of the strings of (26)(a)–(c), was to begin generating the [B]-labels of the objects around him, we should have no means of formulating a rule which would result in his stopping at a particular [B]-label, since the device of getting him to establish a match between a [B]-label and some segment of the presented phonemic string would no longer be available to us.

The best we could do, in fact, with structureless phonemic strings, would be to construct a series of distinct devices, $[C_i]$, $[C_{ii}]$, $[C_{iii}]$, ..., corresponding to the strings in (26)(a)–(c). The rules of $[C_i]$ would instruct the learner, on learning (26)(a), to bring a dog and would do this *directly* (that is, without referring to the rules of any other device); similarly, $[C_{ii}]$ would directly instruct the learner to bring a book on hearing (26)(b), and so on.

That the language consisting of [A], [B], and $[C_i]$–$[C_n]$ would be infertile will easily be seen if we reflect that in order to teach the speaker of that language to bring a type of object which he has not previously been accustomed to bring, it would be necessary to teach him a new [C]-type device, $[C_n]$; whereas in the language consisting of [A], [B], and [C] it would be sufficient merely to teach him the application of a new [B]-label.

It appears, then, that the structure of the basic syntactic schemata of a language (the system of linguistic devices) is not something which is introduced into the language in an arbitrary or *ad hoc* way. Syntactic structure is determined by deeper linguistic considerations: namely, the relationships holding between linguistic devices. And it is absolutely necessary that relationships of the sort which determine syntactic structure should hold between the component linguistic devices of a language, since otherwise the language made up of these devices would not be fertile, that is, would not be a *language* in the sense, made familiar by Chomsky and other linguists, in which that term is properly applicable only to human languages.

Let us return to our discussion of the grammar of the basic sentences of a language. It seems clear that the relationships holding between the devices [B] and [C] will also connect [B] with many other devices. Thus the basic sentences will include such sentences as

(27) (a) Hold book

(b) Read book

(c) Wash dog

In each case, the relationship holding between the device governing the schema 'x ____ ' and [B] will be similar to that holding between [C] and [B]. If we introduce into our grammar the constituents N and V, then this class of relationships between linguistic devices may appear in the grammar as the verb-noun relationship. In other words, the Σ, F grammar of the language consisting just of [A], [B], and [C], together with such further devices as will serve to generate (27)(a)–(c) and their congeners will run as follows:

(28) Σ : S

     F : S ⟶ VN

     V ⟶ *Bring, hold, wash*, etc.

     N ⟶ *Book, doll, dog*, etc.

It seems more than likely, now, that such systematic patterns of relationship among interconnected linguistic devices will result in the occurrence among the base sentences of such pairs of related sentence-forms as

(29) (a) Is John ____ing it?

     (b) John is ____ing it

The relationship between sentences conforming to these patterns is best dealt with in a generative grammar by introducing a singulary transformation. But relationships like that exhibited in (29)(a) and (b) would arise very naturally quite early in the course of the development of a system of linguistic devices. And thus it seems rather probable that the best and simplest description of the grammar of the basic sentences generated by such a system will be one which employs transformational mechanisms.

So far we have considered only sentences formed by filling in the blanks[16] in syntactic schemata with expressions which are not

---

[16] It is perhaps worth emphasizing again that talk of "filling in blanks" in syntactic schemata is merely a shorthand way of summarizing the *effects* of sets of instructions in linguistic devices. The rules of linguistic devices never, of course, expressly *instruct* the language user to "fill in such-and-such a blank with an expression of such-and-such a type."

themselves syntactic schemata (that is, which themselves contain no blanks). There is, of course, no reason why we, or the users of a system of linguistic devices, should maintain this restriction. To see why this is so, we must first notice that the rules of a linguistic device neither expressly require nor expressly forbid the use of any particular class of expressions as fillers for a particular blank in a syntactic schema. The choice of fillers for a particular blank is determined not by stipulation but by the character of the rules of the device in which the syntactic schema in question occurs.

Thus, as we saw in Chapter 9, the question of whether a particular expression can be substituted into a particular blank in a given schema depends entirely on whether or not the linguistic device which governs the schema in question proves to be operable in the context of that particular substitution.

In [C], for example, sentences are initially generated by a process which amounts to instantiating the blank in the schema ' Bring ____ ' with a [B]-label, to yield such sentences as (25)(a)–(c). But it would clearly be possible to operate the device if the blank were to be filled with a [B]-label and a color word, thus:

(30) (a) Bring red book

(b) Bring blue doll

(c) Bring brown dog

The color words will presumably be drawn from a device which we will arbitrarily label [K]. The device [K] will be a labeling device like [B] in that its rules will enable the learner to attach labels, ' red ', ' blue ', and so on, to presented samples, But the instructions of [K] will have a different structure and content from those of [B]: those of [K] will turn on the recognition of resemblances as falling within permissible ranges of degrees of resemblance, defined on a spectrum of continuously and intrinsically related properties; those of [B] will involve checking the presence or absence of intrinsically unrelated properties.

Now, in order to generate a response to (30)(a) (for example) the language user will have to apply the rules of these different devices, [C], [B], and [K] *in sequence*. That is, he must first of all identify a set of objects by applying the rules of [B] to his surroundings. Then, by applying the rules of [K] *to the members of this set*, he must single out one or more of them as *red* books and then, reverting to the rules of [C], perform the bringing operation upon some member of the latter set. It is because the rules of [B], and those of [K], can be applied in sequence to produce results which can be, as it were, *fed into the machinery of* [C], that [K]-labels and [B]-labels can occur as conjoint fillers of the blank in ' Bring ____ '.

But, obviously, there is more than one way in which the rules of [B] and [K] could be applied in sequence to produce results capable of being utilized by the rules of [C]. The language user might, for example, generate a response to (30)(a) by generating the [B]-labels of objects in his vicinity until he obtained a match with the terminal string of (30)(a) and then he would bring the object which produced the match; but if no match occurred, the language user will proceed by generating [K]-labels until a match with the immediately preterminal string occurred and then he would bring the object which produced *that* match. For this user, (30)(a) would be roughly equivalent to

(31) Bring me a book, or failing that, something red

The rules of [C], [B], and [K] evidently do not suffice, then, to fully specify how the user is to set about generating responses to such utterances as (30)(a)–(c). The rules of [C] specify a main sequence of instructions, and they also specify a matching technique by which labeling devices such as [B] and [K] can be made to yield a product (the identification of an object) which can be utilized by the learner at a certain point in the process of carrying out the instructions of the main sequence. But they do not specify how the subordinate labeling devices are to be ordered in generating this product. Are the labeling devices to be applied in a hierarchical series, so that the rules of each are applied only to the class of objects singled out by the application of the rules of the device next highest in the series? Or are they to be applied in sequence, so that each one is brought into play only if all the preceding ones have failed to identify an object? Or in one of a number of other ways?

It will suffice to resolve such difficulties if we admit a new type of rule into our model system of linguistic devices. We shall call such rules *ordering conventions*. An ordering convention will be a rule which specifies, in general terms, certain standard ways in which the application of the rules of linguistic devices of certain types is to proceed when phonemic strings of a given type drawn from these devices occur as blank-fillers in syntactic schemata drawn from other devices.

Thus, we might introduce the following ordering convention (here roughly and schematically formulated) in order to deal with the remaining questions concerning the relationship between [C], [B], and [K].

OC 1: When n labels $l_1, \ldots, l_n$, drawn from m labeling devices, occur in simple juxtaposition as joint fillers of the same blank in a syntactic schema S, where S is such that its rules define a decomposition-and-matching technique T which has the function of interpolating a sequence of instructions drawn from a labeling device into a main sequence defined by the rules of S_1, then T is to be applied to $l_1, \ldots, l_n$ in hierarchical sequence.

Ordering conventions are obviously not *grammatical* rules, either in the rough-and-ready sense of empiricist philosophy (they are not rules governing the combination of signs) or in the linguist's more precise and technical sense; OC 1, for example, could not be made part of either the phrase-structure or the transformational component of a grammar. They belong to a different level of linguistic description, the level upon which a language appears as a system of linguistic devices. However, ordering conventions do not *specify*, or form part of the specification of, linguistic devices: ideally, one should be able to fully specify each and every one of the linguistic devices of a language *before* one set about specifying its ordering conventions.

Ordering conventions, in fact, are concerned only with *relations between* linguistic devices; for any given device, it will be possible to extend the class of expressions which can fill the blank(s) in the syntactic schema which it governs, provided that we can formulate sets of instructions for modifying, in standard ways, the linguistic devices from which they are drawn, in such a way that the main sequence of instructions of the device governing the syntactic schema into which the expressions are to be substituted can accept the rule sequence in question as subroutines. Ordering conventions are just such sets of instructions.

It will sometimes be the case that ordering conventions will apply only to particular devices; but quite often they will refer to *types* of device and will specify in general terms modifications which can be made to the rules of any device of a given type, together with modifications which can be made to any phonemic string generated by a device of that type, prior to inserting it in the receiving syntactic schema, in order to mark the need to apply those rules in their modified form when interpreting the resulting expression. Thus, OC 1 refers to a *class* of labeling devices and to a class of devices which employ a technique T of a given sort and specifies a modification of the rules of the labeling devices—a modification which is to be applied in interpreting expressions which contain phonemic strings of certain sorts.

By adding ordering conventions to a system of linguistic devices, it becomes possible to construct sentences by filling in the blanks in syntactic schemata with modified versions of expressions which have themselves been formed by filling in the blanks of other (or the same) syntactic schemata, and so on indefinitely. Let us call such sentences *complex sentences*. To form, and to understand, complex sentences, it will be necessary to know both the rules of the linguistic devices involved and an appropriate set of ordering conventions.

It would be difficult, without making our model system of linguistic devices much more elaborate, to give a detailed, concrete example of the generation of complex sentences, but the following schematic example may illustrate what I have in mind.

Consider the following sentence:

(32) Bring the cabbage which John brought

We may suppose that (32) is based upon the following linguistic devices:

(33) (a) [C], or some such device governing the schema, 'Bring ____ '.

(b) A device governing the schema, '____$_{person}$ brought the ____$_{object}$'.

(c) A labeling device such as **[B]** whose labels can be inserted in the second blank of the schema of (33)(b).

(d) A device assigning proper names to persons. Its rule will be different from those of (33)(c), and its labels will be substitutable into the first blank of the schema governed by (33)(b).

Now we may suppose that, by using the rules of (33)(c) and (d), we can fill in the blanks of the schema of (33)(b) to yield

(34) John brought a cabbage

We now suppose that there exists an ordering convention operating on devices of the types to which (33)(a) and (33)(b) belong and that this ordering convention modifies the rules of (33)(b) and thus, presumably, the ways in which the subroutines drawn from (33)(c) and (33)(d) are inserted into the main sequence of instructions defined by the rules of (33)(b), in such a way that an expression related to (34) can serve as a filler for the blank in ' Bring ____ '.

Let us suppose that this expression is

(35) the cabbage which John brought

Insertion of this in the blank of ' Bring ____ ' will yield (32).

All of this, no doubt, is very sketchy and programmatic. It is intended only to illustrate, and not to support, the following tentative suggestion. If we are correct, then constructing or understanding a complex sentence such as (32) is a matter of applying to it the rules of a set of linguistic devices, the members of which (or rather, the sets of instructions derived from them) must be applied to the sentence *in a set hierarchical order* determined by the phonemic constitution of the sentence. Thus in our example, we shall derive a main sequence of instructions from (33)(a). Into this we shall interpolate a subroutine derived *via* an ordering convention from (33)(c) and into this, in turn, we shall interpolate sub-subroutines derived respectively from (33)(c) and (d).

Now, in order for sets of linguistic devices to be applied in a set hierarchical order to complex sentences, the phonemic constitution of such sentences must provide the speaker with cues or markers which will immediately identify for him the devices to which he is to refer, their order of application, and the ordering conventions connecting them. Moreover, these cues must be provided in a systematic and principled manner and not on an *ad hoc*, sentence-to-sentence basis; otherwise, the fertility of the language will not be preserved.

We have already seen that, in order for the speaker to solve these problems for the class of sentences formed by filling in the blanks of single syntactic schemata, systematic relations must exist on the phonemic level between different syntactic schemata and that these relations will be represented at the grammatical level of linguistic description in terms of phrase structure and certain classes of trans- formations.

What is needed at the level of complex sentences, then, is that the pre-existing network of phonemic relationships holding between syntactic schemata should have superimposed upon it a further set of systematically ordered phonemic relationships determined by the ordering conventions of the language. These relationships will essentially consist in standardized modifications imposed upon cer- tain classes of syntactic schemata, which have the effect of deriving (from expressions obtained by completing those schemata) other, modified expressions which can serve as fillers of specified blanks in certain other classes of syntactic schemata.

These relationships, since they affect the phonemic constitution of sentences, will necessarily be represented by the grammar of the language; and it seems to me reasonable to suppose that they will turn out to be most simply and systematically represented as general- ized embedding transformations or as whatever formal equivalent of generalized embedding transformations the grammar in question pro- vides. The reason for this is that generalized embedding transforma- tions connect the surface structure of a sentence with a deep structure consisting of (structural descriptions of) other sentences, from which the original sentence has been transformationally derived. The ordering conventions of a language, now, are precisely rules which connect a compound syntactic schema (surface structure) with other syntactic schemata (deep structure) from which it has been constructed.

We may now sum up the argument of this section. The grammar of a body of sentences generated by a system of linguistic devices may reasonably be expected, given the nature of such a system, to exhibit just those formal features which Chomsky and his associates find to be exhibited by the grammar of a natural language. We may expect such a grammar, that is, to possess (1) a phrase structure component, together with a limited range of associated transformations, corresponding to the systematic relationships holding between elements of the syntactic schemata of the language; and (2) a transformational component, corresponding in the main to relationships holding in the system of linguistic devices between syntactic schemata and other syntactic schemata.

Again, within such a grammar, we may expect to find ourselves compelled, for reasons of simplicity and elegance, to introduce a distinction between surface and deep structure, corresponding to the relationship between a complex sentence and the set of syntactic schemata from which it is derived. The set of basic sentences generated by the system of linguistic devices will correspond approximately to the base strings of the grammar. However, the base rules of the grammar will not generate *sentences*, because, even at the level of the basic sentences, there will be some relationships between syntactic schemata (for example, those exhibited by (29)(a) and (b)) which will lend themselves most easily to grammatical representation as transformations.

Finally, only the base strings of the grammar will be semantically interpreted—the rules of the transformational component serving only to relate base strings, by embedding or by other operations, without adding or deleting any semantically significant element. This is because the relationships within the system of linguistic devices which the transformational rules of the grammar reflect, or represent, are invariably relationships holding *between* linguistic devices (for example, those holding in virtue of the existence of ordering conventions) and hence have nothing to do with meaning, which is introduced into the language solely by the rules (that is, the ground rules and instructions) of the linguistic devices themselves.

13.4 It has generally been assumed[17] that the semantic component of a linguistic description of a natural language will contain a dictionary and that the function of this will

[17] Chomsky; Fodor and Katz; Katz and Postal; Katz; *passim.*

LINGUISTIC DEVICES AND GRAMMARS   265

be to assign meanings to the primary meaning-bearing elements of
the language: that is to say, its morphemes and idioms. Meaning,
that is, insofar as it is primary and nonderivative, is conceived of as
entering language solely at the morphemic level; and the fundamental
lexical rules of the language is conceived of as composing a list of
logically discrete items, each member of which associates a single
morpheme—or, in the case of idioms, a single phrase—with a meaning or "reading," which is usually conceived of as a verbal definition
consisting of a string of semantic markers with various attached
notations which serve to determine what morphemes can and cannot
enter particular semantic or syntactic environments. On this view the
dictionary element of the semantic component is not a system of
generative rules, and the fertility of the language—as Chomsky would
say, the possibility of producing original sentences—derives entirely
from the syntactic component. The meaning which a linguistically
competent adult assigns to a sentence must on this view be supposed
to be a resultant of the meanings of the individual morphemes of the
sentence and the rules of the syntactic component of the grammar,
which *are* generative rules. In order to effect this union between syntax and semantics, Fodor, Katz, and Postal introduce into their semantic theory a set of *projection rules*, the function of which are to
amalgamate the meanings of the separate morphemes at each level
of the structural description of a sentence until a derived meaning
is obtained for the sentence as a whole.

At first sight, this combination of a Chomskean theory of grammar,
based upon a radical rejection of empiricist and associationist
theories of language, with an associationist theory of the attachment
of meaning to morphemes and idioms which would be thoroughly
congenial to any holder of the traditional empiricist view of language,
impresses one as illmatched and awkward; and there are, I think,
sound reasons for thinking this impression well-founded.

To begin with, if we treat Fodor and Katz' semantic theory as a
theory of semantic competence in the fullest sense (that is, as an
attempt to state the rules which must be learned if someone is to be
able to understand and to use in discourse with a full awareness of its
meaning, any utterance in a language), then so far as I can see it
commits its holders to some form of the doctrine that all syntactic
structures above the level of morphemes (for example, noun phrases,

verb phrases, sentences) are essentially compound names—that, in fact, "the essence of speech is the composition of names,"[18] Fodor and Katz' projection rules essentially amalgamate selected paths from the trees of readings of two morphemes (or syntactic structures) to form a new tree of readings, which is attached to the syntactic structure composed of the two morphemes (or syntactic structures) in question. But the connection between a morpheme and its tree of readings can be nothing more than the associative linkage beloved of empiricist philosophers of language; and hence, since exactly the same connection seems to hold between a syntactic structure and the amalgamated set of paths produced by the application of a projection rule as holds between a morpheme and its tree of readings, *that* connection cannot be anything more than an associative linkage either.

The notion that the essence of language is the composition of names is an ancient one, which has been held by many philosophers, including Plato and Hobbes; but it is not one that should commend itself to anyone interested in the nature of fertility and originality in the use of language and committed to an attempt to explain it, at least on the syntactic level, in terms of the character of an internalized system of rules constructed by the learner partly through the operation of an innate learning mechanism. Once we accept such a view it will seem highly plausible to argue that just as learning the meaning of a name involves (in associationist theory) merely associating a phonemic string with some feature of the learner's experience, so learning the ' meaning' of a syntactic structure into which names can enter must merely involve associating the patterning of phonemic strings which corresponds to that structure with another feature of the learner's experience: only a more ' abstract' or ' general' feature.[19] What syntax does, in fact, is to enable us to talk about a class of features of our experience which may be exhibited by the features which names, in the ordinary sense, name. The general thrust of the ideas contained in the ETL quite naturally leads, it seems to me, to the

---

[18] See Wittgenstein, *Philosophical Investigations*, I.48f.

[19] 'Logical form' in the *Tractatus* is, I think, just such a feature, although, of course, Wittgenstein does not intend it to be understood in terms of examples drawn from experience.

theory that syntactic rules are second-order semantic rules (using "semantic rule" here in the ETL sense): versions of this view have been independently put forward by both B. F. Skinner and Charles Morris, for example. But, of course, a reverse order of association of connected ideas is equally possible. If we accept the theory that syntax is second-order semantics, other doctrines of the ETL will begin to seem highly plausible. For example, it will begin to appear plausible that all that is necessary to enable a child to learn language is the presentation of a sufficient range of correctly patterned stimuli; that, after all, since the child has merely to locate recurring features of these patterns of stimuli, we need presuppose no innate machinery of language acquisition except the capacity to perform inductive abstraction; that what is acquired by the exercise of this capacity is not a grasp of rules, but a grasp of meanings; and so on.

It seems to me then, that, far from carrying over the insights of Chomskean linguistics into the theory of linguistic meaning, the "amalgamation-of-readings" technique provides, at least in principle, a beachhead from which to conduct an empiricist or "hard" behaviorist counterattack.[20]

So far as I can determine, Fodor and Katz do intend their theory

[20] A beachhead which, indeed, has already been occupied with commendable celerity by W. V. Quine. Thus: "Conditioned response does retain a key role in language learning. It is the entering wedge to any particular lexicon, for it is how we learn observation terms (or, better, simple observation sentences) by ostension. Learning by ostension is learning by simple induction, and the mechanism of such learning is conditioning. But this method is notoriously incapable of carrying us far in language. This is why, on the translational side, we are soon driven to what I have called analytical hypotheses. The as yet unknown innate structures, additional to mere quality space that are needed in language-learning, are needed specifically to get the child over this great hump that lies beyond ostension, or induction. If Chomsky's antiempiricism or antibehaviorism says merely that conditioning is insufficient to explain language-learning, then the doctrine is of a piece with my doctrine of indeterminacy of translation" ("Linguistics and Philosophy," in *Language and Philosophy*, a symposium edited by Sidney Hook (New York: New York University Press, 1969), pp. 96–97). For some reasons why the antiempiricism suggested by Chomsky's work may, far from being "of a piece with," be incompatible with Quine's indeterminacy thesis, see my "Translations and Taxonomies," *Journal of Philosophical Linguistics* (Spring 1970).

to be taken as an attempt to formulate a theory of semantic competence in the fullest sense. Its aim is to exhibit the structure of the semantic component of "a full synchronic description of a natural language"; and "a synchronic description of a natural language seeks to determine what a fluent speaker knows about the structure of his language which enables him to use and understand its sentences."[21] Now, if what we have said so far in this book is correct, a theory of semantic competence will be very much more complex than Fodor and Katz suppose: it will of necessity share the degree of complexity of a transformational grammar, since its rules reflect in some form every distinction which is made by the corresponding grammar. We may therefore ask why Fodor and Katz should suppose that the dictionary component of an adequate semantic theory will merely associate morphemes or idioms with trees of readings. This belief stems, I think, directly from the way in which they define what they regard as the fundamental problem which a theory of semantic competence must solve: the so-called projection problem. A fluent speaker is able to use and understand an infinite set of sentences in his language, although at any given time he has encountered only a finite set of sentences. Hence, Fodor and Katz argue, the speaker must know a set of rules which "project the finite set of sentences of the language." This is harmless enough, but we now find the projection problem for semantics defined as follows.

> Since the set of sentences is infinite and each sentence is a different concatenation of morphemes, the fact that a speaker can understand any sentence must mean that the way he understands sentences he has never heard before is compositional: on the basis of his knowledge of the grammatical properties and the meanings of the morphemes of the language, the rules the speaker knows enable him to determine the meaning of a novel sentence in terms of the manner in which the parts of the sentence are composed to form the whole.[22]

There is no suggestion here that "the meanings of morphemes" might be determined through the operation of some system of rules

---

[21] Katz and Fodor, "The Structure of a Semantic Theory," in *The Structure of Language*, pp. 481–482.

[22] *Ibid.*, p. 482.

known to the learner. Rather, the notion, 'the meaning of a morpheme', is here taken as a primitive notion for the purposes of the
construction of a semantic theory. Reference to *rules* enters the
theory only in connection with the problem of determining how
someone who knows the 'meanings' of the morphemes, and their
grammatical properties, is enabled to attach meaning to sentences.

Thus the central question of semantics, which I take to be not
(or not primarily) the projection problem, but the problem of specifying the nature of the rules which attach meaning to morphemes, is
begged at the outset, and from this point onwards meaning is
implicitly assumed to involve an associative relationship holding
between words and morphemes and some class of extralinguistic
entities. This is a particularly unfortunate subordination of problems,
since it seems obvious that what we say about the projection problem
will depend largely in the end upon what we believe to be the nature
of semantic rules.

Neither Fodor, Katz, and Postal's semantic theory nor the study
of transformational grammars tell us very much about the actual
process of producing and understanding speech. Fodor and Katz
explicitly disclaim any interest in questions concerning the role of
motivation in speech production, the development of fluency, and
so on, which they regard as proper concerns not for a theory of
semantic competence but for a "psychological" theory of speech
production. Similarly, Chomsky makes a sharp distinction between
theories of competence and theories of performance, and speaks of
the "absurdity of regarding the system of generative rules as a
point-by-point model for the actual construction of a sentence by a
speaker."[23]

A competence theory simply describes what a speaker must know
in order to be said to know a language; it does not attempt to
describe the actual process of speech production, which will obviously
involve a host of special neurological, motivational, perceptual and
other factors which are of no concern to the linguist.

The theory of semantic description which I have put forward in
this book is also, and in exactly Chomsky's sense, a competence
theory; a theory of what is learned in learning the semantics of a

---

[23] Chomsky, *Aspects*, p. 139.

natural language. It is important to keep this in mind, since it might seem on the face of it to be a theory of performance. The rules of linguistic devices are rules for generating actual English (or French, or Tamil) sentences, after all, and they involve references to actual perceptual states and to procedures of various types (matching, searching within defined limits, dropping perpendiculars) which actual users are conceived as carrying out. To this extent, indeed, the sort of semantic competence theory which we have outlined here would, it is true, come much closer than a transformational grammar or a semantic description of the sort proposed by Fodor, Katz, and Postal, to representing the actual process of speech production. But it is quite clear, I think, that this representation would be merely an ideal one: that is, it would represent only what the speech production process would have to contain, given that the speech produced was English speech, and thus speech determined by the semantic rules of English. Such a representation merely sets certain conditions which must be met in the speech production process: it does not tell us how—by what neurological or psychological processes they are *in fact* met, and of course it tells us nothing about all the other factors which may affect actual speech production. Theorizing of the sort which has occupied us here may serve to organize empirical studies: it cannot replace them.

The theory that I have proposed is in a general sense a "use theory of meaning." Certain objections to this kind of theory have become commonplace in the literature of generative-transformational linguistics, and it may not be out of place to consider them now.

These objections boil down to two. The first is that ordinary-language philosophy has failed to produce clear explications of such crucial notions as 'use and misuse of language,' 'rule of use,' and so on, relying rather on metaphorical or analogical accounts which themselves require explication. To this Fodor adds the charge that the "ordinary language" philosopher (in particular Ryle[24]) adopts a notion of use according to which only words and not sentences can have uses and that this leads to a "failure to appreciate

[24] In "Use, Usage, and Meaning," *Proceedings of the Aristotelian Society*, supplement vol. XXXV (1961).

the significance of the systematic character of the compositional features of language."[25]

Obviously all that I can do with this objection at this stage is to disclaim the errors which it castigates. I have tried to give a clear and nonmetaphorical account of the concepts which Fodor and Katz rightly regard as crucial for a use theory of meaning. Moreover, I do not think that the explications I have given are merely idiosyncratic; they connect in a good many ways with the practice and the theoretical assumptions of what Fodor and Katz would call ordinary-language philosophy. However, it should be clear that "use" in my sense does not attach only to words. The use of an utterance is defined by the rules of the linguistic device or devices which generate it, and the rules of linguistic devices can operate with equal facility upon single words or syntactic schemata. What I have said in the first half of this chapter, and related material elsewhere in the book, must suffice to rebut the charge that a use theory of meaning must ignore the syntactic and compositional features of language.

The second objection which I have in mind is less of an objection than an attitude of mind. Linguists and psycholinguists who have learned much from Chomsky tend to deprecate any idea that the notion of use might play any significant part in the explanation of language. The reason for this attitude is quite simple. They believe, no doubt rightly, that a theory of language acquisition based upon reinforcement—that is, upon the satisfaction of the child's desires in consequence of its learning how to use language—cannot possibly be correct. It seems to follow, therefore, that any theory which emphasizes the usefulness of language to the child in social situations, which represents language as a box of tools, or a set of problem-solving procedures, must be barking up the wrong tree.

Eric Lenneberg has argued forcefully that the comparative utility of language to the child must be very slight, since congenitally deaf children of two or older manage to get along perfectly well in everyday social intercourse without it, by acquiring a very highly developed set of techniques for communication by pantomine and other forms of sign language: techniques which allow them to freely communicate

[25] Katz and Fodor, Introduction to *The Structure of Language*, p. 11.

"their desires, needs, and even their opinions." Language, says Lenneberg "is extremely complex behavior, the acquisition of which, we might have thought, requires considerable attention and endeavor. Why do hearing children bother to learn this system if it is possible to get along without?"[26]

Lenneberg's answer is, of course, that the child possesses an innate language-acquisition device, and this conclusion is also strongly suggested by the fact that, although the language environment of children appears to vary considerably, the age of onset of various speech and language capabilities remain fairly constant as between different individuals and children in different cultures and social circumstances—along with much other supporting evidence.

An obvious, if incautious, conclusion appears to follow from all this. It is that the usefulness of language is a relatively peripheral aspect of it, and one which is not likely to be of much importance for the theoretical understanding of linguistic phenomena. Psycholinguists and linguists have not been slow in drawing this conclusion. One of the distinguishing features of contemporary writing is, indeed, the tendency of writers to throw as much stress as possible on the *uselessness* of language—the vast and needless complexity of its formation rules, the functional redundancy, and, from a practical point of view, the arbitrariness of its syntactic structures—as a means of throwing into clearer focus the need for an appeal to complex, innate mechanisms to explain its acquisition.

But that this conclusion is unwarranted is evident if one thinks about it carefully. A use theory of meaning need not commit its defenders to any view about the psychological character of language acquisition. A use theory may offer an answer, not to the question "How is a language learned?" but to the question "What is learned in learning a language?" Thus we can say that a given linguistic device has certain rules and that, having these rules, it fulfills a certain social purpose (consider, for example, the conventions of issuing and responding to requests for objects to be brought; of keeping track of events by reference to a calendar) without committing ourselves to any opinion about that mechanism by which the child

[26] Eric H. Lenneberg, *Biological Foundations of Language* (New York: John Wiley and Sons, 1966), p. 140.

acquires the ability to use that device and, in particular, without having to claim that references to the functional aspects of such a device must enter, *via* the mechanisms of "conditioning" or "training," into our account of its acquisition.

Our answer to the question, "What is the child learning in learning language?" is, in fact, "a system of rule systems which simultaneously subserve, and create the possibility of, certain types of human relationship which can only be adequately described by reference to human needs and purposes." Our answer to the question "How are these systems of rules learned?" may well refer to innate structures rather than to training or conditioning. But if we fail to see that not all talk of need and function in connection with language is inimical to a realistic theory of acquisition, we may end by adopting a theory of language which makes it appear that the vast complexity of syntax is virtually irrelevant to the function of language as an instrument of communication and is an arbitrary complexity at least in the sense that all the purposes of communication which are actually subserved by language might in theory be achieved by some very much simpler device.

Some such view appears to be implicit in much of Fodor's and Lenneberg's writing about language. One might infer from some of their remarks that they regard language as a largely decorative accomplishment of vast, but inutile, complexity, which members of the human species are for some unknown reason innately predisposed to master, but whose functions, such as they are, might be subserved in an entirely satisfactory way by some very much simpler form of sign or gesture language. Lenneberg's argument about the communicative powers of the congenitally deaf clearly depends for its force upon some such assumption: the sign language used by the congenitally deaf must be not merely quite effective but *exactly as effective as language* for it to follow that there is no advantage to be gained by the normal child in learning to speak.[27] Fodor, as reported

[27] Similarly, Lenneberg's claim (in *Biological Foundation of Language*) that the child is relatively independent of visual cues is, if true, inconclusive. We could, if we had to, rewrite most of our model linguistic devices in terms of tactile or kinaesthetic or auditory ones. To prove his point conclusively, Lenneberg would require a case of a child's learning language without benefit of *any* sensory input at all.

in one of the discussions in the Miller and Smith *Genesis of Language*, makes the point quite explicitly:

> Fodor's argument was that any attempt to show that each linguistic structure corresponded to a need would rapidly generate the conclusion that human language was the worst possible system for communication. Logicians who had investigated language had started by throwing out almost all its syntactic baggage, essentially because it was enormously complex, mathematically absurd and uneconomical. Nobody in his right mind would attempt to build an artificial language based on phrase structure plus transformations, yet such a system was of necessity brought from one language to another and acquired by every child in learning his first language. Fodor did not think it worthwhile even to try to devise an argument that such syntactic complexities facilitated communication—unless one happened to be an infant human being learning a first language.[28]

This is, to say the least, an argument which can cut both ways. Surely too much water must have flowed under too many philosophical bridges for it to be quite as clear now as it may have appeared in the thirties that everything which can be said in English, or any other natural language, can be said equally well in an artificial language founded upon the twin pillars of formal logic and positivist epistemology. Moreover, the formal languages of logical empiricism were from their inception intended, at least by their more cautious exponents, to represent not the most perfect systems for communication at large, but only a system for communicating what is expressed by the language of science, and especially of physical science. In any event, part of what I have tried to establish in the first two Parts of this book is that language is not functionally equivalent to any of the model systems of communication (sign systems, the Skinnerian 'tact' and 'mand', sets of images) proposed by empiricists in explication of the concept of linguistic meaning, partly because by means of language one can communicate more, and more precisely, than by means of any such systems. In the present chapter I have tried to show that the pattern of phrase structure plus transformations exhibited by the grammars of natural languages can be related more or less

[28] Smith and Miller, *The Genesis of Language*, p. 270.

directly to *functional* exigencies inherent in the nature of systems of linguistic devices considered as systems for fulfilling certain social needs. These arguments must now be left to stand on their own feet.

13.5 It has been customary among linguists to think of the various levels of linguistic description— the "components" (syntactic, phonological, semantic, and so forth) which would make up an integrated theory of linguistic description— as logically quite independent of one another. On the level of speculation about the psychological and neurological processes underlying the acquisition and use of language, this view expresses itself in the construction of flow charts such as the one on page 251. Such diagrams represent the total "language machine" of the human organism as an arithmetical aggregate of subordinate "machines," the only connection being that each box in the diagram accepts the output of one or more other boxes.

The arguments of this book seem to compel us to the conclusion that this view is mistaken in one crucial respect. The semantic component of a language is not a *component* in the above sense: that is, it is false that one could construct a self-contained "semantic machine" which could then be attached to a self-contained "grammar machine" and a self-contained "phonology machine" to yield a machine capable of representing the full linguistic competence of a normal human adult. If we are correct, the semantic component of an integrated theory of linguistic description would state the rules of a system of linguistic devices. But an account of the rules of a language considered as a system of linguistic devices will represent within itself in some form or other not only the whole of the semantics of the language but also the whole of its grammar and the whole of its phonology. No doubt this grammatical and phonological information will be represented in a highly unsystematic and inconvenient way from the point of view of the grammarian or the phonologist. We shall therefore need, for all the usual and obvious reasons, to construct grammars and phonologies of the ordinary kind; and, indeed, without the independent study of grammar and phonology we should lack essential means of checking on the adequacy of our accounts of linguistic devices. But on this view a grammar would not represent a self-contained component of an ideal speaker's total linguistic competence. Rather, the whole of such a speaker's competence would be represented by our account of his language as a system of linguistic devices, and our accounts of the grammar and phonology of his language would, in effect, be abstractions for special purposes of certain types of information already contained in that account.

The relationships of semantics, syntax, and phonology within an integrated theory of linguistic description can, then, on our view, be represented as follows:

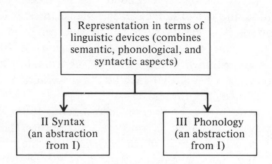

We cannot, however, derive from this diagram a flow chart representing the elements of the speaker's competence. Such a flow chart, if it were possible to draw it, would be a reflection of the detailed contents of box I.

It might be thought that this account of the relationship between syntax and semantics would tend to destroy the autonomy of linguistics, but this is not, I think, the case, for reasons discussed earlier. I am proposing no changes in the methods of linguistics; my concern is purely with the metatheory of linguistics, and in particular, with the relationship between what the linguist discovers and the semantic aspect of language.

I have, however, made—at least by implication—methodological proposals for the study of semantics. What I have tried to do in this direction is to show how the study of linguistic devices might yield a kind of descriptive semantics, which might reasonably hope in time to stand beside generative-transformational linguistics as part of an integrated science of language. Such a descriptive semantics would be free of the vagueness, intuitiveness, and the lack of a clear boundary between its results and those of other forms of empirical inquiry which has characterized much (though not all) philosophical discussion of semantic questions. Its aims would be to represent the semantics of a language in terms of a finite system of clearly and precisely stateable rules. It would make use of the intuitions of native speakers as data, but its results would not themselves be expressions of intuition. It would incorporate, and incidentally provide a theoretical basis for, certain forms of conceptual analysis. And since the theory of linguistic devices enables us to draw a clear and nonmetaphorical distinction between the meaning of a sentence and the truth conditions of a statement, the sort of descriptive semantics which I have in mind would be clearly distinguished from other forms of empirical inquiry as the study of certain systems of human linguistic convention. In short, such a study would parallel structural linguistics in its methodology and its status as an independent branch of inquiry.

There are certain respects in which the task of the linguist might be simplified by the development of this kind of descriptive semantics. A good deal of complex machinery—certain forms of selectional restriction rules and subcategorization rules, for example—has to be introduced into a transformational grammar in order to exclude semantically anomalous expressions, and even then the ground of their anomaly remains quite obscure. If what we said in Chapter 11 is correct, all problems of semantic anomaly could be dealt with quite simply and naturally within a theory of linguistic devices. Such a theory would not only offer us a principled way of distinguishing semantic anomaly from ungrammaticalness but would exclude semantically anomalous expressions from the class of well-formed expressions of a language in a way precisely analogous to the way in which an adequate grammar excludes ungrammatical ones—by simply failing to generate them. We might, then, solve the problem of semantic anomaly for grammars simply by stipulating that the class of expressions all and only whose members must be generated by an adequate grammar is to comprise all and only the expressions generated by the linguistic devices of that language.

The theory of linguistic devices further provides possible explanations of certain abstract features of the grammars of natural languages: notably, of couse, of the salient fact of their division into phrase structure and transformational components. Chomsky addresses himself to this question in his Appendix to Lenneberg's *Biological Foundations of Language*[29] and suggests that one reason why human languages should have a design of this sort is that "the conditions of lexical insertion" are transformational in nature. That is to say, the rules which generate strings of category symbols are simply rewriting rules, whereas the rules which replace category symbols with words are transformational rules. This suggests a semantic basis of some sort for the transformational character of syntax; what we have said here may perhaps take this proposal a little further by suggesting a mechanism by which the semantic structure of language might come to be represented in terms of transformational rules in a grammar, thus explaining successively both the transformational character of the conditions of lexical insertion and the transformational character of grammar.

Again, Chomsky points out[30] that semantic interpretations of sentences must involve cyclic application of interpretative rules to larger and longer segments of the sentence until the whole is interpreted. Thus the semantic interpretation of

(36) The fact that everyone disregarded John disturbed him

depends, in part, on the semantic interpretation of "everyone disregarded John" and would be changed in a fixed way if the latter were replaced by "life seemed to pass him by." But neither (37) nor (38) contains "everyone disregarded John" as a component part, although (36)–(38) must all be assigned essentially the same semantic interpretation.

(37) What disturbed John was being disregarded by everyone

(38) Being disregarded by everyone disturbed John

Hence, Chomsky suggests that the deep structures underlying (36)–(38) must be rather similar, despite the divergencies in surface structure.

---

[29] Lenneberg, *Biological Foundation of Language*, p. 435.

[30] *Ibid.*, p. 416.

If we are right, the process of constructing sentences essentially involves the interpolation of the rules of one linguistic device into another, and sometimes the interpolation of one syntactic schema into another. In either case the semantic interpretation of sentences must necessarily be a cyclic process. Further, it is possible that we might succeed in explaining the gap between the deep and surface structures of (36)–(38), by showing that while the main or dominant syntactic schema of each sentence is different, all three sentences satisfy the same operations. On p. 162 of *Aspects* Chomsky draws attention to such sentence pairs as the following:

(39) (a) John strikes me as pompous—I regard John as pompous

(b) John bought the book from Bill—Bill sold the book to John

He points out that the meaning relations which such sentences exhibit cannot be adequately accounted for in terms of any mechanism available to a transformational grammar and concludes that "consequently, it seems that beyond the notions of surface structures (such as 'grammatical object') and deep structure (such as 'logical subject'), there is some still more abstract notion of 'semantic function' still unexplained."[31]

One notion of "semantic function" which we have developed here may do the trick for cases of this kind. That is, it may be possible to show that the rules governing the use of 'bought' and 'sold' are such that 'John bought the book from Bill' satisfies more or less the same operations as 'Bill sold the book to John'. If we could show this, then we would have shown these two sentences to be functionally (or, as one might equally well say, semantically) equivalent in a perfectly clear sense. Such a demonstration would have the advantage of exhibiting the relationship holding between two such sentences as a semantic relationship (holding in virtue of the rules of language being what they are) and not a factual relationship (holding in virtue of certain statements being contingently true of buyers and sellers), as would be the case with "John was offensive to Bill"–"Bill was offended by John," if it happened to be the case that offensiveness invariably produced offence. We need to notice, in other words,

[31] Chomsky, *Aspects*, p. 163.

that the relationships between the truth values of the initial halves
of (39) and the truth values of the terminal halves are necessary ones.

In general, a semantic theory based upon the notion of a linguistic
device seems to me to offer the only way of conceiving of the internal
relationships (which, as Chomsky remarks,[32] must be supposed to
hold between lexical items) as relationships of a tolerably prosaic
and unmetaphysical kind. Without such a theory we seem to be
confronted by the two equally unfortunate alternatives of, on the
one hand, an atomist theory of meaning, and on the other, some sort
of essentially metaphysical account of such relationships, in terms of
real category differences or the synthetic *a priori*.

One trial Chomskean puzzle may be worth discussing. Chomsky
points out[33] that expressions which deviate from semantic well-
formedness by breaking selectional rules, such as those which pro-
hibit abstract nouns in certain contexts, for example:

(40) (a) the boy may frighten sincerity

(b) misery loves company

are easier to interprete than deviant expressions which break strict
subcategorization rules, such as those by which verbs are strictly
subcategorized as Intransitives, Transitives, Pre-Adjectival, and so
on; for example:

(41) (a) John elapsed that Bill will come

(b) John became Bill to leave

Moreover, such expressions as (40) can usually have an interpretation
imposed upon them by direct analogy with well-formed expressions
which observe the rules which the former break, while no such procedure appears to be available to us in the case of such expressions
as (41). Why, Chomsky asks, is this the case?

An answer might run as follows. Grammatical categories are, if
we are correct, the reflection of relationships holding between the

[32] *Ibid.*, p. 160.

[33] *Ibid.*, pp. 148–149.

parts of syntactic schemata, in virtue of similarities holding between the patterns of rules exhibited by the (similar) linguistic devices to which they belong. In a language there is a finite stock of linguistic devices (though possibly quite a large one). It may be that the distinction between strict subcategorization features and selectional features reflects an underlying distinction between combinations of words which *simply do not constitute an instantiation of any syntactic schema*: that is, which are such that we cannot in their case identify *any* linguistic device by reference to whose rules we might commence the semantic interpretation of the expression in question; and combinations which merely represent improper instantiations of perfectly recognizable syntactic schemata (improper, that is, in the sense explained in Chapter 11).

We may well ask, what could give rise to such an underlying distinction? The answer will probably depend on which words in a given language happen to be the pivots of syntactic schemata. What has happened in (41)(a), for example, seems to be that someone has begun with some such syntactic schema as

(42) ____ believed ____

In (42), the terminal blank can accept a variety of fillers from '(his) mother' to 'the Nicaean Creed', while the initial blank can accept any designating phrase singling out a person ("can," here, means "can, given the nature of the rules of the corresponding linguistic device"). He has then instantiated the initial blank with 'John' and the terminal blank (ungrammatically) with 'Bill will come', to give the reasonably acceptable sentence,

(43) John believed that Bill will come

But he has then removed the *pivot word* (indeed, the only word) of the original syntactic schema, and replaced it by the pivot word of a quite different syntactic schema,

(44) ____ elapsed

which has no terminal blank and whose initial blank cannot accept designating phrases singling out persons. Not surprisingly, we are unable to single out any linguistic device whose rules we might bring to bear on (41)(a). The examples of (40), on the other hand, are not the result of tampering with pivot words but are constructed by inserting inappropriate words (usually nouns; verbs, for reasons which any reader can construct for himself from the contents of previous chapters, seem to me to be most often the pivot words of syntactic schemata) in the blanks of otherwise well-defined (that is, adequately identified) syntactic schemata.

It goes without saying that, in the absence of fully constructed descriptions of systems of linguistic devices, such explanations as the foregoing remain almost wholly speculative, but they may have some value in suggesting possible directions for future work.

14 Linguistic universals and language learning

14.1 The study of generative grammar reveals that a language is an extraordinarily complex structure of rules; and yet a child learns to speak his native language in a very short space of time. His development from his earliest babblings to a more or less complete mastery of normal adult fluency appears to be a smooth and continuous process, whose advance is affected only marginally by differences in type or degree of stimulation or opportunities for practice. Maturational schedules are more or less constant from individual to individual, and no false starts or systematic accumulations of erroneous practices are observed.[1]

Facts such as these have prompted some linguists and psychologists, influenced among other things by the work of ethologists on imprinting and allied phenomena, to suggest that human beings possess a species-specific hereditary, and hence an innate, capacity to acquire mastery of a language in early childhood. Presumably a child is not innately predisposed to learn a particular human language: the notion of an innate capacity to learn Malayalam or Old Faroese

[1] See Eric H. Lenneberg, *Biological Foundations of Language*; Frank Smith and George A. Miller, *The Genesis of Language*, *passim*.

is for various reasons implausible. What has been proposed, therefore, is that all human languages are constructs which share certain general characteristics and that these characteristics are somehow encoded or represented in that part of the child's neurological endowment which corresponds to his innate linguistic ability. Thus, when a child confronts the data—the speech of the adults around him—on which he must base his own linguistic development, he "knows" by reason of this innate endowment that what he is hearing is language and that the language in question will turn out to be a system of a type which is defined already for him by the same innate endowment. Thus his problem is merely to work out *which* of the possible languages of this type is the language of his community.²

These ideas are obviously related to the theories of universal grammar, *characteristica universalia*, and the like developed by the Port Royal logicians, Leibniz, and others in the seventeenth and eighteenth centuries.³ Hence, it is natural that the term *linguistic universals* should have been introduced to describe the contents of the child's presumed innate linguistic endowment. Chomsky has further distinguished between *substantive* and *formal* universals. A claim to have established the existence of a substantive universal would be a claim to the effect that any item of a given sort in any language must be drawn from a finite set of such items whose characteristics can be definitively specified independently of any particular language. Thus the claim that there are a small finite number of phonetic features, characterized in terms of acoustics and articulation, and that these features suffice for the description of the phonetic component of any language, would be a claim of this sort. An example of a claim to have established the identity of a formal universal, on the other hand, would be the claim that any language must contain transformational rules.

Chomsky has put the claims for the existence of "innate knowledge" in a seventeenth-century background, by relating them to the rationalism of Leibniz and Descartes and contrasting them with certain features of Lockean empiricism. This has led to a voluminous

---

² Chomsky, *Aspects*, p. 27f.

³ Chomsky has drawn some of the connections in *Cartesian Linguistics* (New York: Harper & Row, 1966).

philosophical controversy,[4] marked by much mutual misunderstanding and cross-purposes, over the question whether the innateness hypothesis is destructive of "Empiricism." (The idea that entire philosophical outlooks can hang upon the fate of single doctrines or arguments has not been the least important source of confusion in this debate.) It is hence impossible to avoid these issues: accordingly, I shall now deal briefly first with the topic of linguistic universals, and, second with the rationalism versus empiricism debate.

14.2 It seems clear that, since children learn language while animals do not, and learn it quite fast and on a set maturational schedule, there must be *something* relevant to language acquisition which children possess and animals do not. And if we fully understood the nature of what is learned in learning a language—could fully represent a language as a system of rules, that is—it would be quite reasonable to examine the rule structure of all languages to see whether they did not possess some features, perhaps quite abstract features, in common. And then, if we found that such features could not be explained as arising from common characteristics of more fundamental systems of linguistic rules, it would be sensible to see whether we could not explain them in terms of the structure of an innate language-learning mechanism specific to *homo sapiens*. If we were to proceed in this way I think there would be no doubt that we should be employing the notion of a linguistic universal in a perfectly respectable empirical way. And this is, I believe, exactly the sense which the term "linguistic universal" bears in Chomsky's writings.

There seems to me, now, to be nothing hostile to scientific inquiry or empirical method in this suggestion, and nothing to warrant the weight of the philosophical ordnance which has been wheeled out to bombard it. The only further contribution which I have to make to the discussion of this question is this. Some of the features of language

---

[4] The contributions to this debate are now too numerous to be conveniently cited here. A good selection, including the opening salvo from Hilary Putnam and Nelson Goodman, can be found in one or another of two collections of articles: J. R. Searle, ed., *The Philosophy of Language* (New York: Oxford University Press, 1971); and Sidney Hook, ed., *Language and Philosophy* (New York: New York University Press, 1969).

and learning which at present prompt linguists and psychologists to postulate innate structures might turn out to be explicable in terms of the account of language as a system of communication which would be afforded by a semantic description in terms of linguistic devices. And, although it might still be true that some features of systems of linguistic devices might compel us to postulate innate structures and capacities, the character of these might be rather different from those which we might be led to postulate on the basis of the study of syntax and phonology.

Thus, for example, I have already suggested possible semantic grounds for features of transformational grammars, such as principles of cyclic interpretation of sentence structure which figure among the grounds usually offered for the postulation of linguistic universals. Later in this chapter I shall make some similar suggestions about some recent work on children's learning of syntax.[5] It remains to be seen whether explanations of the type proposed would turn out to be satisfactory in detail, but if such a program were to succeed, it might make it considerably easier to see what, in the fabric of language, is likely to depend upon the structure of an innate language-acquisition device. In particular we might hope for some elucidation of the notion, at present obscure, of a semantic universal, conceived as an extrasyntactic constraint of some sort upon the intelligible combination of words.

14.3 No empiricist ever held that learning could take place without benefit of some substratum of innate capacities. What is at issue between empiricism and Chomskean "rationalism" is merely the question whether certain rather parsimonious sets of postulated innate capacities could account for the learning of language, given what the language learner has to learn. The aspect of traditional empiricism which Chomsky's arguments cast into doubt seems to me, indeed, to be not so much its denial of "innate knowledge" (whatever that may mean) as its

---

[5] Some interesting suggestions concerning universal features of color vocabularies have recently appeared in Brent Berlin and Paul Kay, *Basic Color Terms* (Berkeley and Los Angeles: University of California Press, 1969). My book *Form and Content* (forthcoming) contains, among other things, an interpretation of these in terms of linguistic devices.

associationism. I mean by "associationism" the doctrine that our conceptual system is built up from the members of some class of perceptual simples (for example, sense-data, stimuli, impressions) by the repeated application of the members of some small set of extensional operations (for example, contiguity, spatio-temporal concommitance, conditioning relationships, relationships of extensional logic, and so on). What the study of generative-transformational grammar shows is simply that the syntax of a language cannot be described in terms of the sorts of operations which, for some empiricists, have traditionally constituted the glue by means of which the simple constituents of experience were to be made to cohere into a complex conceptual scheme.

What I have tried to do in this book is to carry further this attack upon associationism, by showing, or trying to show, that the sorts of logical construction which have been proposed for essential semantic concepts—of a name, of assertion, of a rule of use, and so on—simply do not construct those concepts. And I have tried also to show that an adequate account of the semantics of a natural language yields a conception of our conceptual scheme as far less extensional— far more characterized by internal relationships—than that suggested by empiricist accounts of the nature of meaning.

Chomsky retains from empiricist conceptions of language the notion that the initial acquisition of a language must be an inductive process. Thus he remarks,

> My own view about the matter of induction is essentially that of Peirce, . . . that while induction may be used for "corrective action," it is the innate principle that "gives a rule to abduction and so puts a limit upon admissible hypotheses."[6]

As we saw earlier, a linguistic device, while it may for convenience be represented as a device for "filling in" a syntactic schema, can always be written out without mentioning any unit of syntax, or indeed any category of linguistic description. What the learner of a linguistic device learns, in fact, is a procedure for communicating with other people in some clearly defined way. It does not seem at all

---

[6] Noam Chomsky, "Comments on Harman's Reply," in *Language and Philosophy*, p. 159.

obvious, now, that the learning of such procedures will be best described as a process of induction inference of linguistic relationships from a body of data provided by the utterances of adult speakers.

For on our view what the learner has to learn is not a set of linguistic relationships, nor even the rules of a generative-transformational grammar, at least in the form in which these are presented by the linguist, but a communicative procedure. And he is not trying to arrive at an understanding of how others, of whom he is merely the spectator, communicate; rather, he is himself constantly enmeshed in the communicative process. It may be, therefore, that a more adequate account of language learning might be founded upon a feedback process of the sort suggested, for example, by Gilbert Harman,[7] than upon any sort of inductive process, even an inductive process "given a rule" by a fairly rich innate language-acquisition device.

14.4 It has become fashionable to employ the concept of linguistic universals in psycholinguistics; and I think that here also we can plausibly argue that an adequate theory of semantic description would remove at least some of the difficulties which at present constitute the grounds for the postulation of particular universals.

A good summary of most recent descriptive studies of children's acquisition of linguistic skill is to be found in David MacNeill's long paper, "Developmental Psycholinguistics,"[8] and I shall mainly discuss this in what follows.

These studies are in the main concerned with the development of the child's understanding of syntax. They have dispensed with the notion that child language is merely an impoverished and error-filled version of adult language, with its correlative assumption that we know all about the grammar of child language because we know the grammar of adult language. Instead, they start from the assump-

[7] Gilbert Harman, "Psychological Aspects of the Theory of Syntax," *Journal of Philosophy*, vol. 64 (1967), pp. 75–87.

[8] In Smith and Miller, *The Genesis of Language*, pp. 15–103.

tion that the child's grammar may not be describable in terms of the categories appropriate to adult grammar and that the child at each stage of his development should be regarded as "a fluent speaker of an exotic language" (MacNeill), whose grammar remains to be discovered. The studies generally involve visiting children at monthly intervals during the period when linguistic growth is most rapid. Tape recorders are used to obtain a complete record of all speech to and from the child.

Between eighteen and twenty-four months, children begin to form simple sentences of two or three words, of a type which Brown and Fraser[9] call "telegraphic" for reasons which are obvious from the following examples:

two boot	put truck window
a gas here	Adam make tower
see truck Mommy	

MacNeill suggests that children's telegraphese is not, however, produced by abbreviating longer sentences. The child possesses a simple grammar whose output is telegraphic speech. The attempt to formulate children's earliest grammars has led several investigators to distinguish between "pivot" and "open" classes of words in the child's vocabulary. The pivot class has fewer members than the open class, and each pivot word is used more frequently than any individual open-class word. Early sentences are formed by juxtaposing a pivot-class word with an open-class word or by juxtaposing two open-class words, but never by juxtaposing two pivot-class words. The following are examples:

Pivot	Open
allgone	boy
byebye	sock
big	boat

[9] R. Brown and C. Frazer, "The Acquisition of Syntax," in C. N. Cofer and B. S. Musgrave, eds., *Verbal Behavior and Learning* (New York: McGraw-Hill, 1963).

Pivot	Open
more	fan
my	milk
pretty	plane
see	shoe
night-night	vitamins

The grammar of a child who constructs out of such materials such sentences as

allgone boy	more plane
more milk	byebye shoe

can be represented as containing the single rule,

$$S \longrightarrow \begin{pmatrix} P \\ O \end{pmatrix} + O$$

where the parenthesis represents optional omission. Both pivot and open class are quite heterogeneous from the point of view of adult grammar, containing adjectives, verbs, pronouns, greetings, interjections, and so on. As the child develops, the privileges of occurrence of the words in the pivot class begin to alter. For example, the child begins to produce sentences like

that a my car

in which 'a' occurs before 'my', and to avoid sentences like

that my car

New rules must be written into the child's grammar to account for the resulting new types of sentence which the child is producing. MacNeill quotes the following developmental sequence:

Time

1    $S \longrightarrow (P_1) + N$

2    $S \longrightarrow (Dem) + (Art) + (P_2) + N$

     $S \longrightarrow (Art) + (Adj) + N_2$

3    $S \longrightarrow \begin{Bmatrix} P_3 \\ \text{Poss Pronoun} \\ \text{Dem} \end{Bmatrix} + N$

     $S \longrightarrow (Art) + N + (Adj)$

It is to be noticed that it is only the words in the pivot class which take part in this development. The pivot class begins to differentiate: in MacNeill's graphic phrase, the categories of adult language are peeled away from the pivot class like successive skins of an onion.

Later, the child begins to produce sentences which appear to require transformational rules for their generation. Thus, for example, a very clumsy and elaborate but apparently nontransformational negation system comes to be systematized and simplified into something much more like the transformational adult negation system.

The facts which we have briefly noted raise a variety of questions, or puzzles, with important theoretical implications. One might list them as follows:

(1) Why is there such a marked statistical imbalance between the numbers of words in the pivot and open classes? It is difficult to see how this could be the outcome of imitation of adults. A similar imbalance exists between what are sometimes called function words and content words in adult speech, but the pivot class contains many adult content words (adjectives, verbs, and so on, as well as some function words).

(2) What is the cause of the pivot-class–open-class division itself?

(3) Why is it that a grasp of adult form classes seems to arise as the result of differentiation of the pivot class only?

(4) The child from a very early age possesses the concepts of noun phrase and verb phrase. That is, it constructs NP's and VP's which have the same privileges of occurrence as single N's and V's and which are treated as units from the point of view of substitution, and in other ways. It is hard to see why the child should arrive at hierarchical structures of this sort.

(5) Why should the child begin to use transformations?

MacNeill suggests answers to these questions which in each case rely heavily on the postulation of linguistic universals. MacNeill's discussion of question (2) will serve as an example. MacNeill argues, reasonably, that a child could not differentiate form classes from a pivot class containing a random selection of words. Nor could the child infer adult classes from parental speech without knowing in advance the range of possible form-class distinctions: as MacNeill acutely remarks, "An ability to infer something about language is the capacity to generalize a distinction once its relevance is noticed. We cannot conceive of it as a capacity to invent the distinctions themselves."[10] Whatever competence the child possesses, which manifests itself in the composition of the pivot class, must initially ignore, but in some sense potentially admit, or embrace, all the adult form classes. The child cannot, for this reason, be using distributional evidence, for distributional evidence drawn from adult speech would yield the adult categories. The solution MacNeill proposes does indeed seem to follow quite strictly from the argument so stated. The child must, for each subdivision of the adult category system, possess at the immediately higher level the information which is criterial for dividing the contents of that level between the wings of the subdivision in question.

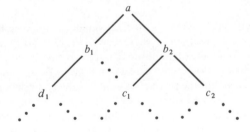

That is, at level a he must already possess whatever information is criterial for dividing the contents of a between b_1 and b_2, at b_2 whatever is criterial for dividing the contents of b_2 between c_1 and c_2, and so on. We must assume, then, that there is a set of distinctions, stateable obviously at a fairly abstract level, which define

[10] MacNeill, "Developmental Psycholinguistics," in Smith and Miller, *The Genesis of Language,* p. 29.

the hierarchy of form classes for any natural language, that a knowledge of this universal hierarchy is part of the child's innate linguistic endowment, and that his problem is thus merely to discover what corresponds in English to each level of the universal hierarchy.

I think that MacNeill is quite right to think that some such position as this follows from his premises, including the known empirical data. But it seems to me that his premises include one extremely important assumption which is not entailed by the empirical data. This is the assumption that the child *infers* whatever grammatical knowledge it acquires from a *body of data* provided by adult speech. One would never guess from reading MacNeill or any other recent writer on linguistics or psycholinguistics that child and adult together form part of the same linguistic community. Their child, like Quine's, is a small anthropologist, who remembers what he hears but who otherwise—at least so far as his learning is concerned—plays no part in the social life of the adult tribe whose usages are the object of his study. This child is a not unfamiliar figure in philosophy, being, in fact, the father of the Lockean individual man: the possessor of the celebrated *tabula rasa*. Linguists and psycholinguists of the recent generation, who have read Chomsky, seem in general to be under the impression that they have broken decisively with the empiricist tradition—Locke included—because they have revived in modern form the doctrine of innate ideas. But Locke, and empiricism, have a good deal more shot in their locker than is expended in the rejection of innate ideas. In particular, there is the Lockean theory of abstraction, which is quite as integral a part of Locke's theory of knowledge as the rejection of innate ideas. What Chomsky and his school have done, in fact, is to assume (1) that inductive abstraction from a body of presented data is the sole method by which a child can learn the structure of his native language; to argue very correctly (2) that this method is grossly insufficient to explain the learning of what manifestly is learned; and to conclude (3) that the child can only abstractively infer its way to the extraordinarily complex syntactic structure of a natural language if it possesses a considerable body of innate knowledge about what sort of structure to expect.

But we need not confine our criticism of empiricism to the revival of innate ideas. We can also look critically at the doctrine of abstraction. What we have done in this book is simply to deny that a child abstractively infers its way to a knowledge of *meanings* or *syntactic structures*: these things are not, in a sense, what it has to learn in learning language. What it does learn—and we can afford to be quite indifferent to the question of whether it learns it in part by abstractive inference or wholly by other means—is a set of techniques, involving vocal utterance, which are socially useful and which consist in the carrying out of sets of instructions. When it has learned a fair number of these, it possesses capabilities of performance which must be described syntactically in terms of a quite complex system of rules; but this is entirely beside the point, for, if we are correct, these rules are not what the child learns (this is why, when he grows up and becomes a grammarian, he finds his work arduous). The techniques, which are what he does learn, are, individually and in themselves, comparatively simple. Thus the child's accomplishment in learning its native language may not be quite as staggering as it has become customary to claim, although no doubt it is still remarkable. We need not therefore suppose, however, that the learning of language is at all likely to prove to be describable in terms of "training" or stimulus-response theory. Whatever is involved in the learning of linguistic devices, it cannot be simply the careful arrangement of stimuli and reinforcements by the adult linguistic community. The child must surely enter into social relationships with adult members of his community, and his acquisition of linguistic devices must bear some relationship to the possibilities for satisfaction and enlargement of his world which can be realized through specific types of communication with others in that community.[11] We know very little, it seems to me, about the actual mechanisms of human learning, and one essential prerequisite for enlarging our knowledge seems to me to be that we drop the picture of the small child as solitary processer of data.

Can we, though, make any headway with the puzzling facts of linguistic development by dropping this assumption? I think that we can, or rather, I think that our theory of linguistic devices will enable us to construct an interpretation of them which is no more speculative than MacNeill's and a good deal simpler.

---

[11] Richard Allen Chase, in his interesting paper "Evolutionary Aspects of Language Development and Function" (Smith and Miller, *The Genesis of Language*, pp. 253–269) argues for a similar position.

To begin with, we can interpret the pivot-class–open-class distinction in terms of the distinction between words which dominate and identify syntactic schemata and words whose role is to be substituted into the blanks in such schemata. On this view, each pivot word corresponds to a linguistic device, and we can easily imagine, for example, how the rules governing 'allgone ____' or 'byebye ____' might run.

In her book *Language in the Crib*,[12] Ruth Weir collects the monologues of her two-and-a-half-year-old son, recorded during the intervals between going to bed and going to sleep. They include sequences, such as the following, which may represent experimental substitutions of words in syntactic schemata.

go for glasses	go for blouse
go for them	pants
go to the top	go for shoes
go throw	

If the pivot-class words are indeed all words with, as it were, invisible blanks associated with them, we would expect the open class to consist of words which either are, or are capable of being treated as, *labels*: that is, words whose rules of use are patterned on the rules of [**B**]. And indeed, if we look at actual samples of pivot- and open-class words, such as the lists given by MacNeill[13] from which our examples on p. 290 are drawn, we find that the open-class words are indeed of this type. One such list consists of

boy	milk	hot
sock	plane	Mommy
boat	shoe	Daddy
fan	vitamins	

---

[12] Ruth Weir, *Language in the Crib* (New York: Humanities Press, 1970).

[13] MacNeill, "Developmental Psycholinguistics," in Smith and Miller, *The Genesis of Language*, p. 22.

We would not, therefore, expect the open class to exhibit differentiation into form classes. All the words in the open class have rules of use of the same general type, and hence (if our view of the semantic basis of grammatical category is correct) belong to the same form class. The words (or syntactic schemata) in the pivot class, on the other hand, will exemplify every other type of linguistic device, or rather, all the linguistic devices other than labeling devices which the child happens to have in his repertoire will be represented in his speech by words which will fall on distributional grounds into the pivot class. At first the rules governing these words will be extremely simple, but soon more complex linguistic devices, related to the initial ones in the kind of ways in which the members of the developing series [A]–[G] are related, will develop around them, and as this happens the syntactic schemata which they dominate, and their emerging relations with other primitive syntactic schemata, will become more complex. These complexities will appear at the level of distributional analysis as new privileges of occurrence, and it will appear that the members of a new form class have split off from the pivot class and taken up an independent existence.

As the child learns more and more of the linguistic devices of adult language, the form-class distinctions distributionally honored in his speech will approximate more closely to the adult classification. But there is no reason to suppose that the child possessed any innate knowledge of these distinctions before he came willy-nilly to observe them as an indirect result of his piecemeal learning of linguistic devices.

This account of the differentiation allows (as indeed does Mac-Neill's) for the fact that children differ in the particular distinctions they draw (some adjectives are treated by some children as open-class words; by others as pivot-class words). A system of linguistic devices can be learned from any of a large number of starting points following numerous different routes.

In principle we can deal with the other puzzles suggested by the analysis of children's speech. Open-class words are more numerous than pivot-class words because it is *prima facie* easier to learn a new label than to add a whole new linguistic device to one's repertoire. Similarly, we would expect hierarchical structures to arise in the child's grammar, since a system of linguistic devices is, for reasons which by now need not be labored further, an inherently hierarchical construct—while the reader can no doubt construct for himself a plausible account of why the child's usage should come to display syntactic patterns which require description in terms of transformations.

All this is, of course, merely speculative. All that one can conclude in the present state of knowledge is that it may be possible to construct an account of what we know about the stages of language learning in which the main weight of explanation is transferred from postulated innate structures to the structure of postulated systems of learned rules of a certain type. In order to discover how fruitful such an account would be we should have to direct our attention not just to the development of children's grasp of grammar but also the development of the semantic, conceptual, and communicative aspects of children's language. This is indeed what is demanded by some of the contributors to *The Genesis of Language*.[14] If their demands have not been met, it is because the whole subject of meaning is surrounded by philosophical difficulties which need to be removed before empirical investigation can get to work. I have tried, in the manner of Locke's underlaborer, to clear away some of this philosophical underbrush in these chapters. It may be that the attempt to construct model systems of linguistic devices to represent children's conceptual schemes and to check them systematically against the facts of child speech viewed in its full social and communicative framework, might produce considerable advances in understanding. But if anything that I have said here were to prove in any way helpful in clearing the road for empirical study, I should be more than content.

---

[14] See, for example, Dan I. Slobin's comments on MacNeill's paper (pp. 85–91), and Slobin's own paper on "The Learning of Russian as a Native Language" (Smith and Miller, *The Genesis of Language*, pp. 129–249).

appendix
The influence of the empiricist theory of language in psychology

I wish here briefly to suggest how I would set about substantiating the claim made in Chapter 1 that the ETL is theoretically indispensable to the formulation of at least some S-R theories of language. The theories I have in mind are mediation theory, in Osgood's and Mowrer's versions, and Skinnerian associationism. The theoretical connection between them and the ETL is simply this. The enterprise of constructing a behavioral theory of the types represented by Mowrer's, Osgood's, and Skinner's is essentially one of conceptual reductionism. The theorist wishes to show that everything that is true of a given body of phenomena can be expressed within the limits of a given conceptual system which employs, ideally, a small number of clearly defined basic concepts whose relationship to less basic concepts within the system is also well-defined with respect to certain criteria. What I wish to claim is that the conceptual revisions proposed by S-R theorists of language would not be remotely plausible unless they could be considered against the background of the assumption that language is, in reality, as it has been described by the long tradition of empiricist writers beginning with Locke (*Essay*, Book III). The plausibility of S-R theories, that is, depends on the assumption that the ETL is not a *theory* at all but a simple and objective description of linguistic phenomena. If this assumption is false, and the ETL is not, as we have suggested, a description of language but a theory about it, and if the ETL is explanatorily vacuous, it follows that S-R theories must be explanatorily vacuous too. It should be clear that I am not objecting here to the *behaviorism* of S-R theories but to the vacuity of certain *philosophical* assumptions implicit in them, which have in themselves nothing whatsoever to do with the issue of behaviorism versus mentalism. Mentalism is not the only disease which honest empirical scientists can catch from philosophers, and an obsessive concern with avoiding it, while no doubt quite right in itself, can blind the possessor to the possibility of succumbing to more subtle theoretical ailments.

OSGOOD

Osgood introduces his account of language[1] by distinguishing his view from that of Charles Morris and from a hypothetical Pavlovian view, and I shall simply summarize his argument.

A naive application of the principles of Pavlovian conditioning might lead us to represent the process by which a sign acquires meaning as one in which the sign is simply conditioned to the reactions originally made to its significatum. Thus the noise 'bull' becomes a sign for me when I am conditioned to make to it the same response I make to the sight of a bull, namely: running. But this theory is manifestly unsatisfactory; I do not respond to the utterance of 'bull', even though I understand the meaning of that word, with wild flight. Again, to use a stock example, the buzzer which Pavlov conditioned to the salivary reaction of his dogs might be considered a sign of food for the dog. But the dog's response to the buzzer is not coextensive with its response to food: the dog does not try to eat the buzzer.

Osgood represents Morris' view as one which avoids the pitfalls of the naive Pavlovian account. This is because the interpretant of a sign for Morris is simply a disposition to make any of the responses previously elicited by the object (significatum). But this view also

[1] C. E. Osgood, *Method and Theory in Experimental Psychology* (New York: Oxford University Press, 1953), pp. 692–699.

has its difficulties, which arise, Osgood argues, because Morris represents the link between sign and significatum as a partial identity between the behavior produced by the significatum and the behavior in which the interpretant (which, we must recall, is a disposition) manifests itself. Osgood suggests that we should instead represent the link between sign and significatum as follows. The sign elicits in the organism some fractional part of its normal behavior towards the significatum. This fractional response Osgood calls a *representational mediation process*. This now itself serves as a (self-)stimulus, eliciting from the organism ("mediating") the behavior which constitutes its full response to (its "taking account of," in Morris' terms) the sign. It is important, I think, to understand the quite literal force which "representational" has for Osgood in this theory:

> Whereas Morris links sign and object through partial identity of object-produced and disposition-*produced* behavior, we shall link sign and object through partial identity of the 'disposition' *itself* with the behavior elicited by the object. *Words represent things because they produce some replica of the actual behavior towards those things.* This is the crucial identification, the mechanism that ties signs to particular stimulus-objects and not to others.[2]

Osgood can now distinguish between examples of ordinary conditioning and sign processes: "What is it that is common to the learning situations that involve sign-processes and yet lacking in those situations that do not? *The distinguishing condition is the presence or absence of a representational process in association with the stimulus.*"

Osgood's theory has been criticized on various grounds by psychologists, but these criticisms are not our immediate concern. What we wish to examine is the relationship of Osgood's theory to the ETL.

To begin with, Osgood retains the notion, crucial to the ETL, that meaning is a *relationship* of some sort between a sign and a thing signified. Again, he accepts the notion that to know "the meaning of" a sign is to possess some determinate item of mental furniture which is able, by its nature, to govern or determine the behavior, including verbal behavior, which manifests one's understanding of that sign. Price, as we have seen, states this view dispositionally: to

[2] *Ibid.*, pp. 695–696 (my italics).

know the meaning of a word 'ϕ' is to possess a concept ϕ (such a concept being a disposition to correctly identify ϕ's as ϕ's); and concepts are what "keep discourse on the rails."

In Osgood's version of the theory, on the other hand, the crucial item of mental furniture, the possession or lack of which makes the difference between someone who knows the meaning of 'ϕ' and someone who does not, is not a disposition but an occurrence; not a concept but a bit of behavior: for example, the clenching of the right hand and the motion of the wrist which, according to Osgood, may sometimes be exhibited by a young child asked for a hammer. This change from a dispositional account of the notion of a concept to an account in terms of occurrent behavior produces, however, certain strains in the theory. In Price's version, the theory answers two main questions: (1) What is the difference between someone who understands a given word and someone who does not? and (2) How is it that someone who understands a given word can use that word in constructing an indefinitely large range of original sentences, make innumerable appropriate responses to its occurrence in the most various verbal and situational contexts, and in general deploy it successfully in a vast variety of new and unforeseeable ways? Price's answer to (1) is that someone who understands a word is able to recognize the things it refers to—in effect, to judge the correctness or incorrectness of applications of it to particular objects; and to (2) his answer is that what guides us in deploying words is a knowledge of the nature of the things they designate. Osgood's behavioristic version of the concept theory will do as well as Price's in answering question (1). Thus, Osgood can say that what makes the difference between someone, A, who understands the word hammer and someone, B, who does not, is that a representational mediation process occurs in A which does not occur in B. And what enables us, in theory at any rate, to identify some one bit of behavior or some specific neurophysical event or events, as *the meaning* of 'hammer' and thus to distinguish it from other bits of behavior or other neurophysical events which just happen to occur in A whenever he hears, or utters, or subvocalizes the word 'hammer', is that the representational mediation process which we thus identify is, in Osgood's special sense, *representational*.

But things are not nearly such plain sailing when we come to consider Osgood's theory as providing an answer to question (2). Let us first consider an example of Osgood's in which the theory does seem to throw some light upon how a representational mediating process might serve to organize the responses of the person in whom it occurred. The example is the word 'spider', which Osgood, for reasons which will be obvious, considers "a largely connotative sign." Osgood argues:

> The stimulus-object (Ṡ), the actual visual pattern of hairy-legged insect body, elicits a pattern of behavior (R_T), *which in this case includes a heavy loading of autonomic 'fear' activity*. Through short-circuiting, 'detachable' portions of this total behavior to the spider-object (particularly 'anxiety') become conditioned to the sign, the word SPIDER. With repetitions of the sign-process, the magnitude of the representational mediation process becomes reduced to some minimally effortful and minimally interfering replica—but still includes the release of those autonomic reactions which literally confer the unpleasant, connotative meaning of threat upon this word. This mediating reaction (r_m) produces a distinctive pattern of self stimulation (s_m) which can elicit a variety of overt behaviors (R_x)—shivering and saying 'ugh!', running out of a room when someone says, 'There's a spider in here'.[3]

There is no doubt, I think, that so far the theory is genuinely explanatory. In effect, it explains why a man may run out of the room when he hears the word 'spider' by telling us that the noise 'spider' elicits in him reactions of fear and anxiety (which are in their origin reduced or truncated parts of his response to the sight of a spider) and that it is *these* which produce the response of running. But now, the question about this situation which corresponds to our question (2) above is: How does the presence of mediating and self-stimulating reactions r_m and s_m, explain the occurrence of certain overt behavioral responses, R_x? And it seems pretty evident that the answer which Osgood would have to give within the context of this example is that the presence of r_m/s_m explains the occurrence of R_x because flight is one natural component of the response of any organism to fear. In other words, the task of rendering intelligible the relationship between representational mediating process and overt behavior in this

[3] *Ibid.*, p. 696.

example is not performed by Osgood's theory but is sidestepped by means of an implicit appeal to a principle which we are prepared to regard as "natural" or "obvious" enough to explain the connection between r_m/s_m and R_x without itself requiring explanation: namely, the principle that a frightened organism may be expected to flee if it can.

The trouble is that in the case of a great many less "connotative" words there appears to be no relationship of this kind to which such an appeal might be made. Thus, Osgood suggests that the sight and feel of a hammer

> elicits in the young child, usually under instructions or imitation of some adult, a total pattern of behavior, including grasping and pounding movements. According to the mediation hypothesis, anticipatory portions of this behavior become short-circuited to the sign HAMMER. The process of reduction is especially important in the case of denotative signs— obviously, overt movements of the hands will interfere with other on-going instrumental behaviors and therefore tend to be extinguished. A young child, however, may actually be observed to clench his hand and move it up and down when asked for a 'hammer'.[4]

Significantly, Osgood does not go on to sketch in the way in which hand clenchings and incipient poundings serve to organize the great variety of behavior which may on occasion form a part or the whole of an appropriate response to some utterance of the word 'hammer' in context. And indeed, it is difficult to see how such a sketch would run, for there is no "natural" or "obvious" connection between incipient and overt behavior of the types in question, and mediation theory itself is at this point explanatorily null.

Osgood's difficulty is precisely that of translating effectively into the language of behaviorism the supposed insight, derived from the ETL, that what organizes an animal's responses to signs is the nature of the objects which the signs refer to. It should be noticed that this problem does not arise in quite the same form for a theorist like Price who has no particular commitment to behaviorism and who is thus quite prepared to talk of people being able to understand the word 'crocodile' because, say, they "know what crocodiles are

[4] *Ibid.*, p. 697.

like" (have seen crocodiles, can form mental images of crocodiles, are aware of various facts about crocodiles, and so forth). But this is only because the theory can depend on the explanatory force which "know" possesses in ordinary usage. It is, for example, "natural" and "to be expected" that someone who knows that bulls are dangerous will not, other things being equal, enter a closed cattle truck marked "bull." In such examples as this we seem to see clearly enough how being acquainted with the referents of signs may serve to organize our responses to the signs themselves; but, as we have seen, the problem of response organization is not absent from, but merely less visible in, nonbehavioral versions of the ETL.

MOWRER

O. H. Mowrer's theory of language[5] reformulates mediation theory in ways which are dictated partly by Mowrer's general position as a learning theorist and partly, it seems to me, by an attempt to remedy, by a tactical retreat towards a more mentalist outlook, the difficulties which we detected in Osgood's theory. If I am right in thinking that the difficulties confronting the notion of mediation as an explanatory concept stem not from the degree of behaviorist rigor, or lack of it, with which such theories are constructed, but from its implicit involvement with the ETL, then we should expect the lines of development which Mowrer pursues to fail to yield a theory of greater explanatory power than Osgood's; and in fact, as I think we shall see, such expectations are justified.

From a theoretical point of view, Mowrer's object is to resolve, by means of the notion of mediation, certain apparent anomalies in learning theory which arise because of the existence of experiments which seem to demonstrate the existence of so-called "latent learning." His suggestion is that a stimulus may produce in an animal a mediating response in the form of an emotion of fear or hope. This emotion may later be aroused in a different situation by the same stimulus and may determine the behavior of the animal in that situation. This latter behavior will then appear as an instance of latent

[5] O. Hobart Mowrer, *Learning Theory and the Symbolic Processes* (New York: Wiley, 1960).

learning: that is, it will not previously have occurred and been subject to strengthening by reinforcement.

In discussing language, Mowrer expands his theory in two directions, first by developing it into an account of the psychological mechanism involved in the understanding of names and sentences, and second by supplementing this account with a theory of cognitive meaning as dependent upon imagery.

Mowrer's discussion of sentences assumes implicitly that "sentence" means "subject-predicate sentence." (The discussion is conducted entirely in terms of the paradigm instance 'Tom is a thief'.) His fundamental point is that the sentence so understood is not merely a complex stimulus, the response to which is a compound of the responses previously conditioned to its parts, but a device for bringing about new learning. This view has as its consequence the thesis that the psychological processes involved in understanding a sentence are essentially the same as those involved in learning the meaning of a word. Thus Mowrer argues,

> the word "Tom" acquired its meaning, presumably, by being associated with, and occurring in the context of, Tom as a real person. Tom himself has elicited in John and Charles and others who have had first-hand contact with him a total reaction which we can label R_T, of which r_T is a component. And as a result of the paired presentation or concurrence of "Tom"-the-word and Tom-the-person, the component or "detachable" reaction, r_T, is shifted from the latter to the former.[6]

In the same way, the mechanism of the sentence involves the transference of a detachable component reaction from the predicate word to the subject word. We may think of 'thief' as acquiring meaning in the same way as 'Tom' and as having as its meaning a detachable component reaction, r_t. Now, if some veracious person says to me, 'Tom is a thief', the r_t reaction will get shifted from the word 'thief' to the word 'Tom', and I shall begin, to put it roughly, to react to Tom as I do to thieves. But we must, as Mowrer points out, be careful here. If we say simply that r_t becomes conditioned to 'Tom', then we shall in effect be saying that the sentence 'Tom is a thief' serves to *change the meaning* of 'Tom', and this is patently absurd. Accordingly, we

[6] *Ibid.*, p. 144.

must instead say that the reaction r_t becomes conditioned (not to 'Tom', but) to the reaction r_T, which constitutes the meaning of 'Tom'. We are now in a position to explain how it is that my behavior toward Tom is changed by my hearing the utterance 'Tom is a thief' from the lips of a veracious friend. When I later meet Tom, the sight of him produces in me the total reaction R_T; a part of this reaction is r_T; and this in turn elicits in me the 'thief' reaction r_t, which has been conditioned to r_T by my friend's utterance.

This development of mediation theory, although it is more complex and subtle than Osgood's version, seems to me to suffer, as a theory of language, from exactly the same defect: it fails to explain the nature of the connection between the mediating responses which according to it constitute the meanings of words and sentences and the overt behavioral and verbal responses which actually manifest someone's understanding of an utterance in a language he knows.

Mowrer might object that this question is not meant to be answered by his theory of the sentence but by his theory of cognitive meaning. We must now explore this possibility.

Mowrer sees that the notion of mediation as he has formulated it in terms of emotion will not account for the cognitive or descriptive components of the meanings of words:

The word "apple" not only carries the implication of something liked or disliked, but also of an object with certain *sensory* qualities. And, thus far, our account of learning contains no provision for explaining *this* as opposed to the purely emotional, evaluative aspect of the meaning reaction.[7]

To fill this gap, Mowrer introduces the notion of images as the mediating responses corresponding to the cognitive meanings of words, which he conceives in a straightforwardly Humian way, as fading vestiges or residues of sensations. We can now understand why Mowrer is not conscious of a gap, in his account of the mechanism underlying the understanding use of 'Tom is a thief', between the occurrence of the mediating response r_t and the subject's overt or behavioral response to the stimulus of seeing Tom. The response r_t

[7] *Ibid.*, p. 164.

is to be understood as an image, the occurrence of which serves to remind its possessor of what thieves are like: being so reminded he knows, naturally, how to behave and speak appropriately to Tom.

To sum up: Mowrer, like Osgood, supplements the explanatory power of mediation theory with an appeal to common sense: that is, to principles which we can all be expected to regard as so "natural" and "obvious" as, themselves, to require no further explanation. In the one example in which Osgood makes this appeal explicit, it is to the principle that flight, cries, and so on, are a natural response to fear. Mowrer makes a more general and powerful appeal of the same kind, and, significantly enough, this appeal is to the principle, central to the ETL, that to be aware of the nature of whatever thing it is that a word refers to is to possess all the understanding necessary to guide one in using and responding to that word in all or most contexts.

It is hardly surprising that Mowrer should be led to cap the edifice of mediation theory with this principle, for most of the other central doctrines of the ETL have already been built into the foundations of the theory. By treating all learning as sign learning, Mowrer has implicitly committed himself to the view that inductive abstraction, or some behavioristic analogue of it, is overwhelmingly the most important and fundamental process operating in the learning by a speaker of his native language. From this it is a short step to the view that names are the fundamental bearers of meaning in language.[8] And finally, Mowrer's belief in the prime significance of the notions of inductive abstraction and naming for any psychological theory of language leads him to a view of the nature of sentences entirely in accord with the ETL. For on Mowrer's view, a sentence is simply a collocation of names so arranged that parts of the meanings of some can be conditioned to the meanings of others. This view implies that the structure of sentences is determined entirely by what sorts of conditioning we want to bring about by conjoining names. This will clearly depend upon what the names in question mean and upon what we want to say about our subject matter: thus, ultimately upon the nature of (or better, perhaps, what happens to be true of) that subject matter. Thus, Mowrer's account of the sentence commits him to a behaviorist reformulation of the view that the syntactic rules of

[8] *Cf. ibid.*, pp. 159–162.

a language are wholly and simply an expression of the empirical nature of the referents of its basic names; or, to put it crudely, that the reason why words can only be inserted in sentential contexts in certain ways is that the things to which they refer are the sorts of things they are.

SKINNER

I shall not attempt to summarise Skinner's elaborate and complex theory and shall assume familiarity with it.[9] It seems worth remarking, however, that Skinner's account of tacts exactly mirrors the traditional theory of ostensive definition. For " controlling stimulus " we can write " paradigm series of ϕ objects "; the generalized reinforcer which serves to condition the disposition to utter a tact can be equated with the word of praise with which we (supposedly) convey to a child that it was right to say ' red ' to a given balloon or bus—more importantly, a tact acquires its meaning purely and simply by *association with* a constant pattern of stimulation. A tact, in effect, is a name, hence naming is as central to Skinner's account of language as to the ETL. Interestingly, Skinner is led by this conception of naming to the view, which we have earlier argued to be characteristic of the ETL, that the act of exhibiting a picture or a physical object can amount to uttering a name: "A man may say, ' *I never go out without carrying my* . . .' and finish by displaying an automatic drawn from his belt. The act of display is verbal according to our definition and is equivalent to the verbal response *automatic*, though much more complete as a description."[10] My reply to this (see Chapter 2) would be that showing the automatic pistol is not a linguistic performance at all, let alone a *description*.

Again, it is only in a context of assumptions drawn from the ETL that Skinner's account of sentence construction makes sense. For Skinner, autoclitics are just second-order tacts—tacts associated, no doubt, with highly abstract properties of first-order tacts and the situations in which they occur, but still tacts. Hence, for Skinner, the ability to construct new and original utterances is to be explained, just as in more traditional formulations of the ETL, by reference to

[9] B. F. Skinner, *Verbal Behavior* (New York: Appleton-Century-Crofts, 1957).

[10] *Ibid.*, p. 124.

the fact that the possessor of such abilities is acquainted with the referents of the basic signs out of which such utterances are to be built (in Skinner's language, the fact that certain tacts are under the control of certain stimuli).

We can now see, I think, that the explanatory vacuity of the concept of stimulus control, with which Chomsky[11] rightly taxes Skinner, is not some idiosyncratic error peculiar to Skinner. Related lapses of explanatory force occur at related points in the work of Mowrer and Osgood, over the question of the nature and location of the mediating responses which (allegedly) constitute the meanings of "denotative" signs and over the even more difficult and fundamental question of how the study of such responses, even if they were locatable, could in principle throw any light on the ability to use and understand words freely in unforseen contexts. And these difficulties arise for them, as related ones arise for Skinner, because they persist in regarding the behavior of a word in discourse as something capable in principle of being determined by the empirical nature of its denotatum. Such a view necessarily constrains anyone who seriously adopts it to spend endless ingenuity in fruitless attempts to explain all linguistic capacities as extensions of the capacity to name objects correctly (whatever technical terminology this unfortunate enterprise is cloaked in).

[11] Noam Chomsky, Review of *Verbal Behavior*, *Language*, vol. 35 (1958), pp. 26–58.

Index

C

Carnap, R., 67, 151
Category
  semantic, 175, 206
  mistake, 8
  conceptual and grammatical, 202–204
  Ryle's criterion of, 204–205
  Chomsky on, 202–206
  "crossing" of, 218–219
  grammatical, 41
Chase, Richard Allen, 294
Chomsky, Noam, 186, 195, 239 ff., 265
  on association and reference, 5–6
  on goals of linguistic theory, 21–22
  on intrinsic lexical relationships, 200–201, 220–221
  on degrees of grammaticalness, 201–202
  on linguistic competence, 106, 269
  on semantic interpretation of sentences, 278
  on semantic function, 279–282
  on linguistic universals, 284 ff.
Cognitive content, 166
Color
  terms, 58–60, 68–69, 70, 224–226, 286
  incompatibilities, 224–227
Colored patch, 74

Competence, linguistic, 106–107, 160–162, 265, 267–270, 284–288
Complementarity, 234
Concepts, 8–11
  basic, 9, 22, 32, 33, 58, 68, 228
  nonbasic, 12
Conceptual model, 4, 102–109
Conceptualism, 8
Conventions, linguistic, 4

D

Day-names, 209 ff.
Degree of grammaticalness, 201–202
Descartes, Rene, 284
Disclaimer clause, 192

E

Epistemological scepticism, 130–132, 135, 137
  and linguistic doubt, 137
  and associationist theory of meaning, 140

72 73 74 75 76   9 8 7 6 5 4 3 2 1

TEXAS WOMAN'S UNIVERSITY
LIBRARY